Classic Bucs

CLASSIC SPORTS

Jonathan Knight, Series Editor

Classic Bucs: The 50 Greatest Games in Pittsburgh Pirates History
  David Finoli

Classic Bucs

THE 50 GREATEST GAMES IN PITTSBURGH PIRATES HISTORY

David Finoli

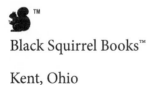

Black Squirrel Books™

Kent, Ohio

© 2013 by The Kent State University Press, Kent, Ohio 44242
All rights reserved
Library of Congress Catalog Card Number 2012048458
ISBN 978-1-60635-160-4
Manufactured in the United States of America

Library of Congress Cataloging-in-Publication Data

Finoli, David, 1961–
    Classic Bucs : the 50 greatest games in Pittsburgh Pirates history / David Finoli.
        pages cm. — (Classic sports)
Includes bibliographical references.
ISBN 978-1-60635-160-4 (pbk.) ∞
1. Pittsburgh Pirates (Baseball team)—History—Juvenile literature. I. Title.
    GV975.P5F56 2013
    796.357′640974886—dc23   2012048458

All photographs appear courtesy of the Pittsburgh Pirates.
All statistics were obtained free of charge from and are copyrighted by Retrosheet. Interested
parties may contact Retrosheet at www.retrosheet.org.

Black Squirrel Books™
Frisky, industrious black squirrels are a familiar sight on the Kent State University campus and
the inspiration for Black Squirrel Books™, a trade imprint of The Kent State University Press.
www.KentStateUniversityPress.com.

17 16 15 14 13   5 4 3 2 1

To my father, Domenic, and the memory of my uncles, Vinnie and Ed, who each helped foster my love of the great game of baseball. And to the boys of Duquesne: Bill R., Bob, Gary, Shawn, Mike, Leo, Bill L., Daryl, Pasquale, and Chris with whom I had the pleasure of experiencing the last Pirates championship in 1979 . . . may our children experience another in the near future.

Contents

Acknowledgments

There are many people who were instrumental in the completion of this book and who deserve a huge amount of appreciation. First, there is my incredible, supportive family that makes my life a true joy: my wife of 26 years, Viv, and our three children, Tony, Matt, and Cara.

Then there is my extended family, which has been there through the highs and lows of my life over the years: my father, Domenic; mother, Eleanor; brother, Jamie; his daughters, Marissa and Brianna; my sister, Mary; her husband, Matthew; and all my loving aunts, uncles, and cousins.

A big thank you also goes to Joyce Harrison and Mary Young of the Kent State University Press, Jonathan Knight, editor of the Classic Sports series, and my copyeditor, Rebekah Cotton, who all made this book a wonderful experience. Also, many thanks to Jim Trdinich of the Pittsburgh Pirates who generously donated the photos in this book.

Additionally, I must recognize the Society of American Baseball Research, which has always provided me with the research opportunities that have been pivotal throughout my writing career. Equally helpful have been the Carnegie Library microfilm department employees, who pointed me in the right direction when I was stuck.

Finally, I offer a huge thank you to my partners in crime, Bill Ranier and Chris Fletcher, who helped with this book when needed and with whom I've had the pleasure of talking about the trials and tribulation of the Bucs since the glory days of the 1970s.

Introduction

When slow-footed former Pirate Sid Bream broke the heart of the Buccos nation in Game Seven of the 1992 National League Championship Series as he slid across the plate in the bottom of the ninth to win it for the Braves and give them the pennant, it began a mind-numbing slide that has now entered its third decade of sub .500 performances. The "Curse of Sid Bream" was born.

With the exception of their surprising run at a playoff spot in 2012, for a generation of Steel City baseball fans, a postseason berth has been a goal that even the most die-hard of young Pirates fans can't even imagine.

But there was a time that a postseason berth wasn't an impossible concept but rather an annual right. From 1970 through 1979, Pittsburgh won six NL Eastern Division crowns and two world championships. While impressive, the 1970s were actually only the second-best era in franchise history. That honor goes to the first decade of the twentieth century when a young, brash Pirates team captured a quartet of pennants and its initial World Series in 1909.

In between those two memorable decades, the club secured a pair of world championships in 1925 and 1960, the latter of which culminated with arguably the greatest contest in the history of the game. It was a memorable fall afternoon on October 13, 1960, when a second baseman known for his defensive prowess became the only man in the history of the game to end the seventh game of the Fall Classic with a home run. Bill Mazeroski had smacked a Ralph Terry pitch over the left field wall to give the Bucs a wild 10–9 victory over the New York Yankees, sending the town into hysterics and forever carving Mazeroski's name into baseball history.

It's that incredible moment, along with so many others, that serves as the inspiration for this book, which chronicles the 50 greatest games in the history of this long-beloved franchise. This list includes not just title-clinchers but the accounts of some legendary individual performances, such as the greatest game ever pitched—Harvey Haddix's 1959 gem—and Rennie Stennett's remarkable seven-for-seven performance in 1975 against the Cubs. There are moments that will bring smiles to the faces of the Pirates faithful and others that may draw tears.

Countless things have changed in Pittsburgh, baseball, and the nation as a whole, but the passion for the Pirates and the desire to reflect on their adventures have remained constant. The stories in this book weave together the wonderful memories of older generations of Pittsburgh baseball fans with today's younger Pirates faithful, a generation that has been looking for its own Mazeroski moment ever since Bream slid across home plate two decades ago.

PIRATES 11, WASHINGTON NATIONALS 6
AUGUST 1, 2009

A Glimpse of the Future

Ever since the fruitful farm system of the Pittsburgh Pirates dried up in the early 1990s, the club had been looking unsuccessfully for homegrown talent that could lead it out of the record-setting funk it had stumbled into since its last playoff appearance in 1992. Superstar players such as Barry Bonds and Bobby Bonilla were replaced by the underwhelming likes of Chad Hermansen and Bobby Bradley.

The first decade of the twenty-first century brought a new commitment to making the farm system fertile again, and young center fielder Andrew McCutchen was to be the centerpiece of that commitment.

A 2005 first-round draft pick out of Fort Meade High School in Florida, McCutchen had shown in the minors that he had the potential to be the man who could lead the parent club out of its doldrums. He hit .284 in the minors between 2005 and 2008, showcasing his incredible speed and defensive prowess along the way. The speedy center fielder did have some chinks in his armor—most notably an average throwing arm and issues with base stealing—but overall the scouts were salivating.

When Pittsburgh general manager Neal Huntingdon began the Andrew McCutchen era on June 3, 2009, by promoting his prize prospect to the majors, Huntingdon hoped that the scouts were right and that his skills would transcend perfectly to the major-league level. It was not a sure thing though. Incredibly, things started off better than anyone had anticipated as the Fort Meade native had hits in 11 of his first 13 games with the Pirates. Then on August 1, 2009, the rookie took it to another level, giving frustrated Pirates fans a glimpse into what the future could be.

On that day, less than two months after his major-league debut, McCutchen etched his name with the likes of Hall of Famers Willie Stargell, Roberto Clemente, and Ralph Kiner with one of the most memorable performances in franchise history. He became only the 10th Pirate to hit three home runs in a game, single-handedly putting the team on his back and beating the Washington Nationals, 11–6.

Facing Nationals rookie right-hander Craig Stammen to lead off the bottom of the first for the Bucs, the young center fielder parked a 1–2 offering just inside the left field foul pole to cut an early Washington lead to 2–1. Two innings later, McCutchen came up again with shortstop Ronnie Cedeno on second and one out. It was here where the speedy rookie showed his versatility by laying down a perfect bunt for a hit and then scored from first base on Lastings Milledge's double to give the Bucs the lead.

It was the bunt that impressed Pittsburgh manager John Russell almost as much as his prestigious power on this evening. "That's something he's been working on," Russell said. "It was nice to see him get one of those down because it's part of his game."[1]

An inning later the young Pirates club put the game away. After plating two runs to make it 5–2, McCutchen struck again, sending a changeup over the left field fence for a two-run homer.

In the sixth, after the Nationals cut the margin to 7–4, McCutchen placed his name in the Pirates' record book by hitting his third round-tripper of the night, a three-run homer almost mirroring his previous long ball, to put an exclamation point on this memorable evening. The throng of 26,855 roared after his third homer and remained standing until McCutchen came out of the dugout to acknowledge their appreciation. The young center fielder would have his shot at immortality with a potential fourth home run in the ninth inning, but he hit into a sharp 6–4–3 double play to close his quest.

Despite the fact that he ended this magnificent effort on a down note, Andrew McCutchen's four-hit, three-homer, six-RBI night was certainly one for the ages in Pirates baseball history. He had never been known as a power hitter in the minors, with only 43 long balls in 511 games, but the young star had proved he had another weapon in his repertoire. After 17 years of frustration, Pirates fans were hopeful they were watching the beginning of a career that could finally lead them out of the landscape of disappointment that had been Pirates baseball since 1992.

| WAS N | 2 | 0 | 0 | 0 | 1 | 1 | 0 | 1 | 1 | – | 6 | 12 | 1 |
| PIT N | 1 | 0 | 2 | 4 | 0 | 4 | 0 | 0 | x | – | 11 | 14 | 0 |

BATTING

Washington Nationals	AB	R	H	RBI
Morgan cf	4	0	3	0
Guzman ss	5	1	2	1
Zimmerman 3b	4	2	3	1
Dunn 1b	4	0	1	1
Willingham lf	2	0	0	0
Villone p	0	0	0	0
Kearns ph	0	1	0	0
Dukes rf	3	0	0	1
Bard c	5	0	2	1
Gonzalez 2b	5	0	0	1
Stammen p	2	0	0	0
Clippard p	0	0	0	0
A. Hernandez ph	1	1	1	0
Kensing p	0	0	0	0
Harris lf	1	1	0	0
Totals	**36**	**6**	**12**	**6**

FIELDING—DP: 3. Gonzalez-Guzman-Dunn, Gonzalez-Dunn, Guzman-Gonzalez-Dunn.
E: Morgan (3).
BATTING—2B: Dunn (21,off Vasquez); Zimmerman (24,off Vasquez); A. Hernandez (9,off Karstens); Guzman (19,off Karstens).
SF: Dukes (1,off Vasquez); Zimmerman (7,off Meek).
HBP: Willingham (11,by Vasquez).
GDP: Dukes (4,off Vasquez).
Team LOB: 12.

Pittsburgh Pirates	AB	R	H	RBI
A. McCutchen cf	5	4	4	6
Milledge lf	4	0	1	2
Jones 1b	4	0	2	0
Doumit c	4	0	0	0
Young 2b	3	1	1	0
Karstens p	0	0	0	0
Pearce ph	1	0	0	0
Veal p	0	0	0	0
Meek p	0	0	0	0
Andy LaRoche 3b	4	2	2	1
Moss rf	4	2	2	1
Cedeno ss	4	1	2	1
Vasquez p	1	0	0	0
Vazquez 2b	0	1	0	0
Totals	34	11	14	11

FIELDING—DP: 1. Cedeno-Young-Jones.
BATTING—2B: Milledge (1,off Stammen); Jones (8,off Villone).
3B: Andy LaRoche (5,off Stammen).
HR: A. McCutchen 3 (6,1st inning off Stammen 0 on 0 out,4th inning off
Clippard 1 on 2 out,6th inning off Kensing 2 on 1 out).
SH: Vasquez (1,off Stammen).
HBP: Vazquez (2,by Villone).
GDP: Doumit (5,off Stammen); A. McCutchen (2,off Villone).
Team LOB: 2.

PITCHING

Washington Nationals	IP	H	R	ER	BB	SO
Stammen L(3–6)	3	8	6	6	0	0
Clippard	2	2	1	1	0	2
Kensing	0.2	3	4	4	1	0
Villone	2.1	1	0	0	0	2
Totals	8	14	11	11	1	4

Stammen faced 3 batters in the 4th inning
HBP: Villone (1,Vazquez).

Pittsburgh Pirates	IP	H	R	ER	BB	SO
Vasquez W(2–5)	5	9	3	3	2	2
Karstens	2	3	1	1	0	2
Veal	0	0	1	1	2	0
Meek	2	0	1	1	2	2
Totals	9	12	6	6	6	6

Veal faced 2 batters in the 8th inning
WP: Meek (5).
HBP: Vasquez (2,Willingham).
Umpires: HP—Adrian Johnson, 1B—Mark Wegner, 2B—Tim Timmons, 3B—Rob Drake
Time of Game: 2:46 **Attendance:** 26,855

PIRATES 5, CHICAGO CUBS 4
JULY 6, 1980

The Marathon

The 1980 season hadn't provided the same kind of magic as it had the year before when the Pittsburgh Pirates surprised everyone by capturing their fifth world championship. Willie Stargell, the leader of the 1979 club who took his team on his back that memorable campaign, suffered a pair of injuries and had missed all but 67 games in 1980. Stalwart pitchers Rick Rhoden and Jim Rooker were out with arm injuries, and the man who was so spectacular on the mound in Game Three of the 1979 National League Championship Series, Bert Blyleven, was angry at his manager, Chuck Tanner, for Tanner's aggressive use of the Pirates' bullpen and opting to use a five-man rotation instead of the then traditional four-man standard.

Heading into the last game before the all-star break, Pittsburgh was wallowing in third place. While they were only 1½ games out of first, their record was a mere 41–37, and they were clearly in need of a spark to turn around their fortunes.

The pitching matchup that day pitted the Bucs' disgruntled hurler, Blyleven, who stood at 2–7 with a 4.11 ERA, against Rick Reuschel of the Chicago Cubs, who was also having a difficult start to the campaign, coming in to the game with a disappointing 5–8 mark.

With the two underachieving clubs facing off, each starting a struggling pitcher, nobody expected this contest to be a classic, but that's exactly what the 25,994 fans at Three Rivers Stadium on that Sunday afternoon were lucky enough to witness.

As the game began, it looked like it was going to be another disappointing performance for Blyleven as the Cubs scored in the first. Pittsburgh evened up the contest in the bottom half of the first when, with two outs, right fielder Dave Parker ripped an 0–2 pitch for his 10th homer of the season.

In the top of the fifth, Ivan DeJesus spurred the Cubs' offense once again with a leadoff single. Two batters later, Buckner gave Chicago a 2–1 lead when he knocked in the Cubs' shortstop with a single to center. The Bucs would not be outdone and bounced right back with three runs in the bottom of the frame, two of them scoring on a single by Blyleven, to take a 4–2 lead. Pittsburgh maintained the two-run advantage until the top of the eighth, when Buckner led off the inning with his fifth homer of the year on Blyleven's first offering to the Cubs' first baseman.

Still leading by one in the ninth, Tanner ironically opted to stay with Blyleven rather than go to his bullpen. His embattled pitcher seemed to make Tanner look like a genius as he retired the first two batters, putting the Pirates one out away from a victory. Unfortunately, Blyleven gave up a pinch-hit home run to Cliff Johnson on an 0–2 pitch to tie the game. In that moment, the game went from the cusp of completion to just getting started as it toiled through a long summer evening.

Both teams came close to ending the contest in extra innings, but neither could get the winning run across the plate. As the game went through the afternoon into evening, the innings went from the 10th to the 11th, eventually turning into the 15th, 16th, and 17th with both teams threatening often, but neither being able to end this marathon.

Chicago almost ended the game in the 18th and 19th innings, putting two men on base each time, but Pittsburgh reliever Jim Bibby, who entered the game in the top of the 18th and was having a spectacular season sporting a 10–1 mark, was able to get out of both jams, keeping the seemingly endless game knotted up at four.

After not mounting any type of serious scoring threat since the 11th inning, Pittsburgh finally broke loose as the game entered the bottom of the 20th inning. Catcher Ed Ott led off with a single and moved into scoring position when short-stop Dale Berra sacrificed him to second. Stargell was intentionally walked and out of options. Tanner inserted reliever Enrique Romo as a pinch runner. Center fielder Omar Moreno then garnered his second hit in nine at bats during this marathon that finally ended the game after 5 hours and 31 minutes.

Cubs skipper Preston Gomez said afterward, "This was one of those games that was good for the fans, but no good for the manager." Conversely, Moreno felt it was worth it. "My feet hurt. My back is stiff, but it feels good to win."[1]

The win turned out to be the catalyst the Bucs were looking for. They went on to win 10 of the next 13 games, vaulting them into first place. While it was a victory that harkened back to the exciting contests Pirates fans enjoyed in

1979, there just weren't enough of them to keep the 1980 team's hopes of a repeat alive. The momentum of this classic marathon was temporary though. Mediocre play returned following the winning streak, and the Pirates finished eight games behind the eventual world champion Philadelphia Phillies.

CHI N	1 0 0	0 1 0	0 1 1	0 0 0	0 0 0	0 0 0	0 0 — 4 17 1
PIT N	1 0 0	0 3 0	0 0 0	0 0 0	0 0 0	0 0 0	0 1 — 5 11 0

BATTING

Chicago Cubs	AB	R	H	RBI
DeJesus ss	8	2	2	0
Randle 3b	9	0	2	0
Buckner 1b	8	1	3	2
Kingman lf	9	0	0	0
Martin cf	9	0	3	1
Vail rf	7	0	3	0
Blackwell c	8	0	1	0
Tyson 2b	3	0	1	0
Biittner ph	1	0	0	0
Kelleher 2b	3	0	1	0
Reuschel p	1	0	0	0
Henderson ph	1	0	0	0
Riley p	0	0	0	0
Johnson ph	1	1	1	1
Sutter p	0	0	0	0
Dillard ph	1	0	0	0
Capilla p	0	0	0	0
Tidrow p	0	0	0	0
Hernandez p	0	0	0	0
Foote ph	1	0	0	0
Caudill p	1	0	0	0
McGlothen ph	1	0	0	0
Lamp p	0	0	0	0
Totals	72	4	17	4

FIELDING—E: Blackwell (3).

BATTING—2B: Tyson (8,off Blyleven); Martin (13,off Blyleven).

HR: Buckner (5,8th inning off Blyleven 0 on 0 out); Johnson (3,9th inning off Blyleven 0 on 2 out).

SH: Reuschel (5,off Blyleven); Blackwell (2,off Jackson).

GDP: Kelleher (3,off Rhoden); Buckner (2,off Jackson).

IBB: Kelleher (1,by Tekulve); Buckner (7,by Bibby).
Team LOB: 15.
BASERUNNING—SB: Randle (16,2nd base off Bibby/Ott).

Pittsburgh Pirates	AB	R	H	RBI
Moreno cf	9	0	2	1
Foli ss	8	0	0	0
Parker rf	6	1	1	1
Milner 1b	6	0	1	0
Easler lf	2	1	1	0
Lacy lf	4	0	1	0
Garner 2b	8	0	1	0
Ott c	7	2	2	0
xBerra 3b	5	1	1	1
Blyleven p	2	0	1	2
Sanguillen ph	0	0	0	0
Tekulve p	0	0	0	0
B. Robinson ph	1	0	0	0
Rhoden p	0	0	0	0
Madlock ph	1	0	0	0
Jackson p	0	0	0	0
Nicosia ph	1	0	0	0
Bibby p	0	0	0	0
Stargell ph	0	0	0	0
Romo pr	0	0	0	0
Totals	**60**	**5**	**11**	**5**

x—reached first on interference.
FIELDING—DP: 3. Foli-Garner-Milner, Ott, Jackson-Foli-Milner.
BATTING—HR: Parker (10,1st inning off Reuschel 0 on 2 out).
SH: Blyleven (5,off Riley); Sanguillen (2,off Sutter); Berra (4,off Lamp).
IBB: Stargell (9,by Lamp).
Team LOB: 10.
BASERUNNING—SB: Lacy (9,2nd base off Tidrow/Blackwell).
CS: Garner (2,2nd base by Reuschel/Blackwell); Moreno (13,2nd base by Reuschel/Blackwell); Parker 2 (5,2nd base by Capilla/Blackwell,2nd base by Caudill/Blackwell); Lacy (4,2nd base by Lamp/Blackwell).

PITCHING

Chicago Cubs	IP	H	R	ER	BB	SO
Reuschel	6	8	4	4	1	3
Riley	2	0	0	0	1	0
Sutter	2	0	0	0	0	3
Capilla	0.1	0	0	0	2	0
Tidrow	0.1	0	0	0	1	0
Hernandez	2.1	0	0	0	1	4
Caudill	5	0	0	0	2	5
Lamp L(9–7)	1.1	3	1	1	1	1
Totals	**19.1**	**11**	**5**	**5**	**9**	**16**

WP: Reuschel (2).

IBB: Lamp (2,Stargell).

Pittsburgh Pirates	IP	H	R	ER	BB	SO
Blyleven	10	9	4	4	1	12
Tekulve	2	2	0	0	1	0
Rhoden	2	1	0	0	1	3
Jackson	3	2	0	0	1	1
Bibby W(11–1)	3	3	0	0	1	2
Totals	**20**	**17**	**4**	**4**	**5**	**18**

IBB: Tekulve (6,Kelleher); Bibby (1,Buckner).

Umpires: HP—Harry Wendelstedt, 1B—Eric Gregg, 2B—Frank Pulli, 3B—Fred Brocklander

Time of Game: 5:31 Attendance: 25,994

PIRATES 14, ST. LOUIS CARDINALS 8
MAY 30, 1939

A Day in the Sun

It had been a whirlwind year for Pirates outfielder Johnny Rizzo. After hitting .358 with 21 homers for the minor-league Columbus Red Birds in 1937, the Houston native burst into the majors with the Pittsburgh Pirates in 1938, setting a team rookie record with 23 homers while knocking in 111 runs and hitting .301. With the Rookie of the Year Award yet to be created, Rizzo had to settle for a sixth-place finish in the National League's MVP race behind a group that included Hall of Famers Mel Ott, teammate Arky Vaughan, and eventual winner Ernie Lombardi, a Cincinnati Reds catcher.

Expectations were very high for Rizzo and the Bucs the following season after the Pirates had a commanding lead in the National League for most of the 1938 campaign before stumbling in September and succumbing to the Chicago Cubs. Even though they got off to a horrendous start in 1939, losing seven of their first eight games, they rebounded in May, standing at 18–17 as they prepared for a doubleheader in St. Louis on the last weekend of the month.

While the team was rebounding, Rizzo continued to slump. He entered the doubleheader in St. Louis, hitting a meager .246 with a single home run. Adding insult to injury, the night before he had hit into what was believed to be the first triple play ever begun with a ground ball.

The first game of this doubleheader was certainly forgettable for the team and its young star. St. Louis thrashed the Bucs 7–2 as Rizzo went 0 for 4, dropping his season average to .239.

The left fielder started the second game, doubling home a run in the first inning to give the Pirates an early 1–0 lead, an advantage they would give away in quick order. The 14,000-plus Cardinal faithful who were in attendance at Sportsman's Park this day saw their beloved team torch Pirates starter Russ

Bauers early on, scoring three runs in the bottom of the second and matching that total an inning later before manager Pie Traynor decided he'd seen enough. He called for veteran hurler Bill Swift who, by 1939, was spending most of his time in the bullpen. Swift immediately gave up another run, putting St. Louis up 7–1 as the third inning came to a close.

The Pirates were now reeling, needing a spark if they were going to exit this doubleheader with some momentum going into Philadelphia, where they would play in the first night game in Phillies history the following day. As Traynor and the Pirates would soon find out, Johnny Rizzo would be that spark.

Rizzo took the Bucs on his back the next two innings. With two on and two out, the Houston native took a pitch from St. Louis hurler Lefty Shoun and parked it in the left field bleachers, cutting the Cards' lead to 7–4. Confidence was now starting to appear for the slumping Pirates star.

Pittsburgh tied the game in the seventh inning with three more runs and then put the game away in the next two innings. While the Pirates' offense had come alive, Swift kept the Cardinal bats at bay and allowed the club to make such a dramatic comeback. After giving up a run in the third, he held St. Louis to five hits and two runs over his 6⅔ innings of relief.

Even though Swift was pitching well, the day belonged to Johnny Rizzo. In the top of the eighth inning with the score tied at seven, Rizzo came up with the bases loaded and ripped Cardinals reliever Bob Bowman's offering so hard off the outfield wall that it bounced past the two St. Louis outfielders who were in pursuit, clearing the bases with a double. The Bucs tacked on another run to give the club an 11–7 lead.

With an inning left to go, Rizzo was already having the game of a lifetime: four hits in five at bats, three runs scored, and seven RBIs. Incredibly, Rizzo wasn't finished. Facing Bowman once again with a runner on first, Rizzo put an exclamation point on his phenomenal afternoon by hitting his second home run of the game, completing an impressive comeback with a 14–8 Pittsburgh victory. Rizzo finished with a remarkable nine RBIs and had accounted for 11 of the 14 Pirates' runs.

In one day Rizzo's batting average shot up 25 points to .264, but it unfortunately would not hold up for the 1939 campaign as a whole. Rizzo finished with a .261 average, hitting only three more home runs. The following year his average fell to .179 before the Pirates dealt him to Cincinnati for Vince DiMaggio.

While Rizzo, who was sent to the Phillies from the Reds before the 1940 season was over, ended up hitting a career-high 24 home runs that year, his major-league career came to a conclusion just two years later. After the 1942 campaign concluded miserably for Rizzo in Brooklyn, he enlisted in the Navy as a seaman. Following World War II, he played four seasons in the minors but was never able to recapture the magic of his rookie campaign in 1938.

Despite the fact that Rizzo wasn't much more than a one-year wonder, his name still remains etched in the Pirates' record books because of that unforgettable day in the sun in St. Louis.

PIT N	1	0	0	0	3	0	3	4	3	—	14	14	1
STL N	0	3	4	0	0	0	0	1	0	—	8	7	1

BATTING

Pittsburgh Pirates	AB	R	H	RBI
P. Waner rf	5	3	2	0
Vaughan ss	3	4	1	0
Rizzo lf	6	4	5	9
Bell cf	2	1	1	0
Berres c	1	0	0	0
Brubaker 2b	5	0	0	0
Suhr 1b	5	0	2	2
Handley 3b	4	0	1	2
Mueller c	3	0	1	0
L.Waner cf	2	0	0	0
Bauer sp	1	0	0	0
Swift p	3	2	1	0
Totals	40	14	14	13

FIELDING—DP: 1. P. Waner-Suhr.
E: Brubaker (10).
BATTING—2B: P. Waner (8); Rizzo 2 (18).
HR: Rizzo 2 (3,5th inning off Shoun 2 on,9th inning off Bowman 1 on).
SH: Berres (3); Handley (3).
Team LOB: 9.

St. Louis Cardinals	AB	R	H	RBI
Brown ss	3	0	0	0
S. Martin 2b	5	1	0	0
P. Martin cf	4	1	0	0
Medwick lf	4	2	2	2
Mize 1b	3	2	1	1
Gutteridge 3b	2	1	0	0
Slaughter rf	4	1	3	4
Franks c	2	0	0	1
Padgett ph	1	0	0	0
Owen c	0	0	0	0
Shoun p	2	0	0	0
Cooper p	0	0	0	0
Davis p	1	0	1	0
Bowman p	0	0	0	0
King ph	0	0	0	0
Totals	31	8	7	8

FIELDING—E: Gutteridge (4).
BATTING—2B: Medwick (8); Slaughter 3 (10).
3B: Mize (1).
SH: Brown (5); Gutteridge (3); Franks (1).
Team LOB: 3.

PITCHING

Pittsburgh Pirates	IP	H	R	ER	BB	SO
Bauers	2.1	2	6	3	3	0
Swift W(1–0)	6.2	5	2	1	1	5
Totals	9	7	8	4	4	5

WP: Bauers (1).

St. Louis Cardinals	IP	H	R	ER	BB	SO
Shoun	4.2	4	4	4	4	3
Cooper	1.2	2	3	3	2	2
Davis L(7–3)	0.2	5	4	4	1	0
Bowman	2	3	3	3	1	3
Totals	9	14	14	14	8	8

Umpires: HP—Babe Pinelli, 1B—George Barr, 3B—Charlie Moran
Time of Game: 2:26 Attendance: 14,178

PIRATES 10, MONTREAL EXPOS 4
SEPTEMBER 25, 1979

The Knockout Punch

It had been a long battle in the National League's Eastern Division in 1979 between the Pittsburgh Pirates and the Montreal Expos. With only eight games left in what had been an exciting campaign, the Expos had traveled to Pittsburgh for a four-game series that would finally decide a race in which the teams had switched places six times in the previous two weeks. After the clubs had split the first two games of this climactic series, Montreal maintained the slimmest of leads: just a half game.

Pirates manager Chuck Tanner chose veteran pitcher Jim Rooker, who just turned 37 two days earlier, to take the mound to try to deliver a victory in this important matchup. A fine pitcher for the franchise during the 1970s after coming over in a trade from Kansas City following the 1972 campaign, Rooker looked like he was coming to the end of his career in 1979, posting a substandard 3–7 record with a 4.47 ERA. *Pittsburgh Post Gazette* columnist Phil Musick noted that "Jim Rooker wanted to feed the 1979 baseball season to the family dog. The summer of his greatest discontent in two decades of pitching baseball for money grew like an odorous weed."[1] Montreal countered with youth on the hill, inserting 23-year-old Scott Sanderson.

The game was delayed for about 10 minutes, not because of the weather but rather the white bandage Rooker was wearing on his right wrist due to a burn he suffered at home. The umpires insisted that he remove the bandage because it could affect the ability of the Montreal hitters to see the ball. Trying to come up with a compromise and still protect his pitcher's wounds, Bucs trainer Tony Bartirome decided to color the bandage brown. The umpires approved the compromise and the game began.

With shortstop Tim Foli on second and two outs in the bottom of the first, up to the plate stepped Willie Stargell, a man who was enjoying quite a resurgence in 1979 in his long and illustrious career. "Pops," as he had affectionately become known to his teammates, had been the leader all season and came through again as he smashed his 30th homer to give the Pirates an early 2–0 lead.

The Expos would not give up their division lead that easily and tied the game in the fourth on a home run by third baseman Larry Parrish. Pops and the Pirates would not be denied, as Stargell lifted an inside fastball for his second home run of the day, putting the Bucs on top once again: 3–2 in the bottom of the fourth. "The first one gave us a lift," Tanner said after the game, "and the second one gave us an even bigger lift."[2]

Pittsburgh failed to break the game wide open in the fourth after loading the bases with one out. Montreal tied the game once again with a run in the top of the fifth. It was at this point that the NL East race took a dramatic turn.

With two outs in the bottom of the fifth, Stargell worked Sanderson for a walk. Milner then followed with a single to left, and third baseman Bill Madlock walked to load the bases. Catcher Ed Ott then ripped a hanging curve to center to put the Bucs ahead once again, 5–3.

Montreal manager Dick Williams called for reliever Bill Atkinson to end the Bucs threat, but second baseman Phil Garner smacked a single to center, scoring Madlock with Pittsburgh's third run of the frame, giving Pittsburgh a three-run lead.

Montreal tried to come back once again in the top of the sixth, cutting the margin to 6–4, but the Pirates' bats once again came alive, scoring four more runs to turn this tense battle into a rout.

There were no comebacks left for Montreal. Pittsburgh reliever Enrique Romo was dominant the last three innings, giving up only one more hit and striking out six batters, including Andre Dawson and Tony Perez, to end the game.

While the Bucs only held a half-game lead now, they would never relinquish it. The next day Pittsburgh smashed Montreal 10–1 and clinched the division four days later with a win over the Cubs. Despite the fact that it was a few days before they made it official, it was this victory against the Montreal Expos that delivered the knockout punch that sent the Pirates to the playoffs in 1979.

MON N	0	0	1		1	1	1		0	0	0	—	4 11 2
PIT N	2	0	0		1	3	4		0	0	x	—	10 13 0

BATTING

Montreal Expos	AB	R	H	RBI
Cromartie lf	5	0	2	0
Cash 2b	5	1	1	0
Dawson cf	5	1	2	0
Perez 1b	3	0	0	1
Valentine rf	4	0	2	1
Parrish 3b	4	1	1	1
Scott ss	4	1	2	0
Dyer c	3	0	1	1
Sanderson p	2	0	0	0
Atkinson p	0	0	0	0
White ph	1	0	0	0
Grimsley p	0	0	0	0
Murray p	0	0	0	0
Hutton ph	1	0	0	0
James p	0	0	0	0
Totals	37	4	11	4

FIELDING—DP: 1. Scott-Cash-Perez.
E: Cash (6), Scott (19).
BATTING—2B: Scott (12,off Rooker).
HR: Parrish (30,4th inning off Rooker 0 on 0 out).
SF: Perez (7,off Rooker).
Team LOB: 9.
BASERUNNING—SB: Scott 2 (37,3rd base off Rooker/Ott,2nd base off Rooker/Ott).

Pittsburgh Pirates	AB	R	H	RBI
Moreno cf	5	1	2	0
Foli ss	5	2	2	0
Parker rf	5	1	1	1
Stargell 1b	4	3	2	3
Milner lf	4	1	1	1
Lois pr	0	1	0	0
B. Robinson lf	1	0	0	0
Madlock 3b	3	1	1	1
Ott c	4	0	2	3
Garner 2b	2	0	2	1
Rooker p	3	0	0	0
Romo p	1	0	0	0
Totals	37	10	13	10

BATTING—2B: Garner (31,off Sanderson).

HR: Stargell 2 (31,1st inning off Sanderson 1 on 2 out,4th inning off Sanderson 0 on 0 out).

SF: Madlock (6,off Murray).

GDP: Foli (8,off Murray).

IBB: Garner 2 (13,by Sanderson,by Murray).

Team LOB: 8.

BASERUNNING—SB: Lois (1,2nd base off Murray/Dyer).

PITCHING

Montreal Expos	IP	H	R	ER	BB	SO
Sanderson L(9–8)	4.2	7	6	6	3	3
Atkinson	0.1	1	0	0	0	0
Grimsley	0.1	3	4	2	0	1
Murray	1.2	2	0	0	1	0
James	1	0	0	0	0	1
Totals	8	13	10	8	4	5

WP: Sanderson (2).

IBB: Sanderson (4,Garner); Murray (16,Garner).

Pittsburgh Pirates	IP	H	R	ER	BB	SO
RookerW(4–7)	5	9	4	4	2	2
RomoSV(5)	4	2	0	0	0	7
Totals	9	11	4	4	2	9

Rooker faced 2 batters in the 6th inning

WP: Rooker (6).

Umpires: HP—Frank Pulli, 1B—Eric Gregg, 2B—Doug Harvey, 3B—Andy Olsen

Time of Game: 3:06 **Attendance:** 31,348

PIRATES 3, CINCINNATI REDS 2
OCTOBER 10, 1990

Stayin' Alive

After a fabulous regular season in which they captured their first division title in 11 years, the Pirates' magical ride of 1990 seemed to finally be coming to a disappointing end. They got off to a good start in the National League Championship Series, rallying to win the first game over Cincinnati, but the Reds came back to win the next three games, taking a commanding lead in the series.

On paper, the Pirates seemed to have the advantage—offensively, defensively, and in the starting pitching—but the Reds had a decisive edge in the bullpen, and they used it well in Games Two, Three, and Four. Rob Dibble and Randy Myers dominated Pirates hitters, and they would finish the series, allowing no earned runs in 10⅔ innings, surrendering only two hits while striking out 17. On the strength of the bullpen, Cincinnati had a chance to end the series and win the pennant in Game Five at Three Rivers Stadium.

While the Reds' bullpen was superb, the Pirates' offense had been disappointing. In the three games that followed its victory, Pittsburgh combined for only seven runs and 22 hits. Their top hitters, Bobby Bonilla and Barry Bonds, were hitting .267 and .214 respectively, while the dangerous Andy Van Slyke was even worse, hitting just .188.

"We've had our chances, but we haven't been able to get any hits," the Pirates' manager Jim Leyland lamented when discussing his club's paltry .156 average with men in scoring position in the National League Championship Series. "We get something going and we can't get that big hit, and that's a backbreaker."[1]

While things looked troublesome offensively for the Bucs as they faced elimination, Leyland still had one trick left up his sleeve: Doug Drabek, who would take the mound to try to keep the season alive.

Drabek was having one of the greatest seasons in Pirates history. He led the National League with 22 wins and posted an impressive 2.76 ERA. For his efforts, the hurler from Victoria, Texas—who was the first piece of the puzzle acquired by general manager Syd Thrift when he put this championship squad together four years earlier—became the first Pirate since Vern Law in 1960 to win the Cy Young Award.

The right-hander had pitched well in a complete-game 2–1 loss in Game Two, and with the poor support Pirates hitters were giving their pitchers, he would have to be close to perfect to keep the Bucs' championship hopes alive.

A wary crowd of 48,221 was further disillusioned early as the Reds took a 1–0 lead in the top of the first. But the Pirates had come too far to go away quietly. Van Slyke laced a triple to right center in the bottom of the first to score a run and tie the game. He then came home on a fielder's choice, giving the Pirates the lead. For Drabek, he settled down and retired the following 13 Cincinnati batters in order.

Pittsburgh added to its lead in the bottom of the fourth as Bonds led off with a walk and went to third on a hit-and-run single by R. J. Reynolds. He then came home on a sacrifice fly by Don Slaught to make it 3–1.

Drabek continued to dominate the Cincinnati hitters into the eighth inning until Reds shortstop Barry Larkin hit a two-out double to cut the Pirates' lead to a single run. Instead of replacing his star pitcher for the ninth, Leyland stuck with Drabek, who would try to finish what he started. The Reds led off the inning with back-to-back singles and had men on second and third when Leyland went to his bullpen and brought in southpaw reliever Bob Patterson, who intentionally walked Chris Sabo to try to set up a force play.

Up to the plate came backup catcher Jeff Reed with a chance for immortality on his bat. Instead, Reed hit a sharp grounder to Bonilla at third. Not known for his defense, Bonilla nonetheless turned a fabulous 5–4–3 double play to end the game and send the large Three Rivers throng into hysterics.

Pittsburgh had held off elimination and would live to play another day, though their superb 1990 campaign would come to an end two days later in an exciting 2–1 defeat in Game Six. While they failed to achieve their goal of getting to the World Series, their Game Five victory showed their loyal fans one last time how special this season had been.

CIN N	1	0	0	0	0	0	0	1	0	—	2	7	0
PIT N	2	0	0	1	0	0	0	0	x	—	3	6	1

BATTING

Cincinnati Reds	AB	R	H	RBI
Larkin ss	4	1	2	1
Winningham cf	2	0	0	1
O'Neill rf	4	0	1	0
Davis lf	4	0	1	0
Morris 1b	3	0	0	0
Sabo 3b	3	0	1	0
Oliver c	2	0	0	0
Oester ph	1	0	0	0
Reed c	1	0	0	0
Duncan 2b	3	0	1	0
Browning p	1	0	0	0
Benzinger ph	1	0	1	0
Mahler p	0	0	0	0
Charlton p	0	0	0	0
Quinones ph	1	1	0	0
Scudder p	0	0	0	0
Totals	**30**	**2**	**7**	**2**

BATTING—**2B:** Larkin 2 (2,off Drabek 2).
SH: Morris (1,off Drabek).
SF: Winningham (1,off Drabek).
GDP: Larkin (1,off Drabek); Reed (1,off Patterson).
IBB: Sabo (1,by Patterson).
Team LOB: 5.

Pittsburgh Pirates	AB	R	H	RBI
Redus 1b	3	0	0	0
Bream 1b	1	0	1	0
Bell ss	2	1	0	0
Van Slyke cf	4	1	2	1
Bonilla 3b	3	0	0	0
Bonds lf	3	1	0	1
Reynolds rf	4	0	2	0
Slaught c	3	0	0	1
Lind 2b	3	0	0	0
Drabek p	3	0	1	0
Patterson p	0	0	0	0
Totals	29	3	6	3

FIELDING—DP: 2. Lind-Bell-Bream, Bonilla-Lind-Bream.
E: Drabek (1).
BATTING—3B: Van Slyke (1,off Browning).
SF: Slaught (1,off Browning).
HBP: Bell (1,by Browning).
Team LOB: 7.
BASERUNNING—SB: Bonds (2,2nd base off Browning/Oliver);
Reynolds (1,2nd base off Scudder/Reed).

PITCHING

Cincinnati Reds	IP	H	R	ER	BB	SO
Browning L(1–1)	5	3	3	3	3	2
Mahler	1.2	2	0	0	0	0
Charlton	0.1	0	0	0	0	1
Scudder	1	1	0	0	0	1
Totals	8	6	3	3	3	4

HBP: Browning (1,Bell).

Pittsburgh Pirates	IP	H	R	ER	BB	SO
Drabek W(1–1)	8.1	7	2	1	1	5
Patterson SV(1)	0.2	0	0	0	1	0
Totals	9	7	2	1	2	5

WP: Drabek (1).
IBB: Patterson (1,Sabo).
Umpires: HP—Jerry Crawford, 1B—Gerry Davis, 2B—Harry Wendelstedt,
3B—John McSherry, LF—Paul Runge, RF—Dutch Rennert
Time of Game: 2:48 Attendance: 48,221

#45

PIRATES 4, PHILADELPHIA PHILLIES 0
JUNE 1, 1965

K's Galore

Baseball in the 1960s was a difficult era to judge pitchers. There weren't radar guns analyzing every pitch, no scoreboard posting pitch speeds and angle degrees, and no box on your TV screen showing the pitch speed. The only tool fans had to understand how hard a pitcher was throwing was their eyes. On a rainy evening at Forbes Field in 1965, the Bucs nation had the opportunity to witness a dominating performance that could be appreciated without the use of any technologies.

Pittsburgh pitcher Bob Veale was an intimidating presence on the mound. At six foot six, the Birmingham, Alabama, native had a powerful fastball as well as a hard curve and an extremely effective slider. What he didn't have was good control and good eyesight—which frightened National League batters more than anything. His vision was so bad that he had to wear glasses when he pitched, and on humid evenings oftentimes they fogged up. On one such night in St Louis, Veale was so concerned about the humidity that he took his glasses off. Hall of Famer Lou Brock was so scared of being decapitated by an errant Veale toss that he refused to step into the batter's box until he put his glasses back on.

After a couple successful seasons in the Pirates' bullpen, Veale joined the starting rotation and had a breakout campaign in 1964, winning 18 games with a 2.74 ERA, while leading the National League in strikeouts with 250; of course he also led the league in walks. He crushed the all-time franchise record for strikeouts in a season, becoming the first Pirates hurler to eclipse 200 in a season and breaking another team record when he struck out 15 batters in a game. Both strikeout records were impressive, but neither would last long as he eclipsed his total of the year before with 276, a record that still stands today. He also topped his single-game mark with a magnificent performance against the Phillies.

Pittsburgh entered the game having won 11 straight games, which was making up for their horrendous 9–24 start to begin the season. Whether or not they would extend their winning streak to 12 depended as much on the weather as it did on how they performed.

Rain had been falling consistently all day, and the opening pitch was delayed. When Veale finally took the mound, he gave no indication of how special this night would turn out, as Philadelphia's Cookie Rojas singled to open the game and then Veale walked a batter. While he was able to get out of the jam, it didn't appear that he had his usual sharpness.

Pittsburgh scored twice in the bottom of the first, but it appeared as if it would all be for naught as the skies opened up, drenching the faithful at Forbes Field. Before this evening would end, there were two more delays that covered two hours, but the umpires eventually let the game continue—allowing Veale to make history.

Pirates manager Harry Walker permitted his starter to remain in the contest, but it did not look like the evening would be anything special for Veale as he struggled through the second, although he did record his first two strikeouts. By then the intimidating Veale caught fire as he blew away Richie Allen and then got his fourth strikeout against former Pirate Dick Stuart. Later Allen would say that night that Veale "was as tough as I've seen."[1]

By the sixth, Veale had amassed 10 strikeouts, and the Pirates had stretched their lead to 4–0 before the frame was over.

With the Bucs now firmly in control, the focus of the game settled on Veale to see how many strikeouts he could accumulate. After fanning pinch hitter Wes Covington in the seventh for his 11th strikeout, Veale's task became simple. To break his own record, he would have to strike out five of the last six Phillies batters, which is precisely what he did.

Following a leadoff single to Rojas to lead off the eighth, Veale mowed down Johnny Callison for the second time and sluggers Allen and Stuart for the third time each. The 10,478 fans who were on hand at Forbes were now going wild at every pitch.

First up in the ninth was Alex Johnson, and Veale quickly made him strike-out victim number 15 to tie the record. He broke it moments later when center fielder Tony Gonzalez struck out swinging to the delight of the Pirates' faithful who had patiently remained in the park through a trio of rain delays. Phila-delphia catcher Gus Triondos avoided extending the record as he grounded out to third to end the game.

It was 12:10 A.M. when the contest finally ended. Veale was jovial, claiming that "it's the first time I ever pitched two days running." But, not surprisingly, the late evening had taken his toll. "I just felt tired, but Jim Pagliaroni kept telling me I wasn't," Veale said.[2] The Pirates' hurler had showed his versatility in striking out nine Phillies on fastballs and seven on curves.

With the performance, he was now getting more notoriety as having one of the best fastballs in the game—maybe the best in the history of the franchise. It was a fastball that allowed Veale to accomplish on that rainy June evening what no other Pirate ever has.

PHI N	0	0	0		0	0	0		0	0	0	—	0	5	1
PIT N	2	0	0		0	0	2		0	0	x	—	4	12	1

BATTING

Philadelphia Phillies	AB	R	H	RBI
Rojas 2b	4	0	2	0
Callison rf	4	0	0	0
Allen 3b	3	0	0	0
Stuart 1b	4	0	0	0
Johnson cf,lf	4	0	1	0
Thomas lf	1	0	0	0
Gonzalez cf	3	0	0	0
Triandos c	4	0	0	0
Amaro ss	2	0	1	0
Mahaffey p	0	0	0	0
Burdette p	2	0	1	0
Covington ph	1	0	0	0
Belinsky p	0	0	0	0
Totals	**32**	**0**	**5**	**0**

FIELDING—DP: 1. Amaro-Rojas-Stuart.
E: Amaro (3).
PB: Triandos (6).
BATTING—GDP: Gonzalez (6,off Veale).
Team LOB: 7.

Pittsburgh Pirates	AB	R	H	RBI
Bailey 3b	4	1	1	0
Virdon cf	4	1	2	0
Stargell rf	3	0	1	1
Lynch lf	3	0	2	1
Mota pr,lf	1	1	0	0
Clendenon 1b	4	0	1	0
Mazeroski 2b	3	1	2	0
Alley 2b	1	0	0	0
Rodgers ss	4	0	2	0
Pagliaroni c	3	0	0	1
Veale p	4	0	1	0
Totals	34	4	12	3

FIELDING—DP: 1. Rodgers-Mazeroski-Clendenon.
E: Clendenon (6).
BATTING—2B: Rodgers (4,off Belinsky).
SF: Stargell (1,off Mahaffey).
GDP: Mazeroski (4,off Burdette).
IBB: Pagliaroni (3,by Belinsky).
Team LOB: 8.

PITCHING

PhiladelphiaPhillies	IP	H	R	ER	BB	SO
MahaffeyL(2–4)	0.1	4	2	2	0	0
Burdette	5.2	6	2	1	0	2
Belinsky	2	2	0	0	1	2
Totals	8	12	4	3	1	4

IBB:Belinsky(2,Pagliaroni).

PittsburghPirates	IP	H	R	ER	BB	SO
VealeW(5–2)	9	5	0	0	2	16

Umpires: HP—Ken Burkhart, 1B—Lee Weyer, 3B—John Kibler
Time of Game: 2:14 Attendance: 10,478

#44

PIRATES 20, ATLANTA BRAVES 10
AUGUST 1, 1970

The Coming-Out Party

Stuck playing in cavernous Forbes Field for the first eight years of his major-league career, the Pirates' Willie Stargell had never been able to unleash his full power-hitting potential, but when Pittsburgh concluded its 61-year run at the legendary ballpark and moved to the friendlier Three Rivers Stadium, a new era for the Bucs' slugger had begun.

Immediately, the new stadium proved to be a good home for Stargell, as he homered in the first game at Three Rivers—the first homer a Pirate would hit in the new stadium. Now that he was playing in this new hitter-friendly facility, Stargell was about to embark on a run of success throughout the 1970s—a run that began at Fulton County Stadium in Atlanta, which was essentially a carbon copy of Three Rivers Stadium.

The Pittsburgh offense started off strong, scoring five runs in the first inning that included an RBI double by Stargell. Atlanta cut the lead to 5–3 in the bottom half of the opening frame, setting the tone for a very wild contest.

The beat went on in the second as Stargell cracked a three-run homer to increase the Pirates' advantage to 9–3. Atlanta never gave up though, as they chipped away at the Pittsburgh lead, making it 10–6 into the seventh. Pittsburgh manager Danny Murtaugh was frustrated with his starters, just as he had been all season. "I'm lucky if I can get five innings out of a pitcher," the Pirates' manager quipped after the game.[1]

As bad as the pitching was, the Pirates' bats once again heated up in the seventh, scoring seven times, including another homer by Stargell to put the game out of reach. Down by 11 runs, the Braves' offense did not give up, scoring four times itself in the bottom of the seventh as the teams combined for a major-league record of five home runs in an inning.

For the Pittsburgh offense, there would be one more onslaught that saw Stargell enter the record book by hitting an RBI double to right, giving him five extra base hits for the game—only the third major leaguer to achieve that feat. Fittingly, Stargell scored the team's 20th run as he came home on a balk.

The box score was full of notable accomplishments for Pittsburgh. Both Bob Robertson and Stargell had five hits, while Pagan finished with four. Every Pirates regular but Gene Alley had a hit, and all but Alley and Dave Cash had multiple hits. The Bucs garnered 22 hits and 47 total bases, while the 20 runs were the most accumulated by a single team at Fulton County Stadium to that point in its brief history.

The most impressive performance belonged to Stargell with his two homers, three doubles, five runs, and six RBIs, marking the beginning of an incredible stretch. He finished the year with 11 more homers, giving him 31 for the year, and went on a phenomenal three-year run, smacking 126 home runs. It was this game in Atlanta that was the catalyst for his incredible decade. Without Forbes Field's distant fences to hide his powerful talent, opponents now had reason to fear Stargell, as much as Braves pitchers did on that Sunday afternoon.

PIT N	5	4	0	0	0	1	7	0	3	—	20	22	2
ATL N	3	1	0	2	0	0	4	0	0	—	10	15	0

BATTING

Pittsburgh Pirates	AB	R	H	RBI
Jeter cf	6	2	2	0
Cash 2b	3	2	1	0
Oliver rf	4	3	2	2
Sanguillen c	6	3	3	3
Robertson 1b	6	4	5	3
Stargell lf	6	5	5	6
Pagan 3b	6	1	4	4
Alley ss	5	0	0	0
Dal Canton p	1	0	0	0
Pena p	3	0	0	0
Giusti p	1	0	0	0
Totals	47	20	22	18

FIELDING—DP: 2. Alley-Cash-Robertson, Pagan-Cash-Robertson.
E: Stargell (4), Pena (3).
BATTING—2B: Stargell 3 (14,off Stone,off Priddy,off McQueen); Pagan 2 (8,off Cardwell 2); Oliver (20,off Priddy); Robertson (10,off McQueen).

3B: Cash (5,off Stone); Jeter 2 (2,off Cardwell,off Priddy).
HR: Stargell 2 (20,2nd inning off Cardwell 2 on 2 out,7th inning off Navarro 0 on 1 out); Robertson (13,7th inning off Navarro 1 on 1 out); Pagan (2,7th inning off Navarro 0 on 1 out).
HBP: Oliver (9,by Stone).
GDP: Oliver (8,off McQueen).
IBB: Alley (5,by Cardwell).
Team LOB: 7.

Atlanta Braves	AB	R	H	RBI
Millan 2b	5	3	3	0
Gonzalez cf	4	3	3	3
H. Aaron rf	4	2	3	5
Aspromonte 3b	1	0	0	0
Carty lf	5	2	2	1
Cepeda 1b	5	0	1	0
King c	4	0	1	0
Boyer 3b	3	0	1	1
McQueen p	0	0	0	0
Garrido ss	4	0	0	0
Stone p	0	0	0	0
Cardwell p	0	0	0	0
Priddy p	3	0	1	0
Navarro p	0	0	0	0
Lum rf	1	0	0	0
Totals	39	10	15	10

FIELDING—DP: 1. Millan-Cepeda-Garrido.
BATTING—2B: Millan (19,off Dal Canton).
HR: H. Aaron 2 (30,1st inning off Dal Canton 1 on 1 out,7th inning off Pena 1 on 0 out); Gonzalez (6,4th inning off Pena 1 on 2 out); Carty (24,7th inning off Pena 0 on 0 out).
SF: Boyer (4,off Dal Canton).
GDP: Garrido (7,off Pena); Boyer (8,off Giusti).
Team LOB: 5.

PITCHING

Pittsburgh Pirates	IP	H	R	ER	BB	SO
Dal Canton	2	5	4	3	2	1
Pena W(1–0)	4	7	6	6	0	2
Giusti SV(18)	3	3	0	0	0	2
Totals	9	15	10	9	2	5

Pena faced 4 batters in the 7th inning

Atlanta Braves	IP	H	R	ER	BB	SO
Stone L(7–8)	0.1	4	5	5	0	0
Cardwell	1.1	6	4	4	2	1
Priddy	4.2	5	4	4	3	2
Navarro	0.2	4	4	4	0	1
McQueen	2	3	3	3	1	2
Totals	9	22	20	20	6	6

WP: McQueen (1).
BK: McQueen (1).
HBP: Stone (6,Oliver).
IBB: Cardwell (3,Alley).
Umpires: HP—Nick Colosi, 1B—Ed Sudol, 2B—Mel Steiner, 3B—Bill Williams
Time of Game: 3:10 **Attendance:** 28,333

PIRATES 12, ST. LOUIS CARDINALS 11
JULY 12, 2008

It Ain't Over Till It's Over

By 2008, it had been 16 years since the Pirates posted a winning record. In that time, Pittsburgh perfected everything that could lead to a poor record—substandard offenses, poor pitching staffs, and questionable decisions by the front office. Just about everything that could lead to a poor record, the Pittsburgh Pirates perfected.

At least from an offensive standpoint, the year 2008 had a different feel as the Pirates' outfield had developed into one of the most potent in the game. Jason Bay had been a dangerous hitter since Pittsburgh acquired him from the Padres in 2003, and he had been joined by Nate McLouth and Xavier Nady, both of whom had been pleasant surprises. McLouth was a 25th-round pick in the 2000 draft and had some success in the minors, but no one could predict the success he would have in 2008. McLouth would hit 26 homers and knock in 94 runs while being selected to his first All-Star game and winning a Gold Glove Award.

Meanwhile, Xavier Nady had begun to live up to the expectations he had as a prospect. After Pittsburgh had traded for him in 2006, he hit 20 homers, and the following year he had put everything together. By mid-July 2008 he'd belted 23 home runs and was hitting .330.

Led by its potent outfield, the Pirates were now hovering around the .500 mark, and there was a real possibility of them posting their first winning record since 1992 when the St. Louis Cardinals came to Pittsburgh for a three-game series.

After the Cardinals silenced the Bucs' bats in the first game of the series 6–0, Pirates manager John Russell sent out heralded prospect Yoslan Herrera for his first major-league start, four years after defecting from Cuba.

Unfortunately for the rookie hurler, his major-league debut was not a memorable one. He struggled through two scoreless innings and then gave up three runs in the third inning to erase an early 3–2 Pirates advantage. "The change was moving a lot, but maybe I threw too many," the young rookie said after the game. Russell concurred, stating, "He's got to use the fastball. He went too soft too soon, and they adjusted."[1]

After St. Louis built a 6–3 lead in the top of the fifth, Russell pulled his rookie starter in favor of relievers T. J. Beam and Sean Burnett. The two hurlers gave up three more runs in the next two innings to increase the Cardinals' advantage to 9–3.

St. Louis maintained its six-run advantage into the eighth, leading 10–4, when Jason Bay hit his second two-run homer of the evening to cut the lead to four. But the Cardinals still carried a comfortable lead into the ninth. After giving up runs to St. Louis in six consecutive innings, Pittsburgh pitchers finally held the Cardinals scoreless in the top half of the frame. The Pirates' relievers kept the Cardinals from adding to their lead, and after the first Pittsburgh batter in the bottom of the ninth was retired, by all appearances, the game was over.

Pinch hitter Jason Michaels coerced a walk from Cardinals reliever Jason Isringhausen, and then Jack Wilson barely beat out an infield hit to put runners on first and second. McLouth continued his breakout season, smacking his 19th home run of the year over the center field fence to cut the St. Louis advantage to a single run at 10–9.

Cardinals manager Tony LaRussa then summoned closer Kyle McClellan from the bullpen to put away the suddenly feisty Pirates club and end the game, but Luis Rivas and catcher Ryan Doumit met the new Cards' reliever with singles to put the tying and winning runs on base. McClellan seemed to get out of the jam when Bay hit into what looked like a perfect double-play grounder. Cards shortstop Cesar Izturis fielded the ball and threw to Aaron Miles at second base for one out, but Miles wasn't able to make the throw to first as Rivas scored, tying the score and sending this once one-sided contest into extra innings.

Not many of the 29,387 fans who came to see this affair were left, but those who did stay were treated to quite a show. At first it seemed like the Pirates' comeback would be for naught when Cardinals slugger Troy Glaus homered in the top of the 10th to put St. Louis up again 11–10.

As defeat once again looked imminent, Pirates catcher Raul Chavez, who came into the game in a double switch in the top of the inning, led off the bottom of the 10th with a single. After Jose Bautista popped up to short, veteran Jason Michaels, whom the Bucs picked up in early May from the Indians, stepped to the plate. Michaels was not having the same success as the other Pirates outfielders, hitting only .242 at the time, but with one swing of the bat he would validate everything that Bay, Nady, and McLouth had done in spearheading the comeback. Michaels sent rookie Chris Perez's 1–0 pitch over the fence, sending the remaining fans in PNC Park into delirium. Michaels later called it the highlight of his career

For one glimmering moment, it appeared that there was a light at the end of the tunnel for this beleaguered franchise. Pirates general manager Neal Huntingdon was convinced, though, his team needed to rebuild its farm system in order to truly compete, so he began to dismantle the newly resurgent Bucs offense. By the end of July, Bay was sent to the Red Sox and Nady was traded to the Yankees. Bautista left a month later in a deal with Toronto. By 2009, LaRoche, McClouth, Wilson, and Freddy Sanchez were gone too. The result was a 17–37 record over the final two months of 2008, and more losing seasons the following four years extended the Bucs' consecutive sub .500 seasons to 20.

Though the future promised more heartbreak, for one night in 2008, this team and the Pirates nation had hope, showcased in one of the most exciting comebacks in the history of the franchise.

STL N	0	0	3		2	1	2		1	1	0		1 —	11	22	0
PIT N	2	0	0		1	0	0		1	2	4		2 —	12	13	0

BATTING

St. Louis Cardinals	AB	R	H	RBI
Miles ss,2b	5	3	2	0
Ludwick lf	5	2	3	4
Pujols 1b	5	1	3	1
Ankiel cf	5	2	2	1
Schumaker cf	1	0	0	0
Glaus 3b	4	2	4	2
Duncan rf	5	0	2	0
Franklin p	0	0	0	0
Villone p	0	0	0	0
Isringhausen p	0	0	0	0
McClellan p	1	0	0	0
Perez p	0	0	0	0
Molina c	6	1	4	1
Wellemeyer p	3	0	0	0
Springer p	0	0	0	0
Mather ph,rf	2	0	1	1
Kennedy 2b	3	0	1	1
Izturis ph,ss	2	0	0	0
Totals	47	11	22	11

BATTING—2B: Ankiel 2 (18,off Herrera,off Beam); Pujols 2 (20,off Herrera,off Beam); Molina (12,off Beam); Miles (9, off Burnett); Mather (2, off Yates).

3B: Ludwick (3, off Herrera).

HR: Ludwick (20, 4th inning off Herrera 1 on 1 out); Glaus (14, 10th inning off D. Bautista 0 on 0 out).

SH: Wellemeyer (7, off Herrera).

SF: Pujols (3, off Herrera).

GDP: Kennedy (9, off Herrera); Molina (14, off Yates).

Team LOB: 12.

Pittsburgh Pirates	AB	R	H	RBI
McLouth cf	4	2	1	3
Rivas 2b	4	2	2	0
Doumit c,1b	5	0	1	0
Bay lf	5	2	2	5
Nady rf	5	0	1	0
D. Bautista p	0	0	0	0
Adam LaRoche 1b	4	2	2	1
R. Chavez c	1	1	1	0
Mientkiewicz 3b	1	0	0	0
J. Bautista 3b	4	0	1	1
Herrera p	1	0	0	0
Osoria p	0	0	0	0
F. Sanchez ph	1	0	0	0
Beam p	0	0	0	0
Burnett p	0	0	0	0
Gomez ph	1	0	0	0
Yates p	0	0	0	0
Marte p	0	0	0	0
Michaels ph,rf	1	2	1	2
Wilson ss	4	1	1	0
Totals	41	12	13	12

FIELDING—DP: 3. Herrera-Doumit-Adam LaRoche, McLouth-Adam LaRoche, Wilson-Rivas-Adam LaRoche.

BATTING—2B: Adam LaRoche (18,off Wellemeyer).

HR: Bay 2 (19,1st inning off Wellemeyer 1 on 2 out, 8th inning off Franklin

1 on 2 out); Adam LaRoche (11,4th inning off Wellemeyer 0 on 2 out); McLouth (19,9th inning off Isringhausen 2 on 1 out); Michaels (4,10th inning off Perez 1 on 1 out).

HBP: Rivas (1, by Wellemeyer).

Team LOB: 4.

PITCHING

St. Louis Cardinals	IP	H	R	ER	BB	SO
Wellemeyer	6.1	4	4	4	1	2
Springer	0.2	0	0	0	0	1
Franklin	0.2	3	2	2	0	1
Villone	0.1	0	0	0	0	1
Isringhausen	0.1	2	3	3	1	1
McClellan	0.2	3	2	2	0	0
Perez L(2–1)	0.1	1	1	1	0	0
Totals	**9.1**	**13**	**12**	**12**	**2**	**6**

McClellan faced 1 batter in the 10th inning

HBP: Wellemeyer (3, Rivas).

Pittsburgh Pirates	IP	H	R	ER	BB	SO
Herrera	4.1	11	6	6	4	4
Osoria	0.2	0	0	0	0	0
Beam	1	4	2	2	0	0
Burnett	1	2	1	1	0	0
Yates	1	3	1	1	0	0
Marte	1	1	0	0	0	0
D. Bautista W(3–1)	1	1	1	1	0	2
Totals	**10**	**22**	**11**	**11**	**4**	**6**

Umpires: HP—Angel Hernandez, 1B—Chad Fairchild, 2B—Eric Cooper, 3B—Marty Foster

Time of Game: 3:39 **Attendance:** 29,387

ALLEGHENIES 6, CHICAGO WHITE STOCKINGS 2
APRIL 30, 1887

The Opening Act

On paper Sam Barkley was a second baseman from Wheeling, West Virginia, who played in only six major-league seasons, the last five of which he hit .248—below the promise he showed in his rookie campaign with Toledo in 1882 when he hit .306 and led the American Association with 39 doubles. But he just may have been the most important player in the history of the Pittsburgh Pirates, for without Barkley there may have been no Pittsburgh Pirates.

The origin of the Pirates' franchise dates back to 1882 when the team began play in the American Association as the Alleghenies. The team went through four mediocre seasons before it finally tasted some success in 1886, finishing second with an impressive 80–57 mark.

Instead of celebration, the season was defined by anger in the front office. The president of the club, William Nimick, and fellow owner Denny McKnight were angry with the American Association over a controversy surrounding the signing of Barkley before the 1886 campaign started.

It began when St. Louis owner Chris Von der Ahe offered Barkley to the first team that was willing to pay Von der Ahe $1,000 for his contract. Baltimore sent the money to Von der Ahe, but in the meantime Pittsburgh signed Barkley.

McKnight had also doubled as president of the American Association and ruled (in what proved to be a clear conflict of interest) that Barkley belonged to Pittsburgh. The case was appealed by Baltimore, and the league decided to fine Barkley $1,000 and suspend him for the season before allowing him to play with the Alleghenies. An angry McKnight refused to tell Barkley. When the second baseman found out, he took the case to court and settled on a $500 fine with no suspension.

After the case was settled, the league fired McKnight. He and Nimick were so incensed over the situation that when a spot opened up in the National League after Kansas City folded, Nimick and McKnight pounced on the opportunity. As a result Pittsburgh became the first franchise to ever shift from the American Association to the National League. It turned out to be a good move for the league as well since it wanted a franchise closer to New York, Boston, and Philadelphia. Pittsburgh fit the bill.

The American Association folded five years later. Had Pittsburgh's owners not been so angered over the Barkley situation, the team likely would have folded with the dying league, and the Pittsburgh Pirates may have never been. Luckily for all Pittsburgh baseball fans, the move was made, and the team commemorated the transition by playing its first game in its new circuit against the defending champion Chicago White Stockings.

Fittingly, it was a festive atmosphere before the contest. A parade ran through the streets on the way to Recreation Park on the north side of the city. As the huge crowd rolled into the wooden facility, the Great Western Band offered an on-field concert. The park had an original capacity of 2,000 fans, but 10,000 showed up for this historic contest and packed every nook and cranny. Thousands filled the park's deep outfield with only a rope separating them from the players.

The large throng would get to see the best team in baseball. Since Chicago had entered the league in 1876, it had won six National League crowns, including two straight and five of the last six. It had stars such as pitcher John Clarkson, who would win 38 games in 1887 and start in this opening game, and the legendary Cap Anson, arguably the greatest player of the nineteenth century.

Facing Clarkson would be the Alleghenies' thirty-year-old hurler Pud Galvin. Galvin only got the start on this day as a last-minute replacement for the younger Ed Morris, who complained of a sore arm just before game time. With the pitching change, manager Horace Phillips also flipped catchers as he put Doggie Miller into the game for Fred Carroll, the man who was famous for having a monkey as a constant companion. When the monkey died in 1887, Carroll had him buried at Recreation Park, below home plate, as part of a pregame ceremony.

Pittsburgh got off to an auspicious beginning as left fielder Abner Dalrymple tripled in the first official National League at bat for the Pittsburgh franchise. He then came home with the team's initial run when the throw from the outfield went awry, and just like that, the Alleghenies led 1–0. Soon after, catcher Doggie Miller walked, went to second on a passed ball, then went to third, and came home on a bad throw.

In the second, the Alleghenies padded their lead when first baseman Alex

McKinnon got his first of four hits of the day, then came home via a triple by third baseman Art Whitney to increase Pittsburgh's advantage to 3–0. Two innings later, McKinnon slashed an RBI triple, then scored himself on a single by Whitney.

After the White Stockings finally broke through with a run in the seventh, Pittsburgh pushed the lead back to five in the eighth when McKinnon completed his fabulous day with an RBI double.

The White Stockings tacked on another run in the ninth, but it was too little too late. Pittsburgh had defeated the defending champions 6–2 in what proved to be the highlight of an otherwise forgettable season that ended with a sixth-place finish and a 55–69 record.

Ironically, Barkley—the impetus for the move—was hitless in four at bats in the opener and went on to hit a paltry .224 in 1887. After the season, he wound up back in the American Association and was purchased by the Kansas City Cowboys.

While it may be hard to justify moving to another league for such an unspectacular player, it was because of Sam Barkley that Pittsburgh was able to secure major-league baseball in the city for more than a century.

CHI N	0	0	0	0	0	0	1	0	1	—	2	9	3
PIT N	2	1	0	2	0	0	1	0	0	—	6	12	0

BATTING

Chicago White Stockings	AB	R	H	RBI
Sunday cf	4	0	1	0
Ryan lf	4	0	1	0
Sullivan rf	4	1	1	0
Anson 1b	4	1	2	0
Pfeffer 2b	4	0	2	0
Williamson ss	4	0	0	0
Burns 3b	4	0	2	0
Daly c	3	0	0	0
Clarkson p	3	0	0	0
Totals	34	2	9	0

FIELDING—E: Sunday, Pfeffer, and Daly.
PB: Daly, 2
BATTING—SH: Burns
2B: Pfeffer, 2, Ryan and Anson
3B: Sullivan
Team LOB: 4.

Pittsburgh Alleghenies	AB	R	H	RBI
Dalrymple lf	5	1	1	0
Brown cf	4	0	1	0
Miller c	4	2	1	0
Barkley 2b	4	0	0	0
Coleman rf	3	1	0	0
McKinnon 1b	4	2	4	2
Whitney 3b	4	0	2	2
Smith ss	4	0	1	0
Galvin p	4	0	2	0
Totals	36	6	12	4

BATTING—SH: Miller
2B: McKinnon
3B: McKinnon, Dalrymple, and Whitney
Team LOB: 4.

PITCHING

Chicago White Stockings	IP	H	R	ER	BB	SO
Clarkson L(0–1)	9	12	6	4	2	5

Pittsburgh Alleghenies	IP	H	R	ER	BB	SO
Galvin W(1–0)	9	9	2	2	1	1

Umpires: Quest

#41

The Mentor and the Prodigy

A young slugger destined for greatness and an aging veteran, one of the greatest power hitters the game had ever seen, came together for one season in 1947.

The young star was Ralph Kiner, a second-year player who'd won the first of what would become seven National League home run crowns in his rookie campaign of 1946, but he'd hit only .247 and the front office felt he was in need of a little polishing. Enter aging superstar Hank Greenberg who'd played 12 Hall of Fame seasons with the Detroit Tigers. His career had already provided some of the greatest numbers in the game's history, even though he'd spent four of his prime years serving his country in World War II.

After the war, Greenberg picked up where he left off, leading the American League in homers with 44 in 1946. But he became embroiled in a contract dispute, and the Tigers angrily sold him to Pittsburgh for $75,000. Reflecting the bitterness of the negotiations, Greenberg heard about the move on the radio, as the Detroit front office didn't tell him personally.

Greenberg was frustrated and contemplated retirement, but the Pirates needed a tutor for Kiner as well as a player who could draw fans into the ballpark. To entice him to come to Pittsburgh, the Pirates not only moved the distant left field fence in 30 feet to 335 feet, creating a bullpen area in front of the wall that became known as Greenberg Gardens, but Pittsburgh also offered to make Greenberg the National League's first $100,000 player. It was too much for the 36-year-old veteran to turn down, so the Bucs got their mentor and a new gate attraction.

Kiner was eager to pick Greenberg's brain for advice on hitting, and Greenberg immediately embraced his new role helping Kiner. The young slugger remembered their first meeting and subsequent relationship quite fondly. "The first day of spring training, all the players had left the field and [Greenberg] said to me 'Hey kid, do you want to stay over and take some extra batting practice?'" Kiner said. "Of course I was impressed with his background and record and said yes. The first thing he said to me was 'You'll never hit a lot of home runs the way you're hitting.' I thought he was putting me on, but he was serious."[1]

Greenberg left Kiner's powerful swing alone, instead opting to teach him a new approach to hitting, showing him how to take the proper pitches as well as changing his position in the batter's box. After an extremely slow start in which Kiner hit only three homers by the beginning of June, the results proved to be astounding. By July 25, Kiner had topped his rookie season, hitting two that day to bring his total to 25. Almost a month later on August 16, he was up to 32 and on an incredible hot streak after smacking a pair against the Cards the day before and hitting four in three days.

On this day, the pennant-contending Cardinals got off to a fast start in front of a meager crowd of 6,435 at Forbes Field. Following a 50-minute rain delay at the beginning of the contest, St. Louis crushed Bucs starter Roger Wolff for four runs in the top of the first.

The St. Louis advantage would not last long as the Bucs quickly stormed back. Greenberg hit a three-run shot with Kiner on board via a walk; then shortstop Billy Cox hit his 10th home run of the campaign to tie the contest. In the third, Kiner and Greenberg hit back-to-back home runs to give Pittsburgh a 6–4 lead. Fittingly, Kiner's homer hit the base of the light tower in Greenberg Gardens.

St. Louis crept back to within one in the fourth, but Kiner blasted a three-run shot high over the large left field scoreboard into Schenley Park, increasing the Bucs' advantage to four. Cox followed with his second of the day, a two-run shot, making it now 11–5.

In the bottom half of the fifth, Kiner also sent his 35th of the year into Schenley Park, marking the Bucs' seventh long ball of the day and the young slugger's fourth homer in four at bats, the first coming the day before.

Besides hitting four home runs in consecutive at bats, Kiner also set three other major-league records that included five homers in two games, six in three contests, and seven long balls in four games.

As a team, the Pirates equaled their own National League mark for homers in a game with seven, which was originally set in 1894 and tied by five other teams. The 10 homers by both clubs also tied a major-league mark for combined long balls in a game.

Following the contest, Kiner and Greenberg, who both hit multiple homers on this memorable day, went in different directions. Kiner became the sixth player ever to eclipse 50 home runs in a season, tying Johnny Mize for the crown with 51. Greenberg, however, only connected twice more in 1947, finishing with 25. The man whom Kiner said knew more about hitting than anyone, including Ted Williams, retired the following year.

Even though his tenure in the Steel City lasted only one season, Greenberg's time in Pittsburgh not only helped the Pirates' young superstar reach his potential but also aided the team financially. His presence helped the Bucs brake the one-million mark in attendance for the first time ever, drawing 1,283,521 fans, despite their seventh-place finish.

Both players eventually were enshrined in the Hall of Fame, but probably the biggest honor for Kiner came after his mentor left the game. It was a passing of the torch, best symbolized by the fact the left field home run area, or Greenberg Gardens, was eventually renamed Kiner's Korner.

STL N	4	0	0		1	1	0		0	1	0	—	7	9	0
PIT N	4	0	2		5	0	0		0	1	x	—	12	16	1

BATTING

St. Louis Cardinals	AB	R	H	RBI
Schoendienst 2b	5	1	2	0
Moore cf	4	1	2	1
Musial 1b	5	1	1	1
Slaughter lf	4	0	1	0
Northey rf	3	1	0	0
Kurowski 3b	4	3	2	4
Marion ss	4	0	0	0
Garagiola c	4	0	1	1
Burkhart p	1	0	0	0
Wilks p	1	0	0	0
Brazle p	1	0	0	0
Medwick ph	1	0	0	0
Grodzick ip	0	0	0	0
Totals	37	7	9	7

FIELDING—DP: 3. Brazle-Musial, Marion-Schoendienst-Musial, Kurowski-Schoendienst.

BATTING—2B: Slaughter (24).

3B: Schoendienst (8); Musial (8); Garagiola (2).

HR: Moore (5,1st inning off Wolff 0 on); Kurowski 2 (19,1st inning off Wolff 1 on, 5th inning off Bagby 0 on).

Team LOB: 5.

Pittsburgh Pirates	AB	R	H	RBI
Rikard rf	5	1	2	0
Russell cf	4	1	1	0
Gustine 3b	5	1	1	0
Kiner lf	3	4	3	5
Greenberg 1b	2	3	2	4
Cox ss	5	2	3	3
Bloodworth 2b	5	0	2	0
Howell c	3	0	1	0
Wolff p	0	0	0	0
Bagby p	2	0	1	0
Totals	34	12	16	12

FIELDING—E: Cox (14).
BATTING—2B: Bloodworth (4); Howell (8).
HR: Kiner 3 (35, 3rd inning off Burkhart 0 on, 4th inning off Wilks 2 on, 8th inning off Grodzicki 0 on); Greenberg 2 (23,1st inning off Burkhart 2 on, 3rd inning off Burkhart 0 on); Cox 2 (11,1st inning off Burkhart 0 on, 4th inning off Wilks 1 on).
SH: Bagby (2).
HBP: Bagby (1).
GDP: Gustine (9); Bloodworth (4).
Team LOB: 8.

PITCHING

St. Louis Cardinals	IP	H	R	ER	BB	SO	HR
Burkhart L(3–5)	2.1	6	6	6	2	0	
Wilks	1	5	5	5	2	0	
Brazle	3.2	3	0	0	3	2	
Grodzicki	1	2	1	1	1	0	
Totals	8	16	12	12	8	2	

HBP: Brazle (2).

Pittsburgh Pirates	IP	H	R	ER	BB	SO
Wolff	0.2	3	4	4	1	0
BagbyW(4–3)	8.1	6	3	2	1	2
Totals	9	9	7	6	2	2

Umpires: HP—Babe Pinelli, 1B—Al Barlick
Time of Game: 2:09 Attendance: 6,435

PIRATES 4, CHICAGO CUBS 1
JUNE 28, 1970

Bringing the Curtain Down on Forbes

When it came to ballparks, Pittsburgh entered the modern era in 1909. In that period, parks were constructed of wood and consequently were often destroyed by fire. Pittsburgh had to prepare for another threat—that of a flood.

There had been three versions of Exposition Park; this one—the third and final version—had been the home of the Pirates since 1891. It was located between where PNC Park and Heinz Field currently stand, right on the banks of the Ohio River. After heavy rains, the river often overflowed into the outfield. On July 4, 1902, more than a foot of water stood in the Exposition Park outfield, but the Bucs decided to play their scheduled doubleheader against Brooklyn that day anyway. The club improvised a special ground rule that all balls hit into the flooded area would be singles.

Fed up with constantly dealing with water on the field, Pirates owner Barney Dreyfuss decided to move inland to the Oakland section of the city where flooding was not a threat. He also decided his stadium would be first-class all the way. Instead of wood, it was to built out of concrete and steel, the first of its kind in the National League. Dreyfuss would call his new baseball palace Forbes Field, after the French and Indian War hero John Forbes.

On June 30, 1909, Dreyfuss opened his fabulous new ballpark before a jam-packed crowd of 30,338. The reviews were universally positive. "It was impossible to properly describe Forbes Field," *The Sporting News* explained. "It requires a personal visit to permit one to understand just how big and magnificent it is."[1]

"Magnificent" also described the park's inaugural season. The Pirates won their first World Series championship in 1909 and went on to win two more while playing in the legendary facility. During its tenure, Forbes Field played host not only to the Pirates but also to the Negro League's Homestead Grays as well as football games for Duquesne University, Carnegie Tech, the University of Pittsburgh, and the Steelers. It also was the site of several boxing events, the most notable being the Jersey Joe Walcott and Ezzard Charles World Heavyweight Championship bout on July 18, 1951, in which the 37-year-old Walcott upset the younger Charles with a memorable seventh-round knockout.

By the end of the 1960s, Forbes Field was starting to decay and become outdated. Many seats had obstructed views and were uncomfortable, and the park often emitted several foul odors.

Like Forbes Field was in 1909, its replacement symbolized a new era for ballparks. Three Rivers Stadium was a multipurpose stadium that would comfortably house both the Pirates and Steelers until 2000.

As the 1970 campaign began, Three Rivers Stadium had yet to be completed, so Forbes Field remained the home of the Pittsburgh Pirates for the first three months of the season. The plan was to close Forbes Field with a three-game series in late June against the Cubs, whom the Pirates were fighting for the NL East Division lead.

The series opener saw the Bucs win in the bottom of the ninth, 2–1, on a single by Al Oliver that knocked in Richie Hebner. The next day would be a doubleheader, the last two games played at Forbes Field.

In the first game of the twin bill, Chicago reliever Phil Regan walked catcher Jerry May with the bases loaded in the bottom of the eighth to give Pittsburgh a 3–2 win. The victory put the Bucs within a game of first place as they prepared for the second game of the twin bill with 40,918 fans jammed into every nook and cranny of the place.

While this would be the final game ever played at Forbes Field, manager Danny Murtaugh would make a couple of surprising moves for the historic event. He decided to start a rookie pitcher by the name of Jim Nelson who had been with the team for less than a month. More unexpectedly, he benched right fielder Roberto Clemente, choosing to rest his superstar in favor of Al Oliver.

Things did not begin on a positive note for Nelson, as the Cubs led off the game with three straight singles to take a 1–0 lead. Murtaugh called for reliever Orlando Pena to warm up in the bullpen just in case things got out of hand. But Nelson was able to get Chicago slugger Jim Hickman to ground into a double play with the lead runner getting tagged out at home and escaping the frame down only one run.

Oliver, who had delivered the game-winning hit the day before, came through again as he tied the game in the bottom of the first with his sixth homer of the year.

Following his shaky start, Nelson was now firmly in control as the game entered the fifth inning; then Pittsburgh added to its lead in the bottom half of the frame. Thanks to an intentional walk and a Cubs error, the Pirates loaded the bases for Matty Alou. Alou knocked in two runs with a two-out single to put Pittsburgh up 3–1.

They added to the advantage in the sixth when the hot-hitting Oliver smacked a leadoff double and came home to score the final run ever at Forbes Field on a sacrifice fly by Bob Robertson. It remained 4–1 through the last three innings when, with two outs in the top of the ninth, Don Kessinger hit a grounder to Mazeroski at second, as the man who hit the most memorable home run in the history of Forbes Field stepped on the base at second to force out Willie Smith and end an amazing era in Pittsburgh history.

Fans poured on to the field to grab any memento they could. "It was like watching a wave of termites descend on a Stradivarius or Attila the Hun loosened on a Sunday school picnic," Phil Musick wrote. "First they dismantled the scoreboard until nothing remained but holes. Then they tore down the ivy, leaving occasional strands hanging on the walls like a grotesque caricature."[2]

Ironically, three decades later, it became in vogue for teams to build ballparks in the style of the older parks. The antiseptic design of stadiums like Three Rivers became outdated, so the new facilities were designed with a nod to Forbes Field and other classic parks. PNC Park, which the Pirates opened in 2001, connects the franchise's future to its past.

CHI N	1	0	0	0	0	0	0	0	0	—	1	7	1
PIT N	1	0	0	0	2	1	0	0	x	—	4	5	0

BATTING

Chicago Cubs	AB	R	H	RBI
Kessinger ss	5	1	2	0
Popovich 2b	3	0	1	0
Williams lf	4	0	3	1
Hickman 1b	3	0	0	0
Santo 3b	3	0	0	0
Callison rf	3	0	0	0
James cf	3	0	0	0
Martin c	3	0	0	0
Pappa sp	2	0	0	0
Beckert ph	1	0	0	0
Gura p	0	0	0	0
Smith ph	1	0	1	0
Totals	31	1	7	1

FIELDING—**E:** Hickman (7).
BATTING—2B: Williams (15, off Nelson).
HBP: James (3, by Nelson).
GDP: Santo (5, off Nelson); Hickman (3, off Nelson).
IBB: Hickman (4, by Nelson).
Team LOB: 9.

Pittsburgh Pirates	AB	R	H	RBI
Alou cf	4	0	1	2
Hebner 3b	4	0	0	0
Oliver rf	4	2	2	1
Stargell lf	4	0	0	0
Giusti p	0	0	0	0
Robertson 1b	2	1	1	1
Alley ss	3	0	0	0
J. May c	3	0	0	0
Mazeroski 2b	2	1	1	0
Nelson p	3	0	0	0
Jeter lf	0	0	0	0
Totals	**29**	**4**	**5**	**4**

FIELDING—DP: 3. Hebner-Mazeroski-J. May-Hebner, Alley-Mazeroski-Robertson, Alley-Mazeroski-Robertson.
BATTING—2B: Oliver (12, off Pappas); Mazeroski (9, off Gura).
HR: Oliver (6, 1st inning off Pappas 0 on 2 out).
SF: Robertson (1, off Pappas).
IBB: Mazeroski (5, by Pappas).
Team LOB: 3.
BASERUNNING—SB: Robertson (3, 2nd base off Pappas/Martin).

PITCHING

Chicago Cubs	IP	H	R	ER	BB	SO
Pappas L(2–3)	6	4	4	2	1	4
Gura	2	1	0	0	0	1
Totals	8	5	4	2	1	5

IBB: Pappas (2, Mazeroski).

Pittsburgh Pirates	IP	H	R	ER	BB	SO
Nelson W(3–0)	8	6	1	1	5	2
Giusti SV(11)	1	1	0	0	0	0
Totals	9	7	1	1	5	2

HBP: Nelson (1, James).
IBB: Nelson (3, Hickman).
Umpires: HP—Ed Vargo, 1B—Paul Pryor, 2B—Dick Stello, 3B—Al Barlick
Time of Game: 2:14 **Attendance:** 40,918

#39

PIRATES 4, NEW YORK METS 2
SEPTEMBER 27, 1992

The Last Title

It had been quite a ride for the Pittsburgh Pirates over the previous 12 seasons. After eight years of decay following the world championship in 1979, manager Jim Leyland and general manager Syd Thrift had put together a powerful squad that in 1990 and 1991 had come so close to a spot in the World Series.

A third consecutive Eastern Division crown was within reach as the Bucs met their division rivals from New York on the final Sunday in September. This impending playoff berth had a different feel to it though. The economic reality of baseball had begun to change. Small markets like Pittsburgh could no longer retain all their talent from year to year. They would have to pick and choose whom to keep and hope they would avoid colossal mistakes that could cripple the franchise for years.

For the Pirates in 1992, the change had already begun as five key members of the back-to-back Eastern Division champions had left, led by Bobby Bonilla, while two of their remaining stars, Doug Drabek and Barry Bonds, would be free agents after the season. Despite the departures, manager Jim Leyland directed his team brilliantly and dominated the competition in the National League East.

Certainly this wasn't the same outfit it had been the previous two years, but as the Pirates came into this series with the Mets, they had a comfortable seven-game lead over the Montreal Expos with just over a week to go. A sweep over the Mets in this series would mean they would have a chance to clinch the division in front of their home fans.

In the first game, pitcher Randy Tomlin won his 14th game of the year, shutting down the Mets in a 3–2 victory. The following night, Pittsburgh hitters combined for 20 hits in a 19–2 lopsided victory over New York. One win away from the postseason, Leyland sent veteran Danny Jackson to the mound to clinch the division.

The Pirates got on the board first in the bottom of the first inning when Barry Bonds—who had been picking up the offensive slack for the team all year in 1992 and who would be named the National League MVP—drove in a run on a sacrifice fly.

As Jackson made Leyland look like a genius by dominating the New York hitters, Pittsburgh added two more runs in the third and one in the fifth to extend their lead to 4–0. It was more than enough support for Jackson. The 30-year-old San Antonio native was dominant, giving up only six hits and one run over seven innings of work before giving way to Danny Cox, who pitched a perfect eighth. Leyland then called on Stan Belinda to close it out.

Vince Coleman delayed the celebration with a single and a stolen base. Coleman scored on a groundout to cut the Pirates' lead to two, but that's as far as the Mets would get.

Belinda then struck out Jeff McKnight to end the game and give Pittsburgh its third consecutive championship. "I was a little nervous in the bullpen, but when I got to the mound it was pure adrenaline," the reliever admitted. "I felt like a big piece of butter melting in a hot frying pan when I saw his hand go up [the umpire's hand signaling strike three]. It is without a doubt the biggest thrill of my career."[1]

For Leyland, it was the most special of the team's trio of division titles. "The first will always have a place in my heart because it was the first," he said. "The second was special because nobody had repeated for so long. But this one is the most satisfying because nobody gave us a chance without Bonilla and Smiley. The club refused to give in to the fact that a lot of people didn't believe in them." Holding back tears he added, "Those people underestimated the talent we have on this team."[2]

It truly was an emotional evening that the team and the 31,217 fans enjoyed to the fullest, knowing that with the likely defections of Bonds and Drabek, this would probably be their last chance to enjoy a title. As it turned out, their worst fears would come to fruition. The Pirates suffered a heart-crushing loss to the Braves in Game Seven of the 1992 National League Championship Series. And over the next two decades there would be no championships or even winning records. For one evening, though, they didn't have to think about the future. They had shocked the baseball world, overcoming quite a few obstructions on the way to the ninth division title in the club's history.

NY N	0	0	0	0	0	1	0	0	1	—	2	7	0
PIT N	1	0	2	0	1	0	0	0	x	—	4	7	0

BATTING

New York Mets	AB	R	H	RBI
Thompson cf	4	0	1	0
Gallagher rf	3	1	1	0
Sasser ph,1b	1	0	0	0
Walker 3b	3	0	0	0
Murray 1b	3	0	2	1
Dozier pr	0	0	0	0
Jones p	0	0	0	0
Bass lf	4	0	1	0
Pecota ss	3	0	0	0
Coleman ph	1	1	1	0
Kent 2b	3	0	0	0
Boston ph	1	0	0	0
Hundley c	4	0	0	1
Schourek p	2	0	0	0
McKnight ph,rf	2	0	1	0
Totals	**34**	**2**	**7**	**2**

BATTING—2B: Gallagher (9,off Jackson).
Team LOB: 7.
BASERUNNING—SB: Coleman (23,2nd base off Belinda/Slaught).

Pittsburgh Pirates	AB	R	H	RBI
Redus 1b	4	2	2	0
Bell ss	3	1	2	2
Van Slyke cf	4	0	1	0
Bonds lf	2	0	0	1
King 3b	4	0	1	1
McClendon rf	3	0	0	0
Espy ph,rf	1	0	0	0
Slaught c	4	0	0	0
Lind 2b	3	0	1	0
Jackson p	1	1	0	0
Cox p	0	0	0	0
Belinda p	0	0	0	0
Totals	**29**	**4**	**7**	**4**

FIELDING—PB: Slaught (6).
BATTING—2B: Redus (7,off Schourek).
SH: Jackson (9,off Schourek).
SF: Bonds (7,off Schourek).
Team LOB: 6.

PITCHING

New York Mets	IP	H	R	ER	BB	SO
Schourek L(5–8)	7	7	4	4	3	3
Jones	1	0	0	0	0	3
Totals	8	7	4	4	3	6

BK: Schourek (2).

Pittsburgh Pirates	IP	H	R	ER	BB	SO
Jackson W(8–12)	7	6	1	1	1	3
Cox	1	0	0	0	1	1
Belinda SV(17)	1	1	1	1	0	1
Totals	9	7	2	2	2	5

Jackson faced 2 batters in the 8th inning
Umpires: HP—Harry Wendelstedt, 1B—Rich Rieker, 2B—Dana DeMuth, 3B—Gary Darling
Time of Game: 2:34 **Attendance:** 31,217

PIRATES 3, BOSTON BRAVES 0
MAY 6, 1951

For One Day

The baseball record books are littered with players who have had less-than-stellar careers. Under ordinary circumstances, they could never stand among the game's greatest names, but for one magnificent day, they were able to lift themselves to heights they never achieved before and never would again. The Pittsburgh Pirates produced one of these unheralded players, a left-handed hurler named Cliff Chambers who for one day was one of the best there was.

A graduate of Washington State University, Chambers was signed by the Chicago Cubs in 1942 and spent his first year in the minors splitting time between the Los Angeles Angels of the Pacific Coast League and the Tulsa Oilers of the Texas League. He joined the Air Force following the season and didn't return to professional baseball until 1946.

After the war the southpaw returned to Los Angeles. While there in 1947, Chambers had his best season as a professional with a 24–9 mark, which earned him a call-up to the Cubs a year later. He was traded to the Pirates following the season and pitched well for the Bucs in 1949, going 13–7 for a team that had a .461 winning percentage.

He was less impressive in 1950 and came into this game on May 6, 1951, with a 2–2 record. Few would have predicted that by day's end he would pitch the second no-hitter in Pittsburgh Pirates history.

It was a Sunday afternoon doubleheader at Braves Field in Boston, and things would not begin well for the visitors in the opener. Future Hall of Famer Warren Spahn shut out Pittsburgh on eight hits in a Braves 6–0 victory.

It looked like things would get worse for the Bucs in the second game as Chambers was unsure he would be able to pitch. He spent the first game resting in the locker room suffering with the flu and trying to decide whether he could play. "I figured I would come to the ballpark and see how I felt," Chambers said after the game. "I sat in the clubhouse during the first game, and didn't feel so badly after all."[1]

His teammates gave him all the support he would need in the top of the first when center fielder George Metkovich smacked a double into center and Gus Bell immediately knocked him in with a single, giving the Pirates an early 1–0 lead.

Chambers strolled to the mound in the bottom half of the frame and immediately walked leadoff hitter Roy Hartsfield but stranded the second baseman as he struck out two of the next three batters. The Pirates' pitcher wiggled out of another jam two innings later, once again walking the leadoff batter, but Chambers proceeded to strike out Hartsfield and got Sam Jethroe to fly out to Bell in right to end the threat.

With one out in the fifth inning, Chambers almost lost his date with history. Boston left fielder Luis Olmo hit a chopper toward the Bucs' pitcher that looked like it might head into center for Boston's first hit of the contest, but Chambers made a great play to snag the ball and throw out Olmo.

The Pirates added an insurance run in the sixth when the Braves' hurler walked in a run to give Pittsburgh a 2–0 lead; although hitless, Boston threatened to score in the bottom half of the inning. Chambers then walked Estock, the Braves' pitcher who went to second on a wild pitch and then to third on a sacrifice with one out. After stranding Estock on third with a ground ball out, Chambers walked another Braves hitter with slugger Bob Elliott strolling to the plate. He retired Elliott on a long fly to right field, keeping his chances for history alive.

In the top of the eighth Chambers helped his own cause with an RBI single but continued to suffer with his control in the bottom of the inning, walking his seventh and eighth batters of the contest. But once again the lefty came through in the clutch, retiring Elliott on a pop-up to the catcher Ed Fitz Gerald.

Now only three outs away from history, Chambers was at his best in the ninth. Sid Gordon grounded out to George Strickland at short for the first out. Catcher Walker Cooper then rifled a Chambers fastball deep to left center that ended up in George Metkovich's glove for out number two. The southpaw then tossed a curveball that Olmo popped up harmlessly to center where Metkovich gloved it to secure the final out and Chambers's place in history. He became the first Pirate in 44 years—the first since Nick Maddox tossed a gem in 1907—to throw a no-hitter.

While Chambers was elated, not all his teammates were impressed with his eight-walk performance. Ralph Kiner called it as ugly a no-hitter as he had ever seen (although it was in fact the only no-hitter Kiner ever participated in). "I don't think there was anything ugly about it at all except that I walked eight," Chambers would later recall. "I was a hard-throwing left-hander and had very good stuff that day. There wasn't anything close to a base hit off me."

Fitz Gerald, who caught the gem, agreed. "He had a real good fastball today," the catcher said afterward. "Sure he was wild, but when he needed that little extra on his fastball, boy, he had it."[2]

Despite the fact that his gem was flawed and far from perfect, it still was a no-hitter. Consequently, Cliff Chambers stands today next to such legendary hurlers as Nolan Ryan, Tom Seaver, and Sandy Koufax. His name may not evoke the same respect as the more famous pitchers in this elite club, but for one Sunday afternoon in Boston, Cliff Chambers could say he was just as good.

PIT N	1	0	0	0	0	1	0	1	0	—	3	9	0
BOS N	0	0	0	0	0	0	0	0	0	—	0	0	1

BATTING

Pittsburgh Pirates	AB	R	H	RBI
Dillinger 3b	5	0	1	0
Metkovich cf	4	2	3	0
Bell rf	4	0	1	1
Kiner 1b	5	0	1	0
Westlake lf	4	1	0	0
Strickland ss	2	0	0	0
Basgall 2b	3	0	1	1
Fitz Gerald c	4	0	1	0
Chamber sp	4	0	1	1
Totals	35	3	9	3

FIELDING—DP: 1. Basgall-Kiner.
BATTING—2B: Metkovich 2 (7,off Estock 2); Kiner (3,off Nichols).
SH: Strickland (2,off Estock).
GDP: Dillinger (4,off Estock).
Team LOB: 11.
BASERUNNING—SB: Bell (1,2nd base off Estock/Cooper).

Boston Braves	AB	R	H	RBI
Hartsfield 2b	1	0	0	0
Jethroe cf	4	0	0	0
Torgeson 1b	1	0	0	0
Elliott 3b	4	0	0	0
Gordon rf	3	0	0	0
Cooper c	4	0	0	0
Olmo lf	4	0	0	0
Kerr ss	2	0	0	0
Estock p	0	0	0	0
Marquez ph	1	0	0	0
Nichols p	0	0	0	0
Totals	24	0	0	0

FIELDING—DP: 1. Elliott-Hartsfield-Torgeson.
E: Estock (1).
BATTING—SH: Estock (1,off Chambers); Hartsfield (1,off Chambers).
GDP: Elliott (4,off Chambers).
Team LOB: 7.

PITCHING

Pittsburgh Pirates	IP	H	R	ER	BB	SO
Chambers W(3–2)	9	0	0	0	8	4

WP: Chambers (2).

Boston Braves	IP	H	R	ER	BB	SO
Estock L(0–1)	8	8	3	3	5	2
Nichols	1	1	0	0	0	0
Totals	9	9	3	3	5	2

Umpires: HP—Frank Dascoli, 1B—Larry Goetz, 3B—Lou Jorda
Time of Game: 2:01 Attendance: 15,492

PIRATES 12, PHILADELPHIA PHILLIES 8
AUGUST 5, 1979

Grand Slam Celebration

Webster defines the art of pinch-hitting as "[batting] in the place of another player especially when a hit is particularly needed." It sounds simple, but it's much easier said than done. A pinch hitter's task can be incredibly difficult, coming off the bench cold in a crucial situation when the game is on the line.

The vast majority of pinch hitters who come in to win a game end in failure. When successful, especially when the games count the most, the pinch hitter can etch his name in the minds of a team's fans forever. Such is the case of John Milner who, on a summer afternoon in 1979, made himself a hero with his pinch-hit heroics in the heat of the pennant race.

The Bucs were facing the three-time defending Eastern Division champion Philadelphia Phillies in a doubleheader and were in the midst of a three-way tussle for the 1979 crown with Montreal and Chicago. The Phillies were a distant fourth, but a sweep of the Pirates would vault them back into contention.

It appeared that the first game would be a pitching duel between two future Hall of Famers—Steve Carlton and Pittsburgh's Bert Blyleven. What should have been a low-scoring affair quickly turned into an offensive showcase.

After the Phillies took an early 2–0 lead, the Bucs made their first comeback in what would become a thrilling contest. An error opened the door for a two-run single by Omar Moreno, and then in the third another Phillies defensive miscue gave the Bucs their third run.

The Pittsburgh lead was short-lived as the Phillies exploded for six runs off Blyleven and reliever Joe Coleman in the fifth. Greg Luzinski led the outbreak with a grand slam to give Philadelphia an 8–3 lead. The defending champs were suddenly alive and well and seemingly gave Carlton more than enough support to seal the victory.

Throughout 1979, things had been different for the Pirates. With their new-found confidence they felt like there was no deficit they couldn't overcome.

Pittsburgh immediately roared back in the bottom of the inning. Following an RBI single by first baseman Bill Robinson, left fielder Lee Lacy ripped a two-run homer to make the score 8–6. An inning later catcher Steve Nicosia smacked a homer off Carlton, cutting the once insurmountable lead to a single run.

While the Phillies' pitching and defense were falling apart, the Bucs' under-rated bullpen was now in control. Coleman, Enrique Romo, and Kent Tekulve completely shut down the Phils' potent attack, yielding only three hits and one run in five innings of work.

Philadelphia's bullpen was not enjoying the same success, as it allowed Pittsburgh to tie the score in the eighth on another clutch hit, this time a single by Tim Foli.

After Tekulve set down the Phillies in order following a leadoff single by McBride, Pittsburgh would have its chance to win the game in the bottom of the ninth.

The game looked destined for extra innings when Phillies reliever Rawly Eastwick retired the first two Pirates batters. Lacy kept their hopes alive with a single before stealing second. Philadelphia then intentionally walked Bill Madlock and loaded the bases when second baseman Phil Garner walked on a 3–2 count. The table was now set for Nicosia, who already had four hits in the game, to add to his heroics.

Pittsburgh manager Chuck Tanner surprisingly pulled the Bucs hot-hitting catcher, replacing him with left-handed veteran John Milner to face the right-handed Eastwick. The lefty still had some power, having hit 11 homers so far in 1979. The decision by Tanner seemed to have some merit until Phillies manager Danny Ozark countered Tanner's move by bringing in his solid left-handed reliever Tug McGraw to swing the advantage back to Philadelphia.

While on paper the Phillies seemed to have the better of the matchup, Milner made it a moot point as he launched a shot over the right field wall for a game-winning pinch-hit grand slam. The crowd of 46,006 went into hysterics as his teammates put Milner on their shoulders and carried him off the field with a dramatic 12–8 win.

"One of the biggest home runs of my career," Milner said following the contest.[1] It was a victory that, coupled with a 5–2 Pirates win in the second game of the doubleheader, vaulted the team into first place and essentially ended Philadelphia's quest for another division title.

For the Pirates, they still had a tough race ahead of them. But they were given a boost by a bench player who had delivered arguably the biggest hit of the season and one of the great moments of a truly memorable season.

PHI N	0	2	0		0	6	0		0	0	0	—	8	9	4
PIT N	0	0	3		0	3	1		0	1	4	—	12	13	1

BATTING

Philadelphia Phillies	AB	R	H	RBI
McBride rf	4	1	1	0
Bowa ss	4	1	0	0
Rose 3b	5	1	1	1
Luzinski lf	3	2	1	4
Anderson lf	0	0	0	0
Gross ph,lf	1	0	0	0
Unser 1b	4	1	2	1
Maddox cf	3	1	1	0
McCarver c	4	0	1	0
Trillo 2b	4	0	0	0
Carlton p	2	1	2	1
Saucier p	1	0	0	0
Eastwick p	0	0	0	0
McGraw p	0	0	0	0
Totals	35	8	9	7

FIELDING—DP: 2. Trillo-Bowa-Unser, Bowa-Trillo-Unser.
E: Luzinski (7), McCarver (1), Trillo (5), Carlton (3).
BATTING—HR: Luzinski (15,5th inning off Blyleven 3 on 0 out); Unser (5,5th inning off Coleman 0 on 0 out).
SF: Carlton (1,off Blyleven).
GDP: Bowa (7,off Coleman).
Team LOB: 5.
BASERUNNING—SB: Maddox (22,3rd base off Blyleven/Nicosia).

Pittsburgh Pirates	AB	R	H	RBI
Moreno cf	5	1	1	2
Foli ss	4	1	3	1
Parker rf	5	0	0	0
B. Robinson 1b	5	1	2	2
Lacy lf	4	2	2	2
Madlock 3b	3	1	0	0
Garner 2b	4	1	0	0
Nicosia c	4	3	4	1
Milner ph	1	1	1	4
Blyleven p	1	1	0	0
Coleman p	0	0	0	0
Sanguillen ph	1	0	0	0
Romo p	0	0	0	0
Stargell ph	1	0	0	0
Tekulve p	0	0	0	0
Totals	38	12	13	12

FIELDING—DP: 1. B. Robinson-Foli-B. Robinson.
E: Foli (9).
BATTING—2B: Nicosia 2 (10,off Carlton,off Saucier); Foli (21,off Carlton).
HR: Lacy (4,5th inning off Carlton 1 on 1 out); Nicosia (4,6th inning off Carlton 0 on 0 out); Milner (12,9th inning off McGraw 3 on 2 out).
SH: Blyleven (11,off Carlton).
GDP: B. Robinson (12,off Saucier); Madlock (7,off Saucier).
IBB: Madlock (6,by Eastwick).
Team LOB: 6.
BASERUNNING—SB: Moreno (50,3rd base off Carlton/McCarver); Lacy (4,2nd base off Eastwick/McCarver).

PITCHING

Philadelphia Phillies	IP	H	R	ER	BB	SO
Carlton	5	9	7	6	1	8
Saucier	3.1	2	1	1	2	2
Eastwick L(1–2)	0.1	1	3	3	2	0
McGraw	0	1	1	1	0	0
Totals	8.2	13	12	11	5	10

Carlton faced 2 batters in the 6th inning

WP: Carlton 2 (8).
IBB: Eastwick (2,Madlock).

Pittsburgh Pirates	IP	H	R	ER	BB	SO
Blyleven	4	5	7	5	4	4
Coleman	2	2	1	1	0	0
Romo	2	1	0	0	0	1
Tekulve W(5–6)	1	1	0	0	0	0
Totals	**9**	**9**	**8**	**6**	**4**	**5**

Blyleven faced 5 batters in the 5th inning
Umpires: HP—Fred Brocklander, 1B—Ed Vargo, 2B—Paul Pryor, 3B—Jim Quick
Time of Game: 3:00 **Attendance:** 46,006

#36

PIRATES 2, BROOKLYN SUPERBAS 1
SEPTEMBER 20, 1907

The First Gem

Often forgotten in the tale of the first Pittsburgh Pirates' hurler to throw a no-hitter was not only the man who performed the feat but how the performance was only part of the phenomenal start to his major-league career.

The man who tossed this memorable gem was a 20-year-old right-hander from Govanstown, Maryland, by the name of Nick Maddox. Maddox was selected by the Pirates in the Rule 5 draft in 1906 and shipped to Wheeling to start the 1907 campaign. The young hurler had compiled a respectable 13–10 mark for the Stogies and had pitched a pair of no-hitters.

When September rolled around, Pirates president Barney Dreyfuss wanted to see what Maddox could do at the major-league level and called him up to join the team late in the season. The results were amazing. In his debut on September 13 against the Cardinals, he tossed an impressive 4–0 shutout victory. Three days later he beat St. Louis once again, 4–2.

Suddenly the rookie seemed to be a fixture in manager Fred Clarke's starting rotation. Next up would be a date with the Brooklyn Superbas at Pittsburgh's Exposition Park.

As good as the Bucs' young hurler was in his first two major-league appearances, he was about to be even better. *The Pittsburgh Press* made the claim that Maddox was so dominant in the game against Brooklyn that he "did not allow his opponents a single hit nor semblance of the same."[1]

Maddox was matched up against Brooklyn's spitball specialist Elmer Stricklett in this game as both teams were held scoreless in the first three innings. In the top of the fourth, the Superbas got on the board first without the benefit of a hit, as two wild throws by the Pirates allowed them to take a 1–0 lead.

An inning later, the Pirates drew even. Stricklett, who would give up only two hits in the game himself, started off the frame by walking Harry Swacina. Third baseman Alan Storke wanted to move the Pirates' first baseman into scoring position with a bunt. Fielding the bunt, first baseman Tim Jordan's throw sailed wide, sending the Bucs' first baseman home and tying the game at one.

In the bottom of the seventh, Pittsburgh was able to scratch out one more run, which was all that Maddox would need. Shortstop Honus Wagner led off the frame with a walk and then went to third when a throw to second on a sacrifice bunt attempt was wild. Catcher George Gibson then hit a grounder to second, scoring Wagner with the go-ahead run.

While both pitchers were dominant, the shoddy defense by both clubs left the game in doubt until the end. Maddox wasn't to be denied, as he cruised through the final two innings completing the first no-hitter in Pirates history. It was the second no-hitter pitched in the city of Pittsburgh, the first being when Matt Kilroy of Baltimore beat the Pittsburgh Alleghenies 6–0 in 1886 in an American Association game at Recreation Park.

On this historic day, no one could have imagined that it would be the last no-hitter pitched in the city of Pittsburgh for 64 years and the last one a Pirate would toss in his home park in 69 years.

While the no-hitter secured Maddox's place in baseball history, it was also the culmination of a whirlwind first month in the majors. He finished his brief season in Pittsburgh in 1907 with a 5–1 mark and a miniscule 0.83 ERA, allowing only 32 hits and 13 walks in 54 innings. In 2004, Alan Schwartz of ESPN.com named Maddox's promotions as the sixth most impressive September pitching call-up in major-league history. It was a prelude to things to come. A year later Maddox went 23–8 and then 13–8 in the world championship campaign of 1909, including a victory in Game Six of the World Series.

By 1910 the magic ran out, and Nick Maddox fell out of the starting rotation, slipping to 2–3 with an ERA 1.12 points higher than he ever had in his short career. He was sold to Kansas City of the American Association.

"I never released a player with more regret than I do in this case," Pirates president Barney Dreyfuss said. "Nick has always been a hard worker. He is a faithful man, he never fails to give the club the best he has in stock, but Nick's best of late has not been good enough for the National League. Players can not be carried on sentiment alone these days and I had to let him go."[2]

Maddox's short but incredible career in the majors was over. After pitching three seasons in the minors, Maddox hung up his spikes and retired to Pittsburgh where he died in 1954. When he was buried, his family had a special designation engraved on his tombstone, one that memorialized the highlight of his career and his most notable achievement in a Pirates uniform: "Pirate pitcher; First no-hitter, 1907."

BRK N	0	0	0	1	0	0	0	0	0 —	1	0	2
PIT N	0	0	0	0	1	0	1	0	0 —	2	2	2

BATTING

Brooklyn Superbas	AB	R	H	RBI
Casey 3b	3	0	0	0
Lewis ss	3	0	0	0
Jordan 1b	3	0	0	0
Hummel 2b	4	0	0	0
Batch lf	4	1	0	0
Burch rf	2	0	0	0
Maloney cf	2	0	0	0
Bergen c	3	0	0	0
Stricklett p	3	0	0	0
Totals	27	1	0	0

FIELDING—E: Jordan 2.
BATTING—SH: Maloney
Team LOB: 4.

Pittsburgh Pirates	AB	R	H	RBI
Hallman rf	4	0	0	0
Leach cf	4	0	0	0
Clarke lf	4	0	2	0
Wagner ss	3	1	0	0
Abbaticchio 2b	3	0	0	0
Swacina 1b	2	1	0	0
Storke 3b	0	0	0	0
Gibson c	2	0	0	1
Maddox p	3	0	0	0
Totals	25	2	2	1

FIELDING—E: Maddox, Wagner
BATTING—2B: Clarke
SH: Storke, Gibson
Team LOB: 5.

PITCHING

Brooklyn Superbas	IP	H	R	ER	BB	SO
Stricklett L(11–14)	8	2	2	1	4	0

Pittsburgh Pirates	IP	H	R	ER	BB	SO
Maddox W(3–0)	9	0	1	0	4	5

Umpires: Klem
Time of Game: 1:30

#35

PIRATES 4, NEW YORK METS 0
SEPTEMBER 20, 1969

Hometown Boy Makes Good

Bob Moose was a young hurler from Export, Pennsylvania, about 20 miles outside of Pittsburgh, and was part of a young contingent of Pirates players that included Dave Cash, Bob Robertson, Al Oliver, Richie Hebner, Manny Sanguillen, and Dock Ellis—players who were expected to put the Bucs back in the title hunt for years to come. The hometown hurler broke into the majors in 1968 and was having a spectacular campaign in 1969 with an 11–3 record, winning eight of his previous nine decisions coming into this late-season game against the Eastern Division–leading New York Mets. The Mets, of course, were putting the finishing touches on one of the most spectacular turnarounds in major-league history, going from one of the jokes of baseball, as they had been since their inaugural season in 1962, to the cusp of their first title.

The Mets had come into this weekend series against Pittsburgh with their magic number to win the NL East at six. The Pirates ripped their Big Apple rivals on Friday night in a doubleheader sweep, beating New York 8–2 and 8–0. But they still were able to reduce their magic number to five when the Chicago Cubs split their doubleheader.

On Saturday 38,784 fans were on hand to see if it they could inch closer to the title, but the Mets would run into a man named Moose who was about to become a part of baseball history, putting a hold on New York's run to glory. The young Pirates' hurler continued the dominance that Pittsburgh pitchers had over the Mets in this series, as he retired the first nine of 10 batters he faced, giving up only a walk to Ed Kranepool.

In the top of the fourth, the Pittsburgh offense came alive, giving Moose all the support he would need. The Pirates loaded the bases with nobody out and then scored twice on a pair of wild pitches by Mets rookie pitcher Gary Gentry. They added a third run on a groundout by Sanguillen.

With Pittsburgh up by three, all eyes turned to the young Pirates' hurler to see if he could continue his quest for history, a quest that almost ended in the bottom of the fourth. New York third baseman Wayne Garrett lashed a long line drive to center field that looked like it would drop in for a hit. Pirates center fielder Matty Alou made a spectacular running grab, keeping the no-hitter alive.

Two innings later in the sixth, Garrett almost put an end to Moose's gem once again. This time he laced a shot to right field that again looked like a certain hit. Unfortunately for the Mets' third baseman, the ball went toward Pittsburgh right fielder Roberto Clemente, who had won eight straight Gold Glove Awards. Clemente made a tremendous leaping grab, keeping New York hitless.

As the game went on, reporters and fans alike wondered if Moose would flirt with history only to come up short like he had the year before. In that game, the young pitcher came within four outs of tossing a no-hitter, only to lose it in the eighth against Houston in Pittsburgh—the latest inning in a game a pitcher would have a no-hitter in the 61-year history of Forbes Field. This was another day, though, as Moose cruised through the eighth and was now only three outs away from his gem.

Pittsburgh tacked on an insurance run in the top of the ninth, thanks to another Mets wild pitch as all eyes were now settled on the second-year Pirates' hurler. Things started off a little shaky when he walked pinch hitter Rod Gaspar to open up the inning. Tommie Agee then popped up to Al Oliver in foul territory, bringing up Garrett, who had come within inches of breaking up the no-hitter twice already. There was no such drama on this at bat, as he grounded out softly to third for the second out.

Art Shamsky would be the Mets' last chance. He got ahead of Moose with a 2–1 count but then rolled a grounder to Cash at second, who tossed it over to Oliver at first, sending the Bucs into a frenzy as they mobbed their 21-year-old teammate, celebrating his momentous achievement, the third official no-hitter in franchise history and the first in 18 years.

Mets fans did have something to celebrate on this day, as the Cardinals held on to defeat the Cubs 4–1, reducing New York's magic number to four. The Mets finished their remarkable climb four days later by clinching the division on the way to a sweep of Baltimore in the World Series. For Pirates fans, though, their enduring memory of Shea Stadium on this day was Bob Moose, who was able to complete his journey, putting his name into the major-league record books as he dominated the Miracle Mets on this September Sunday.

PIT N	0	0	0		3	0	0		0	0	1 —	4	6	0
NY N	0	0	0		0	0	0		0	0	0 —	0	0	0

BATTING

Pittsburgh Pirates	AB	R	H	RBI
Alou cf	5	0	1	0
Cash 2b	2	1	0	0
Stargell lf	4	1	1	0
Jeter lf	0	0	0	0
Clemente rf	3	1	0	0
Oliver 1b	3	0	1	0
Sanguillen c	4	1	2	1
Hebner 3b	4	0	1	0
Patek ss	4	0	0	0
Moose p	3	0	0	0
Totals	32	4	6	1

BATTING—HBP: Oliver (12,by Gentry).
Team LOB: 6.
BASERUNNING—SB: Cash (2,3rd base off Gentry/Martin); Stargell (1,2nd base off Gentry/Martin).
CS: Oliver (5,2nd base by Gentry/Martin).

New York Mets	AB	R	H	RBI
Agee cf	4	0	0	0
Garrett 3b	4	0	0	0
Shamsky lf	4	0	0	0
Boswell 2b	3	0	0	0
Kranepool 1b	2	0	0	0
Swoboda rf	2	0	0	0
Martin c	3	0	0	0
Harrelson ss	3	0	0	0
Gentry p	1	0	0	0
Gosger ph	1	0	0	0
McGraw p	0	0	0	0
Gaspar ph	0	0	0	0
Totals	27	0	0	0

BATTING—Team LOB: 3.
PITCHING

Pittsburgh Pirates	IP	H	R	ER	BB	SO
Moose W(12–3)	9	0	0	0	3	6

New York Mets	IP	H	R	ER	BB	SO
Gentry L(11–12)	6	4	3	3	3	2
McGraw	3	2	1	1	1	3
Totals	9	6	4	4	4	5

WP: Gentry 2 (9), McGraw (7).

HBP: Gentry (5,Oliver).

Umpires: HP—Augie Donatelli, 1B—Mel Steiner, 2B—Bob Engel, 3B—Dick Stello

Time of Game: 2:08 **Attendance:** 38,784

PIRATES 4, SAN DIEGO PADRES 3
AUGUST 25, 1979

Roberts Chokes the Padres

In every championship season there comes a defining moment that demonstrates the team has what it takes to be a champion. For the 1979 Pittsburgh Pirates, that moment came on a late summer evening in San Diego in a six-hour marathon that saw the Bucs hang on time and time again when defeat seemed imminent, only to fight through to win a game they rightfully should have lost. It was a victory that was an important catalyst in their capturing a tight division race and one that every Pirates fan who stayed up into the early hours of the morning to witness on television will not soon forget.

On that warm evening in San Diego, the two clubs sent out pitchers who were destined for the Hall of Fame: Gaylord Perry of the Padres and the Pirates' Bert Blyleven. The pitching matchup lived up to its billing as runs were at a premium. The Padres scored the only two runs in the first eight innings, taking advantage of a wild pitch and an error in the third. With the dominance Perry was displaying this night, it looked like the two runs would be more than enough for San Diego.

After the Padres went down in the eighth, San Diego manager Roger Craig decided to let Perry go for the complete game shutout and sent him out in the ninth. Pittsburgh would show its comeback ability for the first time in this game, as Pirates right fielder Dave Parker laced a one-out double. After going to third on a groundout, Pittsburgh was down to its last chance. Left fielder John Milner got on board on a walk and was replaced by Pirates manager Chuck Tanner, who inserted the speedy Matt Alexander. Third baseman Bill Madlock then laced a single to score Parker. Madlock got into scoring position on the unsuccessful throw to third to try to get Alexander.

Craig had seen enough at that point and summoned another future Hall of Famer, reliever Rollie Fingers, to close out the game. Unfortunately, Fingers's first pitch got past Padres catcher Bill Fahey, which scored Alexander to tie the game. After giving up two more walks to load the bases, Craig brought in Mark Lee, who fanned Bill Robinson to end the Bucs' threat. After Pirates closer Kent Tekulve got San Diego's Dave Winfield to ground into a force play with the bases loaded in the bottom of the ninth, the game went into extra innings.

The game remained tied until the top of the 12th, when the Pirates pushed across the plate what they hoped would be the winning run, as center fielder Omar Moreno smacked a single to bring across second baseman Phil Garner, giving Pittsburgh a 3–2 lead. The lead would not last; San Diego tied the score in the bottom half on a two single by pinch hitter Dan Briggs.

With the score tied 3–3 through 14 innings, both managers were running out of options. After Steve Nicosia batted for reliever Grant Jackson in the 15th, the Pirates were out of position players. Tanner brought in his sixth pitcher at that point, Dave Roberts, the 10th man on a 10-man staff, who had mostly performed in mop-up situations since coming over in a midseason trade. But on this night he would be the star. San Diego constantly threatened to get to Roberts, but each time he was up to the challenge.

In the 16th, the Padres loaded the bases with two out as Roberts fell behind his counterpart, San Diego pitcher John D'Acquisto, three balls and no strikes. As Roberts stepped off the mound, he looked to second base and saw Winfield giving him the choke sign. The gesture lit a fire under Roberts, who struck out D'Acquisto on three straight pitches, sending it to the 17th inning.

An inning later the Padres once again were on the brink of victory, loading the bases, but Roberts escaped as the game tolled into the night. Finally in the top of the 19th, Pittsburgh took the lead when shortstop Tim Foli laced a two-out single to score Bill Robinson with the go-ahead run. The Padres would not go down quietly as once more San Diego threatened putting a man on third with two outs, setting up a climactic showdown with Roberts facing the Padres' Jay Johnstone. At 1:20 A.M., 4:20 A.M. in Pittsburgh, Johnstone lifted a lazy fly ball to Robinson in left, ending what had been the longest game in Padres history.

Though mentally and physically exhausted, the Pirates knew this was a special win. "It was all worthwhile," Parker said afterward, "because it keeps us out in front."[1]

The marathon victory turned out to serve as a spark for the Pirates as they went on to win six of the remaining seven games of their final West Coast trip of the year. Most importantly, it was a game that also proved—to themselves and their fans—that they were indeed tough and resilient enough to win the pennant.

PIT N	0 0 0	0 0 0	0 0 2	0 0 1	0 0 0	0 0 0	1 — 4	14 4
SD N	0 0 2	0 0 0	0 0 0	0 0 1	0 0 0	0 0 0	0 — 3	14 0

BATTING

Pittsburgh Pirates	AB	R	H	RBI
Moreno cf	5	0	1	1
Foli ss	7	0	2	1
Parker rf	9	1	2	0
Stargell 1b	7	0	2	0
Milner lf	3	0	1	0
Alexander pr	0	1	0	0
Tekulve p	0	0	0	0
Lacy ph	1	0	0	0
D. Robinson p	0	0	0	0
Sanguillen ph	1	0	0	0
Jackson p	0	0	0	0
Nicosia ph	1	0	0	0
Roberts p	1	0	0	0
Madlock 3b	5	0	1	1
Stennett 2b	3	0	1	0
Ott c	6	0	2	0
Garner 2b,3b	7	1	1	0
Blyleven p	2	0	0	0
Easler ph	1	0	0	0
Romo p	0	0	0	0
B. Robinson ph,lf	4	1	1	0
Totals	63	4	14	3

FIELDING—E: Foli (13), Milner 2 (7), Garner (19).

BATTING—2B: Parker (35,off Perry); Garner (26,off Rasmussen); Ott (17,off D'Acquisto); B. Robinson (15,off D'Acquisto).

SH: Ott (4,off Mura); Foli (14,off D'Acquisto).

GDP: Stargell (7,off Perry); Madlock 2 (12,off Perry 2); Milner (5,off Perry); Foli (5,off Rasmussen).

IBB: Ott (6,by Fingers); Moreno 2 (9,by D'Acquisto 2).

Team LOB: 14.

BASERUNNING—SB: Moreno (57,2nd base off Perry/Fahey).

San Diego Padres	AB	R	H	RBI
Richards lf	3	0	0	0
Briggs lf,1b	2	0	1	1
Mura p	0	0	0	0
D'Acquisto ph,p	3	0	0	0
Smith ss	9	1	3	0
Dade 3b	9	0	3	0
Tenace 1b	2	1	1	0
Tolan ph	0	0	0	0
Gonzalez 2b	4	0	0	0
Johnstone rf,cf	9	0	3	1
Wilhelm cf	4	0	1	0
Turner ph,lf	4	0	0	0
Fahey c	7	0	2	0
Almon 2b	3	0	0	0
Winfield ph,rf	2	1	0	0
Perry p	2	0	0	0
Fingers p	0	0	0	0
Lee p	0	0	0	0
Bevacqua ph	1	0	0	0
Rasmussen p	0	0	0	0
Kendall ph,1b	3	0	0	0
Totals	**67**	**3**	**14**	**2**

FIELDING—DP: 6. Almon-Smith-Tenace, Smith-Almon-Tenace, Smith-Tenace, Smith-Almon-Tenace, Smith-Gonzalez-Briggs, Smith.
PB: Fahey (3).
BATTING—2B: Smith (14,off Blyleven); Tenace (13,off Blyleven).
3B: Wilhelm (3,off Blyleven).
SH: Perry 2 (11,off Blyleven,off Romo); Tolan (3,off Tekulve); Turner (2,off Roberts); Dade (7,off Roberts).
IBB: Richards (6,by Romo); Johnstone (3,by Tekulve); Fahey (3,by Tekulve); Winfield (18,by Roberts); Kendall (2,by Roberts); Gonzalez (9,by Roberts).
Team LOB: 26.
BASERUNNING—SB: Richards (14,2nd base off Blyleven/Ott).
CS: Tenace (4,2nd base by Blyleven/Ott).

PITCHING

Pittsburgh Pirates	IP	H	R	ER	BB	SO
Blyleven	7	6	2	1	6	7
Romo	1	1	0	0	1	1
Tekulve	2	0	0	0	2	0
D. Robinson	2	2	1	1	1	0
Jackson	3	1	0	0	1	1
Roberts W(2–3)	4	4	0	0	3	3
Totals	**19**	**14**	**3**	**2**	**14**	**12**

WP: Blyleven (8).
IBB: Romo (7,Richards); Tekulve 2 (14,Johnstone,Fahey); Roberts 3 (7,Winfield,Kendall,Gonzalez).

San Diego Padres	IP	H	R	ER	BB	SO
Perry	8.2	7	2	2	4	1
Fingers	0	0	0	0	2	0
Lee	1.1	0	0	0	0	2
Rasmussen	2	2	1	1	1	1
Mura	2	1	0	0	0	2
D'Acquisto L(8–12)	5	4	1	1	3	3
Totals	**19**	**14**	**4**	**4**	**10**	**9**

WP: Perry (6).
IBB: Fingers (8,Ott); D'Acquisto 2 (4,Moreno 2).
Umpires: HP—Dave Pallone, 1B—John McSherry, 2B—Paul Runge, 3B—Dick Stello
Time of Game: 6:12 **Attendance:** 14,607

PIRATES 10, BROOKLYN SUPERBAS 0
OCTOBER 17, 1900

The Postseason Tradition Begins

Since the Pittsburgh Alleghenies played the franchise's first game in the American Association in 1882, the club has participated in 17 postseason series. While many Pirates fans are aware of the 16 World Series and National League Championship Series in which Pittsburgh has appeared, few realize that their initial venture into the championship waters actually occurred before the World Series was created. In 1900 the top two teams in the National League squared off in a best-of-five series called the Chronicle-Telegraph Cup.

Named for the Pittsburgh *Chronicle Telegraph* newspaper, which donated a silver cup to be awarded to the winner, the series pitted the first-place Brooklyn Superbas against the hometown second-place Pittsburgh Pirates. The Chronicle-Telegraph Cup was the third attempt to establish a postseason championship series. The first was the Dauvray Cup, a series between the National League and American Association champions between 1882 and 1891. The Dauvray Cup ended after the American Association disbanded in 1892 and was replaced by the Temple Cup, named after Pirates president William Temple, a series that brought the top two finishers in the National League together. The Temple Cup ended in 1897 due to a lack of interest following four very one-sided series.

After two seasons without a postseason championship series, the new version would be played entirely at the Pirates' Recreation Park.

The 1900 Pirates boasted a plethora of impressive young talent, strengthened by the merger between the Louisville Colonels and the Bucs in the previous off-season. The club was led by Honus Wagner, Fred Clarke, Tommy Leach, Jesse Tannehill, and one of the best pitchers in the history of the franchise, Deacon Phillippe.

Meanwhile, Brooklyn had captured back-to-back pennants and had a potent offense that boasted a quartet of .300 hitters, including the legendary Wee Willie Keeler.

The Superbas had taken the first two contests, 5–2 and 4–2, and were looking to finish off the Pirates in the third game. Brooklyn manager Ned Hanlon tabbed little-used pitcher Harry Howell to put an end to the series, deciding at the last minute to keep star hurler "Iron Man" Joe McGinnity and his 28–8 mark on the bench in case there was a Game Four. Pirates manager Fred Clarke had no room for error and called on Phillippe in an effort to give the franchise its first-ever postseason win on a chilly mid-October afternoon.

While the pitching matchup may have favored the Bucs, they could only take advantage if their defense stabilized. It had been horrendous the first two contests, committing 10 errors. Luckily for the hometown crowd in Game Three, a sweep was not in the cards for Brooklyn—and this was apparent from the outset.

The Bucs broke out on top in the first, giving Phillippe all the support he would need. Stringing together four consecutive singles, Pittsburgh broke out to an early 3–0 lead. They extended it to 4–0 in the second and never looked back.

While the Pittsburgh offense was battering Brooklyn, Phillippe was dominant. He limited the regular season champions to six hits—five of them singles—keeping the Superbas off the board.

In the fifth, Pittsburgh tacked on two more runs off an RBI single by Honus Wagner. Then with the team up 7–0 in the eighth, Pittsburgh put the icing on the cake by taking advantage of a sloppy Brooklyn defense, scoring three more runs, the last of which came on a double steal, to give the Bucs a 10-run lead.

Brooklyn went down quietly in the top of the ninth, and Pittsburgh had cut the Superbas' advantage in the series to two games to one.

Brooklyn was able to close it out the next day, winning the first and last Chronicle-Telegraph Cup when McGinnity shut down the Pirates 6–1 aided by three more Pirates errors. It would be the last postseason series victory for the Brooklyn franchise for 55 years, when the Dodgers finally upset the Yankees for their first and only World Series championship while residing in the borough of Brooklyn.

For the Pirates, the victory in Game Three of the Chronicle-Telegraph Cup was the start of something special. The team would go on to win 41 postseason games over the next century, including five world championships, but it was this victory that helped them establish their championship tradition.

BRK N	0	0	0		0	0	0		0	0	0	—	0	6	3
PIT N	3	1	0		0	2	0		1	3	x	—	10	13	1

BATTING

Brooklyn Superbas	AB	R	H	RBI
Jones cf	4	0	0	0
Keeler rf	4	0	2	0
Jennings 1b	4	0	1	0
Kelley lf	3	0	1	0
Cross 3b	4	0	1	0
Daly 2b	3	0	0	0
Dahlen ss	4	0	0	0
McGuire c	4	0	1	0
Howell p	3	0	0	0
Totals	**33**	**0**	**6**	**0**

FIELDING—E: Cross, McGuire, Howell
BATTING—3B: Cross

Pittsburgh Pirates	AB	R	H	RBI
Leach lf	4	4	3	0
Beaumont cf	4	2	3	1
Ritchey 2b	4	1	1	2
Wagner rf	4	0	2	3
O'Brien 1b	4	0	0	0
Williams 3b	4	0	0	0
Zimmer c	3	1	1	0
Ely ss	3	1	3	0
Phillippe p	4	1	0	0
Totals	**34**	**10**	**13**	**6**

FIELDING—E: Williams
BATTING—SB: Beaumont, Wagner 2, Ely
SH: Beaumont

PITCHING

Brooklyn Superbas	IP	H	R	ER	BB	SO
Howell L(0–1)	8	13	10	5	2	3

Pittsburgh Pirates	IP	H	R	ER	BB	SO
Phillippe W(1–0)	9	6	0	0	2	5

Umpires: Hurst and Swartwood
Time of Game: 3:00

PIRATES 2, SAN DIEGO PADRES 0
JUNE 12, 1970

Flawed Perfection

"I didn't think I had good enough stuff to throw a no-hitter," said Pirates hurler Dock Ellis after tossing the fifth no-hitter in Pirates history.[1] On a fateful night in San Diego on June 12, 1970, Ellis walked eight Padres batters but remarkably gave up no hits. What made this feat more incredible was a revelation he made in his autobiography years later. He explained that he tossed the no-hitter while under the influence of LSD.

A pitcher known just as much for his off-field antics and opinions as he was for his phenomenal talent, this game epitomized Dock Ellis.

Most people didn't realize just how close Ellis came to missing the contest. In a 2008 interview with American Public Media shortly before he passed away as a result of a liver ailment at the age of 63, Ellis told his incredible tale. In Los Angeles visiting friends, Ellis didn't realize he was supposed to start the first game of a doubleheader that evening in San Diego. He had spent the night before with friends smoking marijuana and drinking screwdrivers. When he woke up the next morning, he dropped some acid, thinking he would not pitch until the next day. Lucky for him, a friend of Ellis had read in the paper that the Bucs were playing in San Diego that night—and that Ellis was the starting pitcher in the first game.

It was 1:00 P.M. when Ellis heard the news; the game would begin in five hours. He was dropped off at the Los Angeles airport and arrived in San Diego at 4:30. He made it to the ballpark and looked for a lady in the stands whom he said, "Always had the bennies for me."[2] He popped out of the dugout to meet the lady, who handed him a gold pouch full of the drug. He swallowed the pills and then went out to take the mound.

With a fine mist falling that day, Ellis started off wildly walking two San Diego batters in the first before stranding them both.

Understandably, the young pitcher's mind was all over the place. As the game went on and he continued to hold the Padres hitless, his teammates left him alone in the time-honored tradition of staying away from a pitcher during a no-hitter. Ellis mistook his teammates' silence as disapproval of his drug-induced state. He would constantly dig mud from his cleats in frustration. After the game, he told reporters that night, "I thought about the no-hitter from the fourth inning. I know guys who don't want to talk about it, but if you're going to throw it, you're going to throw it."[3] Years later he disputed that, claiming he had no idea he was pitching a no-hitter until much later in the game.

Ellis was unable to focus on the hitters. "All I could tell was if they were on the right side or the left side," he said. "The catcher [Jerry May] put tape on his fingers so I could see the signals." He added that he "zeroed in on the catcher's glove, but I didn't hit the glove too much. The ball was small sometimes, the ball was large sometimes. Sometimes I saw the catcher, sometimes I didn't. Sometimes I tried to stare down the hitter and throw while I was looking at him."[4]

He also recalled that at times he saw Jimi Hendrix in the batter's box and that Richard Nixon was calling balls and strikes. While the hallucinations were bizarre to say the least, in reality he was dominating.

Ellis continued to struggle with his control, giving up at least one base runner between the third and sixth innings, including walking two in the fifth and sixth, but he continued to hold the Padres hitless. San Diego pitcher Dave Roberts was almost his equal but gave up two home runs to Pittsburgh slugger Willie Stargell in the second and seventh innings, giving Ellis all the support he would need.

In the bottom of the seventh, the Padres came as close as they would to breaking up the no-hitter when San Diego's Ramon Webster led off the inning with a sharp line drive, but second baseman Bill Mazeroski made a spectacular leaping grab to keep Ellis's quest for history alive.

Finally settling down after Maz's brilliant grab, Ellis retired eight of the next nine batters, permitting just one more walk in the eighth. He struck out pinch hitter Ed Spiezio to end the contest, placing his name in the record books—albeit somewhat infamously.

It truly was as odd a moment as baseball has ever experienced, a strange tale that, even four decades later, still seems impossible to believe.

PIT N	0	1	0		0	0	0		1	0	0	—	2	5	0
SD N	0	0	0		0	0	0		0	0	0	—	0	0	0

BATTING

Pittsburgh Pirates	AB	R	H	RBI
Alou cf	4	0	0	0
Alley ss	4	0	1	0
Clemente rf	4	0	0	0
Robertson 3b	3	0	0	0
Pagan 3b	1	0	0	0
Stargell lf	3	2	2	2
J. May c	3	0	0	0
Oliver 1b	3	0	2	0
Mazeroski 2b	3	0	0	0
Ellis p	3	0	0	0
Totals	31	2	5	2

BATTING—HR: Stargell 2 (12,2nd inning off Roberts 0 on 1 out,7th inning off Roberts 0 on 1 out).
Team LOB: 2.
BASERUNNING—CS: Alley (1,2nd base by Roberts/Cannizzaro).

San Diego Padres	AB	R	H	RBI
Campbell 2b	3	0	0	0
Huntz 3b	1	0	0	0
Ferrara lf	4	0	0	0
Colbert 1b	2	0	0	0
Brown rf	3	0	0	0
Murrell cf	3	0	0	0
Cannizzaro c	3	0	0	0
Dean ss	3	0	0	0
Kelly ph	1	0	0	0
Roberts p	2	0	0	0
Webster ph	1	0	0	0
Herbel p	0	0	0	0
Spiezio ph	1	0	0	0
Totals	27	0	0	0

BATTING—HBP: Murrell (3,by Ellis).
Team LOB: 9.
BASERUNNING—SB: Murrell (2,2nd base off Ellis/J. May); Campbell (9,2nd base off Ellis/J. May); Colbert (2,2nd base off Ellis/J. May).

PITCHING

Pittsburgh Pirates	IP	H	R	ER	BB	SO
Ellis W(5–4)	9	0	0	0	8	6

HBP: Ellis (6,Murrell).

San Diego Padres	IP	H	R	ER	BB	SO
Roberts L(4–3)	7	5	2	2	0	7
Herbel	2	0	0	0	0	0
Totals	9	5	2	2	0	7

Umpires: HP—Tony Venzon, 1B—Frank Secory, 2B—Bob Engel, 3B—Harry Wendelstedt
Time of Game: 2:13

Control Pitcher Extraordinare

When Charles "Babe" Adams made his debut with the Pirates in 1909, few would have predicted that he was going to be the hero of the Bucs' first World Series championship that same season. If that surprised Pirates fans, they would have been stunned if someone had told them he would become not only one of the game's best control pitcher but arguably the greatest hurler ever to don a Pirates uniform. Yet that's exactly what Adams became over his long career in the Steel City.

Born in Tipton, Indiana, in 1882, Adams was sold to the Bucs in 1907 and in limited action lost two games with a 6.95 ERA. After a year in the minors at Louisville, Adams returned to Pittsburgh in 1909 and was a remarkably different pitcher. He went 12–3 with a miniscule 1.11 ERA, helping lead the Bucs to their fourth National League pennant. Adams then was the hero of the 1909 World Series, winning three games over Detroit.

It was the beginning of a long, successful career. He went 18–9 in 1910 and won 22 the following year, becoming a fixture in the Pittsburgh rotation. He was also among the most accurate hurlers. Between 1910 and 1913, he constantly was at the top of the league in fewest bases on balls allowed per nine innings, almost always below two walks per game.

In 1914 the Pirates were suffering through a less-than-stellar campaign and hovered near the bottom of the National League standings. With little at stake, Adams put his control on display on a July afternoon in one of the most remarkable games ever played to that point and still one of the best ever pitched.

It was truly a classic pitchers' duel. Adams was matched up against one of the best left-handers ever in future Hall of Famer Rube Marquard. While 1914 had not been kind to Marquard as he struggled with a 12–12 record, on this day he was spectacular and had to keep up with Adams.

In a contest that would be dominated by pitching, both teams scored early. Forty-year-old Honus Wagner ripped an RBI triple in the bottom of the first inning to give Pittsburgh a 1–0 lead. Two innings later New York equalized the game on a single by Giants second baseman Larry Doyle. It would be an incredible 18 innings before another run would score.

Each team would have several opportunities to score. The most memorable threat came in the sixth for the Bucs. Wagner singled and went to third base on a hit by second baseman Jim Viox. On the throw to third to get Wagner, the ball disappeared, and third baseman Milt Stock desperately looked for it. Wagner sprinted home with what appeared to be the go-ahead run, but as he was about to cross the plate, the ball fell from his armpit. Marquard scooped it up and tossed it to third, but Viox slid under the toss safe, and Pittsburgh appeared be ahead 2–1 with a man on third.

Giants manager John McGraw came out to argue with umpire Bill "Lord" Byron claiming that Wagner—who said the ball was stuck under his uniform—purposely picked up the ball and should be called out and that Viox should return to second. Byron agreed with McGraw and called the Bucs' Hall of Famer out due to interference and sent Viox back. Pittsburgh manager Fred Clarke then protested vehemently but to no avail. Byron's decision stood, and Clarke was ejected from the game.

In the 10th, the Pirates had a chance to win the game with two outs and a runner on third, but the Pirates' Mike Mowry failed to hustle to first on a grounder to third that was bobbled. Had Mowry run at full speed, he would have easily beat the throw, and the Bucs would have won the game, but he was out, and the game continued.

As the contest went further into extra innings, Adams was compiling an amazing feat as his control was on display issuing no walks.

Both hurlers continued to dominate as the game toiled into the 21st inning, the longest game in National League history at that time. Finally after 17 innings since the last run was scored, the Giants broke through as Doyle lofted a long shot over the head of Pirates center fielder Joe Kelly for a two-run homer to give New York a 3–1 advantage.

The Pirates managed only a single in the bottom half of the inning and lost the heartbreaking contest. Clarke was furious at his team for not providing the proper support for Adams, who had pitched spectacularly and not allowed a walk in the long affair. "Babe pitches his heart out," he said afterward. "He don't give a base on balls for 21 innings and you so-and-so's let him down and score only one run for him."[1]

As bad as the loss was, it was insignificant. The Pirates' season was a lost cause and the defeat paled significantly to the record Adams achieved, pitching 21 innings without giving up a walk—a record that has never been challenged nor likely ever will be.

For Marquard, the 21-inning victory took its toll on the pitcher. He went on to lose 12 consecutive games in what would be his worst professional campaign. Though he lost, Adams's performance got his name etched in the record books. Ironically, had Wagner not pulled the hidden-ball trick, or had Mowry hustled to first base earlier in the game, Adams would have won the game, but the contest would have long been forgotten. Instead, as the losing pitcher, he holds a record that most likely will remain in the major-league record books in perpetuity.

NYG N	0	0	1	0	0	0	0	0	0	0	0	0
PIT N	1	0	0	0	0	0	0	0	0	0	0	0

NYG N	0	0	0	0	0	0	0	0	2	—	3	12	2
PIT N	0	0	0	0	0	0	0	0	0	—	1	15	2

BATTING

New York Giants	AB	R	H	RBI
Bescher cf	9	2	3	0
Doyle 2b	8	1	2	3
Burns 1b	8	0	2	0
Robertson rf	8	0	0	0
Fletcher ss	8	0	2	0
Merkle lf	8	0	0	0
Meyers c	6	0	3	0
Murray ph	1	0	0	0
McClean c	2	0	0	0
Stock 3b	5	0	0	0
Snodgrass ph	1	0	0	0
Grant 3b	1	0	0	0
Marquard p	8	0	1	0
Totals	73	3	12	3

FIELDING—DP: 1. Fletcher to Doyle to Merkle.
BATTING—HR- Doyle
SB-Burns 2, Bescher 2, Fletcher
SF- Stock, Burns
Team LOB: 9.

Pittsburgh Pirates	AB	R	H	RBI
Mensor lf	7	1	1	0
Mowry 3b	7	0	1	0
Wagner ss	9	0	3	1
Viox 2b	7	0	2	0
Konetchy 1b	8	0	2	0
Mitchell rf	8	0	1	0
Kelly cf	8	0	2	0
Gibson c	4	0	1	0
Carey pr	0	0	0	0
Coleman c	4	0	1	0
Adams p	7	0	1	0
Totals	69	1	15	1

FIELDING—DP: 1. Viox to Wagner to Konetchy
BATTING—3B: Wagner
SF: Mowry, Adams, Viox, Mensor
Team LOB: 15.

PITCHING

New York Giants	IP	H	R	ER	BB	SO
Marquard	21	15	1	1	2	2

HBP- Marquard

Pittsburgh Pirates	IP	H	R	ER	BB	SO
Adams	21	12	3	3	0	6

Umpires: Byron and Johnson
Time of Game: 5:42

#30

PIRATES 16, LOS ANGELES DODGERS 2
MAY 3, 1985

The Gunner Comes Home

October 30, 1975, had been among the darkest days in the history of the Pittsburgh Pirates. It was the day that Bob Prince, the "Voice of the Pirates," was surprisingly fired after 28 years behind the microphone.

At odds with Pirates general manager Joe L. Brown, who wanted the legendary broadcaster to promote the team more and stick to the action, Prince loved to tell stories during the contest and oftentimes toward the end of his career would veer off course of the play-by-play while telling his stories. Prince indignantly kept broadcasting games the way he wanted to. Westinghouse Broadcasting, the parent organization of the Pirates' radio flagship KDKA, was also irritated at his refusal to listen to management. Prince didn't realize he was in danger of losing his job until it was too late. Later he said, "I never dreamed that meant, 'If you don't, you're out.'"[1]

Controversy swirled around the city immediately following the dismissal. It was originally reported that all three organizations that had a vote in such decisions (the Pirates, Westinghouse, and sponsor Iron City Beer), had unanimously agreed that Prince and his partner, former Pirates pitcher Nellie King, should be removed from the booth. KDKA received approximately 600 phone calls in a six-hour period immediately following the firings, the vast majority criticizing the decision. Iron City Beer announced they were in fact against firing Prince and King. Company officials, in a statement sent to the *Pittsburgh Post Gazette*, stated that "Officials of the Pittsburgh Brewing Company expressed extreme disappointment about the dismissal of Pirate broadcasters Bob Prince and Nellie King. Pittsburgh Brewery. . . had expressed very strongly to the other parties its desire to renew the Prince-King contracts. Unfortunately, as minority rights holders, Pittsburgh Brewing said it was not the controlling factor."[2]

Regardless of whether or not it was unanimous, the fact was that the announcer who had manned the Pirates' booth for 28 seasons was gone and the city was stunned. A competing radio station in Pittsburgh, WEEP, arranged a parade to honor the dismissed broadcasters, one that more than 10,000 Pirates fans attended, including several members of the current team. Despite the fact that the majority of fans seemed to be very critical, Westinghouse did not relent, instead bringing in Milo Hamilton and a young broadcaster by the name of Lanny Frattare to man the booth.

Prince was devastated. According to his wife, Betty, "It took the life out of him. He retreated to the bedroom for three days right after. He had the drapes drawn in the bedroom and kept the door closed."[3]

Prince wouldn't be out of work for long as many job offers soon followed. He received offers to be the Houston Astros' broadcaster, to join Bob Uecker and Al Michaels as the original trio in ABC's *Monday Night Baseball* booth, and to be the television voice for the Pittsburgh Penguins. But none of those jobs worked out for the man they called "The Gunner."

Eventually Prince would return to call Pirates cable telecasts on the Home Sports Entertainment Network. At the time, cable television was still a fledgling enterprise, so this was considered a big step down from his past radio duties.

Three years later, the broadcasting legend was diagnosed with cancer of the mouth and underwent an operation to remove the tumor. Meanwhile, KDKA was formulating plans to finally make things right and bring Prince back to the Pirates' radio booth.

Sickly and emotional at the press conference to announce the three-year contract he had signed, Prince stated tearfully, "Other than my family, you've given me back the only other thing I love in the world."[4] He would begin his new tenure on May 3 at Three Rivers Stadium when the Pirates hosted the Los Angeles Dodgers.

Though Pittsburgh was in the midst of one of the most disappointing seasons in franchise history, 17,628 fans came out that night for the event, and thousands more were glued to their radios eagerly waiting for the fourth inning when Prince would take over the play by play.

The game, to that point, was a back-and-forth affair. The Bucs started things off scoring in the first inning on two errors to lead 1–0. The Dodgers battled back with two of their own in the top of the third, before the Pirates surged ahead by a run in the bottom of the frame.

As the game moved to the top of the fourth, the fans were about to hear what they had waited nine long years for: the return of Bob Prince to the Pirates' radio booth. The future Hall of Fame announcer was certainly not at his prime. *Pittsburgh Press* writer Bill Modoono described him as having "trouble wrapping up the hits, runs, errors and men left on base at the end of innings. Frequently, his listeners had no idea where the ball was going once it left the bat. One play that involved one Dodger error and one misplay that resulted in a Pirate run was just completely ignored by Prince."[5] Pitcher Larry McWilliams retired Los Angeles in order in the top half of the inning and—as if in a tribute to Prince—the Pirates' bats were about to put on a memorable show in the bottom half.

It was a scoring onslaught that almost didn't happen. After a leadoff strike-out and Bill Almon doubled but was thrown out stealing third for the second out, Jim Morrison singled and stole second, Bill Madlock walked, and George Hendrick hit a ground ball to shortstop Bill Russell, who tossed the ball away, allowing Morrison to score. Jason Thompson walked, and catcher Tony Pena ripped a two-run single. After a balk and another two-run hit by Sixto Lezcano, it was 8–2, and the Pirates weren't done yet.

The bizarre inning continued with another balk and then a two-run double by Bucs pitcher McWilliams, prompting Prince to scream "that a baby, Mac" on the air. The Pirates went on to score three more runs in a nine-run outburst to make the score 12–2 in Prince's first inning back.

There was more excitement in the bottom of the fifth when Jason Thompson came to bat with a man on first. Prince told his audience, "Well, we've had everything else. Jason might as well ding one." As if on cue, Thompson launched a home run, capping two of the most symbolic innings in the history of the franchise.

After the fifth, an exhausted Prince called it a night, only doing two of the three innings he was scheduled to broadcast. Though it ended early for Prince, it was truly a night to remember in a 16–2 Pirates victory.

Unfortunately, though, this proved to be one of his last broadcasts. After announcing two more games, Prince fell ill during a long rain delay on May 20 and was taken to the hospital suffering from dehydration and pneumonia. He died on June 10 at the age of 69.

While the town and team were saddened by his passing, they at least were comforted in the knowledge that before he died, they had one last chance to hear his golden voice in the Pirates' booth again, where it always belonged.

LA N	0	0	2	0	0	0	0	0	0	—	2	8	4
PIT N	1	0	2	9	2	0	2	0	x	—	16	15	1

BATTING

Los Angeles Dodgers	AB	R	H	RBI
Reynolds lf	4	0	1	1
Russell ss	2	1	0	0
Bailor 2b	1	0	0	0
Maldonado cf	4	0	1	1
Guerrero 3b	4	0	1	0
Marshall rf	3	0	1	0
Yeager c	4	0	1	0
Brock 1b	4	0	0	0
Ramsey 2b,ss	3	1	1	0
Honeycutt p	0	0	0	0
Brennan p	0	0	0	0
Castillo p	1	0	1	0
Whitfield ph	1	0	1	0
Howe p	0	0	0	0
Diaz p	0	0	0	0
Oliver ph	1	0	0	0
Totals	32	2	8	2

FIELDING—DP: 1. Honeycutt-Brock.

E: Russell 3 (6), Ramsey (1).

PB: Yeager (1).

BATTING—2B: Ramsey (1,off McWilliams); Maldonado (2,off McWilliams); Marshall (3,off McWilliams).

SH: Honeycutt (1,off McWilliams).

Team LOB: 7.

BASERUNNING—CS: Guerrero (2,2nd base by McWilliams/Pena).

Pittsburgh Pirates	AB	R	H	RBI
Almon ss,3b	6	2	3	2
Morrison 2b	3	1	1	1
Ray ph,2b	3	0	1	1
Madlock 3b	3	2	1	0
Belliard ss	1	0	0	0
Hendrick rf	2	2	1	0
Frobel pr,rf	1	2	1	0
Thompson 1b	2	2	2	4
Mazzilli 1b	1	1	1	0
Pena c	5	1	1	2
Lezcano lf	4	1	2	3
Orsulak cf	4	1	0	0
McWilliams p	5	1	1	1
Totals	40	16	15	14

FIELDING—DP: 1. Pena-Morrison.

E: Pena (2).

BATTING—2B: Almon (3,off Honeycutt); Hendrick (5,off Honeycutt); Mc-Williams (1,off Brennan); Ray (6,off Castillo); Lezcano (1,off Howe).

HR: Thompson (4,5th inning off Castillo 1 on 0 out).

IBB: Lezcano (2,by Honeycutt); Orsulak (1,by Brennan).

Team LOB: 7.

BASERUNNING—SB: Almon (2,2nd base off Honeycutt/Yeager); Morrison (1,2nd base off Honeycutt/Yeager).

CS: Almon (1,3rd base by Honeycutt/Yeager).

PITCHING

Los Angeles Dodgers	IP	H	R	ER	BB	SO
Honeycutt L(1–2)	3.2	6	7	2	5	3
Brennan	0	4	5	5	1	0
Castillo	2.1	2	2	2	1	0
Howe	1	3	2	2	0	1
Diaz	1	0	0	0	0	1
Totals	8	15	16	6*	7	5

*—Team earned runs does not equal the composite totals for all pitchers due to instances in which provisions of Section 10.18 (i) of the Scoring Rules were applied.

WP: Howe (2).
BK: Brennan 2 (3).
IBB: Honeycutt (1,Lezcano); Brennan (2,Orsulak).

Pittsburgh Pirates	IP	H	R	ER	BB	SO
McWilliams W(3–1)	9	8	2	2	3	5

WP: McWilliams (2).
Umpires: HP—Joe West, 1B—Eric Gregg, 2B—Frank Pulli, 3B—Doug Harvey
Time of Game: 2:45 **Attendance:** 17,628

PIRATES 9, SAN FRANCISCO GIANTS 4
OCTOBER 3, 1971

Robertson Blasts the Giants

Things did not look good for the Pittsburgh Pirates in the 1971 National League Championship Series. The team blew a two-run lead in the opener to lose the game and had lost 11 of their past 14 games at the Giants' Candlestick Park. Pittsburgh manager Danny Murtaugh knew if they left San Francisco down two games in the best-of-five series against a team that included four future Hall of Famers, odds were that the improvement the Bucs made during this memorable campaign would be for naught.

For this crucial contest, Murtaugh tapped his controversial right-hander Dock Ellis to try to even up the series. The 26-year-old Ellis, who was as well known for his off-field antics as he was for his accomplishments on the mound, was having a breakthrough season. He finished the campaign with a team-high 19 wins and had the distinction of being the first African American hurler to start an All-Star Game, an honor he shared with Vida Blue, who got the nod as the starter for the American League the same season.

While many thought that a Pirates victory in Game Two would hinge on the right arm of Ellis, it turned out to be the bat of a slugging first baseman by the name of Bob Robertson that gave this team all the momentum it needed. For Robertson it would be one of the greatest postseason performances in baseball history.

Things did not begin well for the Bucs when the Giants grabbed a quick 1–0 lead and threatened to blow it open in the top of the first on a walk and three hits. Ellis bore down and kept the damage to one run after facing the bases loaded with one out.

In the second, Robertson began his game for the ages with a leadoff double and came home on a Manny Sanguillen hit to tie the game. San Francisco surged back ahead in the bottom of the frame, but then Ellis and Robertson simply took over.

Ellis found his rhythm and shut down the Giants' potent offense, giving up only a walk over the next three innings. In the top of the fourth, Robertson continued his magical game, sending a John Cumberland pitch toward the right field wall where Dave Kingman, the Giants' six-foot-six right fielder jumped up for the catch. The ball caromed off his glove, bouncing against the foul screen for Robertson's first homer of the game and tying the game once again. After the home run came two more hits, the second an RBI single by the Pirates' light-hitting shortstop Jackie Hernandez, who sandwiched around a stolen base to put Pittsburgh in front for good, 3–2.

Pirates center fielder Gene Clines, who had hit only one home run in his first two seasons and five in a 10-year career, hit his only postseason homer to give Pittsburgh a two-run advantage.

Following a failed Giants threat in the sixth, the Pirates blew the game open in the seventh on the strength of Robertson's second homer of the game, a three-run shot, giving Pittsburgh a 7–2 lead. Two innings later, the Pirates' first baseman joined Babe Ruth as only the second player to hit three home runs in a postseason game, smacking the ball over the center field fence.

The Giants scored two meaningless runs in the bottom of the ninth, but the Pirates had done what they had set out to do: split the first two games at Candlestick Park. Three days later, the Pirates won their first National League pennant in 11 years, a victory that may not have happened if not for an amazing performance by Bob Robertson on this afternoon.

PIT N	0	1	0	2	1	0	4	0	1	—	9	15	0
SF N	1	1	0	0	0	0	0	0	2	—	4	9	0

BATTING

Pittsburgh Pirates	AB	R	H	RBI
Cash 2b	5	1	3	0
Clines cf	3	1	1	1
Oliver ph,cf	1	1	1	0
Clemente rf	5	1	3	1
Stargell lf	5	0	0	0
Robertson 1b	5	4	4	5
Sanguillen c	5	1	2	1
Pagan 3b	1	0	0	0
Hebner ph,3b	3	0	0	0
Hernandez ss	4	0	1	1
Ellis p	3	0	0	0
Miller p	1	0	0	0
Giusti p	0	0	0	0
Totals	41	9	15	9

FIELDING—DP: 1. Hernandez-Cash-Robertson.

PB: Sanguillen (1).

BATTING—2B: Robertson (1,off Cumberland); Cash (2,off Carrithers).

HR: Robertson 3 (3,4th inning off Cumberland 0 on 0 out,7th inning off Bryant 2 on 1 out,9th inning off Hamilton 0 on 1 out); Clines (1,5th inning off Barr 0 on 0 out).

HBP: Hebner (1,by Bryant).

Team LOB: 7.

BASERUNNING—SB: Sanguillen (1,2nd base off Barr/Dietz).

CS: Cash (1,2nd base by Cumberland/Dietz).

San Francisco Giants	AB	R	H	RBI
Henderson lf	3	0	1	1
Fuentes 2b	5	2	2	0
Mays cf	5	1	2	3
McCovey 1b	3	0	1	0
Rosario pr	0	0	0	0
Kingman rf	4	0	1	0
Dietz c	4	0	0	0
Gallagher 3b	4	0	0	0
Speier ss	3	1	2	0
Cumberland p	0	0	0	0
Barr p	1	0	0	0
McMahon p	0	0	0	0
Duffy ph	1	0	0	0
Carrithers p	0	0	0	0
Bryant p	0	0	0	0
Hart ph	1	0	0	0
Hamilton p	0	0	0	0
Totals	34	4	9	4

FIELDING—DP: 1. Dietz-Fuentes.

BATTING—2B: Mays (2,off Ellis); Speier (1,off Ellis); Fuentes (1,off Miller).

HR: Mays (1,9th inning off Miller 1 on 0 out).

SH: Cumberland (1,off Ellis).

HBP: Gallagher (1,by Ellis).

GDP: Hart (1,off Miller).

IBB: McCovey (2,by Ellis).

Team LOB: 12.

BASERUNNING—SB: Henderson (1,2nd base off Ellis/Sanguillen).

PITCHING

Pittsburgh Pirates	IP	H	R	ER	BB	SO
Ellis W(1–0)	5	6	2	2	4	1
Miller	3	3	2	2	3	3
Giusti	1	0	0	0	0	0
Totals	9	9	4	4	7	4

Ellis faced 2 batters in the 6th inning
Miller faced 3 batters in the 9th inning
HBP: Ellis (1,Gallagher).
IBB: Ellis (1,McCovey).

San Francisco Giants	IP	H	R	ER	BB	SO
Cumberland L(0–1)	3	7	3	3	0	4
Barr	1	3	1	1	0	2
McMahon	2	0	0	0	0	2
Carrithers	0	3	3	3	0	0
Bryant	2	1	1	1	1	2
Hamilton	1	1	1	1	0	3
Totals	9	15	9	9	1	13

Cumberland faced 2 batters in the 4th inning
Barr faced 2 batters in the 5th inning
Carrithers faced 3 batters in the 7th inning
HBP: Bryant (1,Hebner).
Umpires: HP—Shag Crawford, 1B—Lee Weyer, 2B—Andy Olsen, 3B—Dick Stello, LF—Satch Davidson, RF—Tom Gorman
Time of Game: 3:23 **Attendance:** 42,562

PIRATES 2, ST. LOUIS CARDINALS 0
SEPTEMBER 30, 1990

Dynasty in the Making
10 Years Later

In the 1980 version of Zander Hollander's *The Complete Handbook of Baseball,* he had a rosy outlook for the recent world champion Pittsburgh Pirates. "The Bucs have it all, including a manager who maintains enthusiasm from the first day of the season till the last. . . . If the Bucs are close to contention in August, there's a good chance they'll go all the way—and their chances seem even better now than they did a year ago. This is simply the best all around club in baseball."[1] For most of the baseball world, the Pirates looked like a dynasty in the making.

As August ended and September began in 1980, the Bucs were indeed in contention and had a half-game lead over Philadelphia and Montreal. Hollander's forecast unfortunately was off the mark as Pittsburgh floundered in the final month, limping across the finish line with a 13–19 mark over the last five weeks of the campaign, to finish at 83–79, in third place in the division. The September swoon was a harbinger of things to come.

The Eastern Division championships of the 1970s were replaced by sub-.500 finishes; a potential bankruptcy that endangered the club's future in the Steel City; and a drug trial involving several members of the 1979 world champions, which threatened to destroy all the good will that the memorable club gave the town. The 1980s were among the darkest days in the franchise's history.

Things started to stabilize when a group of local investors, led by then Mayor Richard Caliguiri, purchased the team, which allowed the franchise to stay in Pittsburgh. In 1985, the club tabbed a former scout for the team who had been out of baseball since the mid-1970s; Syd Thrift would be its general manager. Thrift made several pivotal moves that put together the pieces of what would become a championship team. In 1986 he made his greatest maneuver, selecting a minor-league manager with no major-league experience to lead the Bucs out the basement. His name was Jim Leyland.

With a bevy of young talent Thrift brought to the team, including Andy Van Slyke, Barry Bonds, Bobby Bonilla, and Doug Drabek, Leyland was able to transform the Pirates into contenders. By 1990 they were fighting with the New York Mets to retake the National League East title that had seemed like their birthright in the 1970s.

After being locked in a tight battle with the Mets all season, the Pirates were able to open up a little cushion by late September. When they went to St. Louis the last weekend of September, the Bucs knew that a sweep of the Cardinals and at least one loss by the Mets would mean Pittsburgh would clinch the division. Pittsburgh won the first two games of the series and, coupled with a New York loss, was now one win away.

On the mound for the Pirates was Doug Drabek, who had ascended to the top of the baseball world. He came into this contest with a 21–6 record, becoming the first Pittsburgh pitcher since John Candelaria in 1977 to win 20 games. Drabek was the prohibitive favorite to capture the Cy Young Award and would put an exclamation point on his memorable campaign.

Drabek was on top of his game and after stopping two St. Louis threats in the second and third, he hit his stride, allowing only one hit over the next four innings. Unfortunately for the Pirates, Cardinals pitcher Joe Magrane also was pitching superbly as the game went into the eighth scoreless.

With the game winding down, it was becoming apparent that the Pirates' offense would need a spark quickly if it were to win the division on this day. Pittsburgh finally caught that spark in the top of the eighth when Don Slaught and Jose Lind singled to start the inning. Drabek then beat out a two-strike bunt to load the bases. Gary Redus finally broke the ice on this scoreless game with an RBI sacrifice fly to center. Then Van Slyke hit into a fielder's choice, scoring another to make the game 2–0. It would be all the run support Drabek would need.

Drabek was dominant over the last two innings. As pitching coach Ray Miller simply put it, "He wasn't going to let anyone on base." After retiring the Cards in order in the eighth, Drabek got two quick outs in the ninth and then faced pinch hitter Denny Walling, who grounded to Lind at second for the final out, giving Pittsburgh its first division championship in 11 years.

The players were ecstatic, especially those who had experienced the lean years of the 1980s, like R. J. Reynolds. "I have laughed for five minutes then cried for five minutes, and I've done it for the last hour," he said in the jubilant locker room. Relief pitcher Bob Kipper, who had also been with the Bucs since 1985, noted, "It looked like there would not even be a franchise here in 1990."[2]

But Jim Leyland was the most emotional, taking in his first championship as a major-league manager. "Everyone is on our bandwagon today," he said. "It was not always that crowded. Five years. A lot of heartaches, a lot of tough times."[3]

Now the tough times were over. The Pirates finally won the division championship that Hollander had predicted for them so long ago and erased a miserable era the franchise wanted to forget.

PIT N	0	0	0		0	0	0		0	2	0 —	2	6	0
STL N	0	0	0		0	0	0		0	0	0 —	0	3	0

BATTING

Pittsburgh Pirates	AB	R	H	RBI
Redus 1b	2	0	0	1
LaValliere c	0	0	0	0
Bell ss	3	0	0	0
Van Slyke cf	4	0	1	1
Bonilla rf	4	0	1	0
Bonds lf	3	0	0	0
King 3b	4	0	1	0
Slaught c	3	0	1	0
Cangelosi pr	0	1	0	0
Bream 1b	1	0	0	0
Lind 2b	4	1	1	0
Drabek p	4	0	1	0
Totals	32	2	6	2

BATTING—2B: King (17,off L. Smith).
SF: Redus (5,off Magrane).
Team LOB: 7.
BASERUNNING—CS: Redus (5,2nd base by Magrane/Pagnozzi).

St. Louis Cardinals	AB	R	H	RBI
Gilkey lf	3	0	0	0
Walling ph	1	0	0	0
O. Smith ss	3	0	0	0
Lankford cf	3	0	0	0
Guerrero 1b	3	0	0	0
Pendleton 3b	3	0	1	0
Thompson rf	3	0	1	0
L. Smith p	0	0	0	0
Pagnozzi c	3	0	0	0
Oquendo 2b	3	0	1	0
Magrane p	1	0	0	0
Collins rf	1	0	0	0
Totals	**27**	**0**	**3**	**0**

BATTING—2B: Pendleton (20,off Drabek).

SH: Magrane (9,off Drabek).

Team LOB: 1.

BASERUNNING—CS: Thompson (5,2nd base by Drabek/Slaught).

PITCHING

Pittsburgh Pirates	IP	H	R	ER	BB	SO
Drabek W(22–6)	9	3	0	0	0	2

St. Louis Cardinals	IP	H	R	ER	BB	SO
Magrane L(10–17)	8	5	2	2	3	3
L. Smith	1	1	0	0	0	1
Totals	**9**	**6**	**2**	**2**	**3**	**4**

Umpires: HP—Tom Hallion, 1B—Joe West, 2B—Randy Marsh, 3B—Ed Montague

Time of Game: 2:09 Attendance: 32,672

PIRATES 5, BROOKLYN SUPERBAS 4
SEPTEMBER 27, 1901

The Dawn of a Dynasty

There are some trades that can mean the difference for a team between just missing out on their championship dreams and achieving them. Other trades can take a club from the brink of a title and plummet them to the realm of mediocrity. As the nineteenth century came to an end, a trade between the Louisville Colonels and the Pittsburgh Pirates not only was the difference between a few wins and losses, but it created the game's first dynasty of the next century.

On December 8, 1899, Pittsburgh sent Jack Chesbro, George Fox, Art Madison, John O'Brien, and $25,000 to the Colonels. It was a lot to give up, but what they got in return was a once-in-a-lifetime bonanza: Bert Cunningham, Mike Kelley, Tacks Latimer, Tommy Leach, Tom Messitt, Deacon Phillippe, Claude Ritchey, Rube Waddell, Jack Wadsworth, and Chief Zimmer. Just those players alone would have made the deal tremendous, but the Pirates also received two players that made this trade legendary: Honus Wagner and Fred Clarke, both of whom would be enshrined in the Hall of Fame.

A closer inspection showed that it wasn't as much a trade as it was a moving of assets. The National League was about to contract teams, including Louisville, and Colonels owner Barney Dreyfuss struck a deal where he would take less money from the league for eliminating Louisville if it gave him an opportunity to buy half of an existing franchise, a team that turned out to be the Pittsburgh Pirates. Once Dreyfuss purchased his half of the Pirates, he brought back the just-traded Chesbro, making this perhaps the most one-sided deal in the history of baseball.

The results were immediate. In 1900, for the first time since joining the National League, the Pirates finished above fifth place, finishing second and securing a spot in the postseason Chronicle-Telegraph Cup against the first-place Brooklyn Superbas. While they lost to Brooklyn four games, it would be a sign of things to come.

Able to hang on to their star players while most of the National League rosters were being raided by the upstart American League, the Pirates enjoyed a memorable 1901 campaign. After a subpar 16–15 start, they went on a 13–2 run, seizing first place following a 7–0 victory over the Giants on June 20, a game in which Wagner became the first player in the new century to steal home plate twice in the same game. Pittsburgh would relinquish the top spot only for a short time on July 4, holding on to it for the rest of the season.

By the time they came to play Brooklyn on September 27 at Exposition Park, they had a nine-game lead over the Philadelphia Phillies with nine left to play. The Pirates realized a win over the team that defeated them in the postseason series a year earlier would be poetic justice. Appropriately, one of the Louisville Colonels who helped make the Pirates so successful was 20-game winner Deacon Phillippe.

After a scoreless first inning, the Superbas broke out on top, 1–0, in the top of the second on a miscue by Bucs first baseman Ginger Beaumont. Pittsburgh tied the score in the bottom half of the frame on a Brooklyn error and took the lead an inning later when Beaumont made amends for his first-inning blunder with an RBI single.

Phillippe kept Brooklyn under control until the top of the sixth when Brooklyn struck back to tie the game and then took a 4–2 lead an inning later on back-to-back RBI singles by the Superbas' Jimmy Sheckard and Cozy Dolan. It looked like Pittsburgh would have to put its pennant-clinching celebration on hold.

The Pirates' Lefty Davis led off the eighth by hitting a long drive into center field that was over the head of Dolan. With the speedy Davis running, it looked like it would be an inside-the-park home run, but as the Bucs' right fielder passed second, he tripped and fell. He was able to get up and make it to third safely. After Clarke walked to put the tying run on base, Ginger Beaumont hit a bouncer to the mound as Davis broke for home, costing the Bucs a run, but he stayed alive long enough to allow the other two Pirates to get into scoring position. Up to the plate stepped Honus Wagner, who promptly smacked a two-run single to center, tying the score at four. Wagner, who pulled into second on the throw home, scored a batter later with the go-ahead tally when Kitty Bransfield lined a single to left.

Pittsburgh was now three outs away from its first National League pennant, but Brooklyn wouldn't go down easily, putting men on first and second with no outs. Pittsburgh then snuffed out a sacrifice attempt for the first out, and then Brooklyn superstar Willie Keeler hit a soft liner that looked like it might go over Wagner's head, but the shortstop moved into position to catch the ball for the second out. Sheckard then came to the plate and hit a ground ball to second baseman Claude Ritchey. Ritchey grabbed the ball and tossed to Wagner at second for the pennant-winning out.

The fans at Exposition Park were ecstatic. The town planned a big celebration, and Dreyfuss put together one of his own. He threw an expensive celebration for his players at the Schenley Hotel, handed them $2,000 to split, and had solid gold pins shaped like a pennant made for them. It was that kind of generosity that helped keep the team together as it began a three-year run as National League champions. It was also the twentieth century's first baseball dynasty, one that never would have happened if not for a very one-sided deal two years before.

| BR N | 0 | 1 | 0 | 0 | 0 | 1 | 2 | 0 | 0 | — | 4 |
| PIT N | 0 | 1 | 1 | 0 | 0 | 0 | 0 | 3 | x | — | 5 |

BATTING

Pittsburgh Pirates	AB	R	H	RBI
Davis rf	3	0	1	0
Clarke lf	3	1	0	0
Beaumont cf	4	1	1	1
Wagner ss	4	2	2	2
Bransfield 1b	4	0	2	1
Ritchey 2b	4	0	2	0
Leach 3b	1	0	0	0
Burke 3b	3	0	0	0
Zimmer c	3	1	1	0
Phillippe p	2	0	1	0
Totals	31	5	10	4

FIELDING

E: Wagner, Burke 2, Zimmer

BATTING—3B: Davis

SF: Phillippe

BASERUNNING—SB: Beaumont, Wagner

Brooklyn Suberbas	AB	R	H	RBI
Keeler rf	5	1	0	0
Sheckard lf	5	0	1	1
Dolan cf	4	0	2	1
Kelley 1b	4	1	1	0
Daly 2b	4	0	1	0
Dahlen ss	4	1	2	1
Irwin 3b	3	0	0	0
Farrell c	4	0	1	0
Kitson p	4	1	2	1
Totals	37	4	10	4

FIELDING—E: Dolan, Dahlen
BATTING—2B: Dolan, Daly
SF: Irwin
BASERUNNING—SB: Kelley

PITCHING

Pittsburgh Pirates	IP	H	R	BB	SO
Phillippe W(21–12)	9	10	4	0	2

Brooklyn Superbas	IP	H	R	BB	SO
Kitson L(19–11)	8	10	5	2	2

Umpires: Emslie
Time of Game: 1:55

PIRATES 3, WASHINGTON SENATORS 2
OCTOBER 13, 1925

Down But Not Out

The first four games of the 1925 World Series for the Pittsburgh Pirates had been very disappointing. The once-confident National League champions had seen their potent lineup held at bay by the Washington Senators and their Hall of Fame pitcher Walter Johnson.

Johnson started off the series by handcuffing the Bucs in a 4–1 victory in the opener. The Pirates won the next contest 3–2, before blowing a two-run lead in Game Three. Johnson tossed a shutout in Game Four as Washington built what seemed to be an insurmountable 3–1 lead, a deficit that no team in major-league history had ever come back from to win a World Series.

Facing elimination, the Pirates scored four times in the last three innings in Game Five to keep their season alive with a 6–3 win. With the victory, Pittsburgh's hopes brightened as they would now have home-field advantage, with the final two games at the friendly confines of Forbes Field.

A throng of 43,810 optimistic but anxious fans packed the ballpark as the Pirates started longtime minor-league pitcher Ray Kremer, who the Pirates acquired the year before. Kremer proved to be a key element in the Bucs' run to the 1925 National League crown. He won 18 games his rookie season in 1924 and followed it up a year later with a 17–8 mark. The right-hander pitched well in his first World Series start in Game Three, but he gave up two runs in the seventh for a tough 4–3 defeat.

The game did not start off well for the Pirates' pitcher as Kremer gave up a first inning homer to future Hall of Famer Goose Goslin, his third home run of the series, before allowing another tally in the second to give the Senators an early 2–0 lead. To keep their championship hopes alive and stave off elimination, the Pittsburgh bats would need to come alive, which they did in the third.

After a walk and a Washington error led to a Pirates' run off Clyde Barn-hart's groundout, Pittsburgh tied the game at two as Pie Traynor looped a short two-out single over second base to score center fielder Max Carey.

With the game now tied, Kremer hit his stride cruising through the fifth as the Bucs broke the stalemate when second baseman Eddie Moore smacked a long home run into the center field seats in front of the scoreboard, putting the Pirates ahead 3–2, a lead that Kremer would not relinquish. The Pirates' pitcher continued to stymie the Washington bats until he ran into trouble in the eighth.

Senators catcher Hank Severeid led off the frame with a long single to left as Washington manager Bucky Harris replaced his catcher with the faster Earl McNeely at first. McNeely promptly stole second, but Kremer bore down to retire the next three Senator batters to keep the game at 3–2.

An inning later, the Pirates' pitcher stopped another Washington threat as Kremer stranded right fielder Joe Harris, who hit a one-out double to the deepest part of the park in center, to close out the game and remarkably tie the series at three games apiece.

Only two days before, the team's championship hopes looked grim. Now they were on the precipice of making history as they forced a Game Seven. The Bucs had all the momentum now as they would complete the turnaround with a dramatic Game Seven victory. Somewhat lost in the dramatic climax was the performance of Ray Kremer in his Game Six masterpiece that was pivotal in them getting there.

WAS A	1	1	0	0	0	0	0	0	0	—	2	6	2
PIT N	0	0	2	0	1	0	0	0	x	—	3	7	1

BATTING

Washington Senators	AB	R	H	RBI
Rice cf	4	0	0	0
B. Harris 2b	3	0	0	0
Veach ph	1	0	0	0
Ballou p	0	0	0	0
Goslin lf	3	1	1	1
J. Harris rf	4	0	1	0
Judge 1b	4	0	1	0
Bluege 3b	4	1	1	0
Peckinpaugh ss	3	0	1	1
Severeid c	3	0	1	0
McNeely pr	0	0	0	0
Adams 2b	0	0	0	0
Ferguson p	2	0	0	0
Leibold ph	1	0	0	0
Ruel c	0	0	0	0
Totals	32	2	6	2

FIELDING—DP: 1. Judge.

E: Peckinpaugh (6), Severeid (1).

BATTING—2B: Peckinpaugh (1,off Kremer); J. Harris (1,off Kremer).

HR: Goslin (3,1st inning off Kremer 0 on 2 out).

Team LOB: 4.

BASERUNNING—SB: McNeely (1,2nd base off Kremer/Smith).

Pittsburgh Pirates	AB	R	H	RBI
Moore 2b	3	2	2	1
Carey cf	2	1	0	0
Cuyler rf	3	0	0	0
Barnhart lf	3	0	1	1
Traynor 3b	4	0	2	1
Wright ss	3	0	0	0
McInnis 1b	4	0	1	0
Smith c	4	0	1	0
Kremer p	3	0	0	0
Totals	29	3	7	3

FIELDING—E: Kremer (1).
BATTING—2B: Barnhart (1,off Ferguson).
HR: Moore (1,5th inning off Ferguson 0 on 0 out).
SH: Carey 2 (2,off Ferguson 2); Cuyler (2,off Ferguson).
Team LOB: 8.
BASERUNNING—SB: Traynor (1, 2nd base off Ferguson/Severeid).

PITCHING

Washington Senators	IP	H	R	ER	BB	SO
Ferguson L(1–1)	7	7	3	3	2	6
Ballou	1	0	0	0	1	0
Totals	8	7	3	3	3	6

Pittsburgh Pirates	IP	H	R	ER	BB	SO
Kremer W(1–1)	9	6	2	2	1	3

Umpires: HP—Brick Owens, 1B—Barry McCormick, 2B—George Moriarty, 3B—Cy Rigler
Time of Game: 1:57 Attendance: 43,810

10 Years Later

It had been 10 years since Bill Mazeroski hit his memorable home run against the New York Yankees to win the 1960 World Series and the Pirates hadn't tasted glory since. They had a young core of players that year and felt that the 1960s would be their decade. While there were close calls in 1962, 1965, and 1966, they were never able to achieve the lofty heights again that they did in 1960.

As the core of the 1960s team was aging, the front office looked toward an impressive crop of young players to get the Bucs back on top. By the end of the decade, prospects like Dave Cash, Bobby Robertson, Al Oliver, Richie Hebner, Manny Sanguillen, Dock Ellis, Luke Walker, and Bob Moose were on their way up through the system, starring for the Bucs' AAA team in Columbus.

In 1969, the seeds of the minor-league system began to take root at the major-league level. Entering the 1970s, it was hoped that these young players, when mixed with veterans Willie Stargell, Roberto Clemente, and the fabled Mazeroski, would propel the Bucs into championship contention. Fittingly, this new era would play out on a new stage, Three Rivers Stadium, which opened midway during the 1970 season.

To lead this core of young Pirates into the future, general manager Joe L. Brown tabbed Danny Murtaugh, the man who led the Bucs to the world championship 10 years earlier but retired after the 1964 campaign for health reasons. His health concerns now apparently not an issue, Murtaugh performed miracles in 1970 overcoming such obstacles as spotty starting pitching, several losing streaks, and myriad injuries to lead the club to the brink of their first NL East title as the season was coming to an end. A victory over the defending world champion New York Mets on this evening would mean the end of Pittsburgh's championship drought.

The largest crowd in the short history of Three Rivers Stadium—50,469 elated Pirates fans—hoped to witness the long-awaited celebration.

New York scored in the first inning to take an early lead off Pirates starter Dock Ellis. But the Bucs tied the game in the third when Cash singled to lead off the inning, went to third on a Clemente double, and then came home on a sacrifice fly by Robertson, making the contest 1–1. An inning later Pittsburgh loaded the bases and took a 2–1 lead when Cash smacked a sacrifice fly to Mets center fielder Tommie Agee, which scored Hebner and gave Ellis all the support he would need.

The lead did not look like it would last for long, as the Mets loaded the bases in the fifth with nobody out. Ellis, who had thrown a no-hitter earlier in the year while under the influence of LSD (see game #32), was able to get out of the jam on a pair of grounders, the first forcing out New York pitcher Jim McAndrew at the plate and the second forcing an inning-ending double play.

Like his eight-walk no-hitter against the Padres, Dock Ellis was not at his sharpest, but he found a way to stave off several Met threats throughout the game to keep the game at 2–1.

With two on and one out in the eighth, Murtaugh wanted to end this pennant race now, so he called on the one man who had been the only sure thing on the Bucs' pitching staff all season, closer Dave Giusti.

The Bucs' reliever did not get off on the right foot. After getting Harrelson on a ground, he walked pinch hitter Dave Marshall to load the bases. He was now facing Agee with two outs. The Mets' center fielder, who was two for three on the day, ripped a grounder up the middle. The ball, which looked like it was going for a sure hit to give New York the lead, hit the Pirates' reliever on the right calf and bounced up to the left of the mound into Giusti's glove. He threw it to Robertson at first; what had looked like a play that would put New York ahead became the Mets' third out.

"I made a bad pitch to Agee," Giusti would later say. "When the ball hit my leg and came down to me like it did, I knew it was our day. I said to myself they'll never beat us now."[1]

Giusti needed only five pitches to close out the ninth. When the Mets' Art Shamsky hit a roller to Robertson at first that looked like it might go foul, the Bucs' husky first baseman grabbed the ball in fair territory, touched the bag, and sent Giusti leaping high in the air as the championship drought finally ended. The large crowd went into delirium.

In the locker room afterward, Murtaugh reflected on the overall teamwork necessary to turn 1970 into a championship season. "I can tell you this and I'm saying it without being trite," he said. "This was a team effort, all the way."

He also felt that instead of hampering the team, the injuries actually brought them together. "I believe that all those injuries which seemed to be hurting us actually made a more closely knit team. That is the one ingredient which brought us this far."[2]

A decade removed from their last title, the 1970 Pirates had indeed come a long way, finally winning the championship that had been predicted so many years before.

NY N	1	0	0	0	0	0	0	0	0	—	1	10	2
PIT N	0	0	1	1	0	0	0	0	x	—	2	8	1

BATTING

New York Mets	AB	R	H	RBI
Agee cf	4	0	2	0
Garrett 3b	5	1	2	0
Jones lf	4	0	0	0
Shamsky rf	4	0	0	0
Clendenon 1b	4	0	1	1
Boswell 2b	4	0	2	0
Grote c	3	0	1	0
Weis pr	0	0	0	0
Dyer c	0	0	0	0
Harrelson ss	4	0	1	0
McAndrew p	2	0	1	0
Kranepool ph	1	0	0	0
Ryan p	0	0	0	0
Marshall ph	0	0	0	0
Herbel p	0	0	0	0
Totals	**35**	**1**	**10**	**1**

FIELDING—E: Garrett (12), Boswell (2).
BATTING—GDP: Boswell (13,off Ellis); Jones (24,off Ellis).
Team LOB: 12.
BASERUNNING—SB: Agee (31,2nd base off Ellis/Sanguillen).
CS: Grote (1,2nd base by Ellis/Sanguillen).

Pittsburgh Pirates	AB	R	H	RBI
Alou cf	4	0	1	0
Cash 2b	4	1	1	1
Clemente rf	4	0	2	0
Oliver lf	3	0	0	0
Robertson 1b	2	0	1	1
Sanguillen c	4	0	1	0
Hebner 3b	4	0	2	0
Alley ss	3	1	0	0
Ellis p	3	0	0	0
Giusti p	1	0	0	0
Totals	32	2	8	2

FIELDING—DP: 2. Cash-Alley-Robertson, Hebner-Sanguillen-Robertson.
E: Cash (8).
BATTING—2B: Clemente (22,off McAndrew); Hebner (23,off McAndrew).
SF: Robertson (6,off McAndrew); Cash (2,off McAndrew).
HBP: Alley (3,by McAndrew).
IBB: Oliver (8,by McAndrew); Alou (3,by Herbel).
Team LOB: 12.

PITCHING

New York Mets	IP	H	R	ER	BB	SO
McAndrew L(10–13)	5	7	2	2	1	5
Ryan	2	0	0	0	1	2
Herbel	1	1	0	0	1	0
Totals	8	8	2	2	3	7

HBP: McAndrew (2,Alley).
IBB: McAndrew (5,Oliver); Herbel (6,Alou).

Pittsburgh Pirates	IP	H	R	ER	BB	SO
Ellis W(13–10)	7.1	10	1	1	4	2
Giusti SV(26)	1.2	0	0	0	1	0
Totals	9	10	1	1	5	2

Umpires: HP—Ed Sudol, 1B—Ed Vargo, 2B—Al Barlick, 3B—Augie Donatelli
Time of Game: 2:30 Attendance: 50,469

714

It had been eight years since the great Babe Ruth last played in Forbes Field. The year was 1927, and things were a lot different for the Bambino. He was at the pinnacle of his career then, coming off a season in which he led what is arguably the greatest team ever assembled to the American League pennant. Along the way, Ruth had hit a record 60 home runs, a mark that would stand for the next 34 years. After taking the first two games of the 1927 World Series, the Yankees came to Pittsburgh and helped New York sweep the Pirates. When he returned to Forbes Field in 1935, it was a very different situation.

His magnificent 15-year career in New York had come to an end following the 1934 campaign; the legendary athlete was a shell of himself. Rather than retire, the out-of-shape Ruth had signed on with the Boston Braves for $20,000 plus a share of the Braves' profits. The man who was once the greatest player to ever step on the diamond was nothing more than a sideshow.

He was hitting under .200 with only three homers on the season when the Braves came to Forbes Field for a three-game series. The Babe was a mere one for eight in the first two games and naturally not much was expected for the finale.

While his better days may have been behind him, Ruth still loved the fans, especially children. He not only arranged for many of the *Pittsburgh Sun Telegraph* newsboys to be his guests at the game, but he made sure a sick child from McKeesport got an autographed ball after he received a note from the boy's mother in the locker room before the game.

It was a perfect sunny day with no wind, which would prove fortuitous for the Bambino. Ruth came up in the top of the first to face Pirates pitcher Red Lucas with a man aboard and smacked a ball into the right field stands for a two-run homer, putting the Braves in front 2–0. He was just getting started.

In the third inning Ruth put the Braves up 4–0 when he launched another majestic shot in the upper deck in right field against Pirates reliever Guy Bush, who surrendered the Babe's legendary "called shot" homer in the 1932 World Series in Chicago's Wrigley Field.

The Pirates rallied in the fourth inning to tie the score, but in the top of the fifth, Ruth knocked in his fifth run of the game, this time with a single, to put the Braves up again 5–4.

Even though Babe Ruth was putting on a performance for the ages, the Pirates would not be outdone. They tacked on three more runs in the bottom of the fifth on a Pep Young homer to take the lead for the first time on this memorable day, 7–5.

Two innings later Ruth would put a legendary exclamation point on his memorable performance. He came up in the seventh for what would be his last at bat of the game and sent a slow curveball by Bush to a place that was previously thought to be unattainable—over the right field roof at Forbes Field—for his third homer of the game. The ball traveled an estimated 600 feet and landed on a roof of a house outside the ballpark.

As Ruth rounded third, he was tired and knew he was done for the day. He went into the Pirates' dugout by mistake, sat next to rookie pitcher Mace Brown, and then took himself out of the game.

With the homer, Ruth became the first player to hit three home runs in a game in both the American and National Leagues. More importantly, the long ball would prove to be the 714th and last home run of his illustrious career.

It would have been truly appropriate had he retired at that point with his 600-foot home run as the last at bat of his career. In fact, Ruth wanted to quit at that point, but he was talked out of it by the Braves' management. He floundered for six more games, finally hanging it up after a doubleheader loss to the Phillies on May 30.

While the Bucs did score four more runs in their last two at bats to give them an 11–7 victory, their win was all but forgotten by the joyous throng. Similarly, the career game by the Pirates' Tommy Thevenow, who had a double, triple, and five RBIs, was ignored. The day belonged to Babe Ruth, the greatest slugger ever to play the game, ending his career with an exclamation point and giving the city of Pittsburgh a baseball gift it would never forget.

BOS N	2	0	2		0	1	0		2	0	0	—	7	13	1
PIT N	0	0	0		4	3	0		3	1	x	—	11	14	0

BATTING

Boston Braves	AB	R	H	RBI
Urbanski ss	3	1	0	0
Mallon 2b	4	2	1	0
Ruth rf	4	3	4	6
Mowry rf	1	0	1	0
Berger cf	5	1	3	0
Moore 1b	4	0	2	0
Lee lf	5	0	0	1
Coscarart 3b	4	0	2	0
Spohrer c	4	0	0	0
Betts p	2	0	0	0
Cantwell p	1	0	0	0
Whitney ph	1	0	0	0
Benton p	0	0	0	0
Totals	38	7	13	7

FIELDING—DP: 1. Urbanski-Mallon-Moore.

E: Mallon (4).

BATTING—2B: Mallon (9).

HR: Ruth 3 (6,1st inning off Lucas 1 on,3rd inning off Bush 1 on,7th inning off Bush 0 on).

SH: Mallon (4).

GDP: Lee (4).

Team LOB: 8.

Pittsburgh Pirates	AB	R	H	RBI
L. Waner cf	5	2	3	0
Jensen lf	4	1	2	0
P. Waner rf	4	2	2	0
Vaughan ss	4	2	2	1
Young 2b	3	1	1	3
Suhr 1b	3	2	2	1
Thevenow 3b	4	1	2	5
Grace c	4	0	0	1
Lucas p	0	0	0	0
Bush p	3	0	0	0
Hoyt p	1	0	0	0
Totals	35	11	14	11

FIELDING—DP: 1. Vaughan-Young-Suhr.
BATTING—2B: Thevenow (2).
3B: L. Waner (3); Suhr (3); Thevenow (2).
HR: Young (1,5th inning off Betts 2 on).
SH: Jensen (2); Young (2).
GDP: Young (1).
Team LOB: 5.

PITCHING

Boston Braves	IP	H	R	ER	BB	SO
Betts	4.2	9	7	7	1	1
Cantwell L(1–5)	2.1	3	3	3	2	0
Benton	1	2	1	1	0	0
Totals	8	14	11	11	3	1

Pittsburgh Pirates	IP	H	R	ER	BB	SO
Lucas	0.1	3	2	2	1	0
Bush	6	8	5	5	2	0
Hoyt W(3–5)	2.2	2	0	0	0	2
Totals	9	13	7	7	3	2

Umpires: HP—Beans Reardon, 1B—George Magerkurth, 3B—Charlie Moran
Time of Game: 2:14 Attendance: 10,000

#23

PIRATES 3, BROOKLYN DODGERS 2
MAY 28, 1956

The Streak

One of the best things about baseball is that the record book is not exclusively filled with the legends of the game. For every Babe Ruth, Ty Cobb, and Hank Aaron, there are names like Owen Wilson, Bob Horner, and Dale Long, from Springfield, Missouri, who for a short period of time in the spring of 1956, was the talk of the baseball world.

A two-sport star in high school, Long excelled in both football and baseball and was offered contracts by both the Pittsburgh Pirates and the Green Bay Packers. He chose baseball, but shortly after he made his major-league debut in 1951, the club waived him.

Long found success in the minors, winning the Pacific Coast League's Most Valuable Player Award in 1953, hitting 35 homers with the Hollywood Stars. Two years later he was back in the majors, getting a second opportunity with the Pirates. He made the most of his second chance, hitting 16 homers with a league-high 13 triples in 1955, cementing his spot as the Pirates' starting first baseman. A year later he would etch himself into baseball history with a home run streak that temporarily vaulted him among the game's best power hitters.

The streak began on May 19 when he hit his 17th homer of the year against Cubs hurler Jim Davis. The following day the Milwaukee Braves came in for a doubleheader, and the Pirates' first baseman hit home runs in each game, accounting for seven RBIs in the twin bill.

Long continued his torrid streak, smashing long balls in each of the next three games, tying the major-league mark of home runs in six consecutive games, a record he then shared with Lou Gehrig and Ken Williams.

All eyes were focused on the slugger the next evening in Philadelphia as he tried to make history against knuckleball pitcher Ben Flowers. While Long certainly was swinging well, his hits were falling just short of the fence. In the first inning he smacked a long ball that hit a foot below the top of the fence for a double, and then he belted a 380-foot sacrifice fly in the third. With one at bat left for the slugger in the eighth, Long came through in dramatic fashion, slugging a long home run at Connie Mack Stadium and putting his name in the record books with a home run in his seventh consecutive game.

Long was now a celebrity. His 13 home runs were ahead of Babe Ruth's then record pace of 60 homers in 1927. The story of his quest for glory was chronicled in *Life* magazine, he was a guest on the *Ed Sullivan Show,* and general manager Joe L. Brown gave him a $2,500 raise on the spot after he eclipsed the mark.

Dale Long was on top of the world, and he would attempt to extend his historic run two days later against the defending world champion Brooklyn Dodgers. A crowd of 32,221 eager Pirates fans filed into Forbes Field to see if their new hero could keep the streak going.

Brooklyn got off to a quick start when center fielder Duke Snider hit a towering homer over 500 feet to give the Dodgers a first inning 2–0 lead. Dodgers hurler Carl Erskine kept the Bucs scoreless in the first, retiring Long on a ground ball to shortstop Pee Wee Reese in his first at bat.

Pittsburgh cut the lead to one in the next frame when right fielder Lee Walls tripled, and third baseman Gene Freese brought him home with a sacrifice fly.

The score remained 2–1 until the fourth, when Erskine faced Long once again, trying to put a halt to the record streak that had baseball fans everywhere mesmerized. The Bucs' first baseman came through again, belting a long shot to right field that cleared the fence and extended his record home run blitz to eight consecutive games.

The Forbes Field crowd erupted. *Pittsburgh Post Gazette* baseball writer Jack Hernon exclaimed, "Never before has a Pirate received such a tremendous ovation."[1] The large throng demanded that the first baseman come out of the dugout for an encore after he crossed home plate. Long did just that and tipped his cap to the cheering fans.

After Long's homer tied it, the Pirates went on to win the game 3–2 on a single by Bob Skinner that knocked in Hank Foiles in the fifth inning. The victory gave Pittsburgh ace Bob Friend his fifth-straight win and his eighth triumph in the year, but the night truly belonged to Dale Long.

Unfortunately, Long's moment in the sun faded quickly. His average slipped to .263 by season's end, and he hit only 13 more home runs the rest of the campaign that included a one-for-50 dry spell. Things got worse when he became embroiled in an argument with Brown, feeling he was being treated poorly by the Bucs' general manager since he was no longer performing like a star.

Long was dealt to the Cubs the next season and hit only 99 home runs over the final eight seasons of his career. He did return to Forbes Field in 1960, playing with the Yankees in the World Series where he stroked a ninth-inning pinch-hit single in the seventh game.

While he never became the star slugger many thought he'd become following his memorable streak, Dale Long was able to set a record that over five decades later still stands. Don Mattingly and Ken Griffey Jr. tied the impressive mark, each hitting homers in eight consecutive games in 1987 and 1993, respectively, but Long's streak remains in the record book. For 10 days in May of 1956, there was no better power hitter in the game.

BRO N	2	0	0	0	0	0	0	0	0	—	2	2	1
PIT N	0	1	0	1	1	0	0	0	x	—	3	8	0

BATTING

Brooklyn Dodgers	AB	R	H	RBI
Gilliam 2b	3	1	1	0
Reese ss	3	0	0	0
Snider cf	3	1	1	2
Campanella c	4	0	0	0
Hodges 1b	3	0	0	0
Robinson 3b	1	0	0	0
Amoros lf	3	0	0	0
Furillo rf	3	0	0	0
Erskine p	2	0	0	0
Jackson ph	1	0	0	0
Labine p	0	0	0	0
Totals	26	2	2	2

FIELDING—DP: 1. Erskine-Reese-Hodges.

E: Gilliam (2).

BATTING—HR: Snider (7,1st inning off Friend 1 on 1 out).

GDP: Furillo (8,off Friend); Campanella (7,off Friend).

Team LOB: 3.

BASERUNNING—CS: Robinson (3,2nd base by Friend/Foiles).

Pittsburgh Pirates	AB	R	H	RBI
Virdon cf	4	0	1	0
Groat ss	4	0	0	0
Long 1b	4	1	1	1
Thomas lf	4	0	2	0
Clemente pr,lf	0	0	0	0
Walls rf	4	1	1	0
Freese 3b	3	0	0	1
Foiles c	2	1	1	0
J. O'Brien 2b	1	0	0	0
Skinner ph	1	0	1	1
Roberts 2b	1	0	1	0
Friend p	2	0	0	0
Totals	30	3	8	3

FIELDING—DP: 2. Groat-J. O'Brien-Long, Groat-Roberts-Long.
BATTING—2B: Roberts (4,off Erskine).
3B: Walls (5,off Erskine); Foiles (1,off Erskine).
HR: Long (14,4th inning off Erskine 0 on 0 out).
SH: Friend (4,off Erskine).
SF: Freese (1,off Erskine).
GDP: Groat (1,off Erskine).
Team LOB: 6.

PITCHING

Brooklyn Dodgers	IP	H	R	ER	BB	SO
Erskine L(2–4)	7	7	3	3	1	3
Labine	1	1	0	0	0	1
Totals	8	8	3	3	1	4

Pittsburgh Pirates	IP	H	R	ER	BB	SO
Friend W(8–2)	9	2	2	2	6	3

Umpires: HP—Lee Ballanfant, 1B—Artie Gore, 2B—Bill Jackowski, 3B—Shag Crawford
Time of Game: 2:13 **Attendance:** 32,221

A winner of 20 games five times during his 12-year career with the Pirates, Charles "Deacon" Phillippe had the honor of winning the franchise's first postseason game. In Game Three of the Chronicle-Telegraph Cup, a series pitting the top two finishers in the National League, Phillippe shut out Brooklyn 10–0 to cut the Superbas lead to two games to one. Three years later Phillippe would also have the honor of winning the first World Series game ever played, 7–3 against Boston. (Courtesy of the Pittsburgh Pirates.)

As a late season call-up in 1907 for the Pirates, Nick Maddox broke into majors in a big way. He went 5–1 in September with a 0.83 ERA, but it was his third major league start against Brooklyn on September 20 that forever etched his name in Pirates history. That day the young rookie pitched the franchise's first no-hitter and defeated the Superbas 2–1. (Courtesy of the Pittsburgh Pirates.)

Widely considered one of the 20 greatest players in major-league history, Pirates shortstop Honus Wagner's career nonetheless had a stigma surrounding it: his failure in the 1903 World Series where he hit only .222 in the Bucs' eight-game loss to Boston. Six years later Wagner finally rid himself of that earlier black mark by leading Pittsburgh to the 1909 World Series championship, hitting .333 against Detroit—including a clutch two-run triple in the seventh and deciding game. (Courtesy of the Pittsburgh Pirates.)

Pictured above is the 1909 Pittsburgh Pirates. Led by Hall of Fame shortstop Honus Wagner (pictured in the bottom row below the 19), who won his seventh National League batting title with a .339 average, the Pirates won a franchise record 110 games en route to their first World Series title. (Courtesy of the Pittsburgh Pirates.)

One of the few people in baseball history to have the credentials to be elected to the Hall of Fame as both a manager and player, Fred Clarke led the Pittsburgh Pirates to four National League pennants and a World Series title in 1909. Clarke won 1,602 games as a manager while hitting .315 with 2,703 hits. He was elected by the Veteran's Committee to the Hall of Fame in 1945. (Courtesy of the Pittsburgh Pirates.)

One of the greatest control pitchers in the history of the game, Babe Adams won 194 games for the Pirates in his 19-year major-league career while walking an average of only 1.29 batters per nine innings, the 18th best mark in baseball history. His control was best on display during a game on July 14, 1914, when he tossed a 21-inning contest against the Giants where he did not issue a walk. The game is the longest in major-league history in which a pitcher did not yield a base on balls. (Courtesy of the Pittsburgh Pirates.)

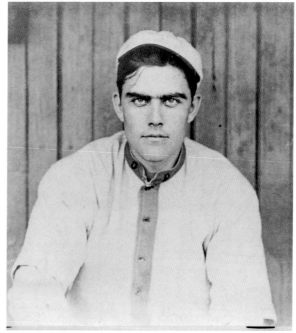

Best Wishes from — "Hank" Greenberg

Hall of Fame slugger Hank Greenberg was at the end of his major-league career when Pittsburgh Pirates owner John Galbreath made him the National League's first $100,000 player. Galbreath brought Greenberg to Pittsburgh to help tutor his young slugger Ralph Kiner. The mentor truly helped his student, as Kiner had his first great season in 1947 with a league-leading 51 homers. Following the 1947 campaign, Greenberg retired after hitting 23 home runs in his only season in Pittsburgh. (Courtesy of the Pittsburgh Pirates.)

On May 26, 1959, Pirates pitcher Harvey Haddix etched his name into the record books in a heartbreaking manner. That evening in Milwaukee against the Braves, Haddix pitched perhaps the greatest game in major-league history. He retired 36 Braves in a row, pitching 12 perfect innings, the only pitcher to ever take a perfect game beyond nine innings. Unfortunately, he gave up a run in the 13th, losing the greatest game ever pitched 1–0. (Courtesy of the Pittsburgh Pirates.)

One of the greatest power pitchers in Pirates history, six-foot-six left-hander Bob Veale put his awesome fastball on display against the Philadelphia Phillies on June 1, 1965. Despite several rain delays, Veale set a team record that night by striking out 16 Phillies in a 4–0 shutout victory. Veale went on to break his own franchise mark that same season by striking out 276 batters in 1965. (Courtesy of the Pittsburgh Pirates.)

In one of the strangest games in baseball history, Pittsburgh Pirates pitcher Dock Ellis tossed a no-hitter against the San Diego Padres on July 12, 1970, 2–0. He was uncharacteristically wild that game, walking eight Padres batters. What made this game so unique was that Ellis later admitted he was under the influence of LSD when he tossed his gem. (Courtesy of the Pittsburgh Pirates.)

A grave digger from Boston, Richie Hebner was the Pirates fine-hitting third baseman in the early 1970s. Perhaps his most memorable home run came in the 1971 National League Championship Series. Following a clutch homer in a Game Three win, Hebner was even more impressive in Game Four against San Francisco, when he blasted a three-run shot to bring the Bucs back from a three-run deficit en route to a 9–5 pennant-winning victory. (Courtesy of the Pittsburgh Pirates.)

The most revered athlete in the history of Pittsburgh, Roberto Clemente smacked a double off the left center field wall at Three Rivers Stadium on September 30, 1972, against New York Mets pitcher Jon Matlack for his 3,000th career hit. It would turn out to be his last major-league regular season at bat, as he was killed in a plane crash off the coast of Puerto Rico while delivering supplies to earthquake-ravaged Nicaragua on New Year's Eve 1972. (Courtesy of the Pittsburgh Pirates.)

On August 19, 1976, Pittsburgh Pirates pitcher John Candelaria tossed a no-hitter against the Los Angeles Dodgers, 2–0, at Three Rivers Stadium. The no-hitter was the first pitched by a Pirates pitcher in Pittsburgh since Nick Maddox tossed a gem against Brooklyn in 1907. (Courtesy of the Pittsburgh Pirates.)

After defeating the Cincinnati Reds 7–1 in Game Three of the 1979 National League Championship Series and capturing their first pennant since 1971, Pirates greats Willie Stargell and Dave Parker embrace. Parker hit .333 for the series while Stargell was awarded the National League Championship Series MVP Award, hitting .455 with two home runs. (Courtesy of the Pittsburgh Pirates.)

Sitting on home plate is Pirates left fielder Bill Robinson, who was hit by a pitch by Baltimore hurler Dennis Martinez with the bases loaded, scoring Omar Moreno (18) in the top of the ninth inning of Game Seven in the 1979 World Series to give Pittsburgh a 4–1 lead. The Pirates hung on to their three-run advantage to capture their fifth World Series championship. (Courtesy of the Pittsburgh Pirates.)

Among the many exciting moments for the Pittsburgh Pirates in their world championship run in 1979, perhaps the most exciting came in the first game of a doubleheader
against the Philadelphia Phillies on August 5. With the score tied 8–8 in the bottom of
the ninth, the Pirates loaded the bases as manager Chuck Tanner called on pinch hitter
John Milner. Milner launched a grand slam to beat their rivals 12–8, and his excited
teammates carried him off the field. (Courtesy of the Pittsburgh Pirates.)

While he certainly had a wonderful career before injuries caused some less-than-stellar seasons in the late 1970s, his renaissance in 1979 at 38 years old is one of the greatest stories in Pirates history. His efforts that season not only earned him the Most Valuable Player triple crown—MVP in the regular season, National League Championship Series, and World Series—but helped lead the Bucs to the World Series title. Perhaps one of his most memorable moments that season was his game-winning three-run homer in Game One of the National League Championship Series. (Courtesy of the Pittsburgh Pirates.)

After 11 years since their last postseason appearance, the Pittsburgh Pirates won their seventh National League Eastern Division championship on September 30, 1990, 2–0 against the St. Louis Cardinals. Pictured above is pitcher Doug Drabek, who tossed a three-hit shutout against the Cardinals that day for his 22nd victory of the season. Drabek went on to become the second Pirate to win the Cy Young Award following the 1990 campaign. (Courtesy of the Pittsburgh Pirates.)

Coming to the Pirates in 1998 from the Cleveland Indians, Brian Giles became one of the top home run hitters in team history, slugging 165 homers in five seasons in Pittsburgh. Perhaps his most memorable home run with the Pirates came on July 28, 2001, when he slammed a game-winning two-out grand slam against Houston to win the game 9–8. The grand slam capped a record-tying seven-run, ninth-inning comeback by the Bucs as they were down 8–2 to Houston with two outs. (Courtesy of the Pittsburgh Pirates.)

#22

Overcoming Obstacles

After a decade of frustration at the hands of the Cincinnati Reds, the Pittsburgh Pirates were on the brink of finally climbing over the hurdle that had consistently prevented them from winning the National League crown. Fresh off two exciting extra-inning victories over the Reds in Cincinnati to take a commanding 2–0 lead in the best-of-five National League Championship Series, Pittsburgh was coming home to try to win one more game and capture its long-awaited pennant.

It was far from a sure thing, though. A well-placed hit here or there by the Reds and it could have easily been Cincinnati with the 2–0 lead, and this talented Reds team was certainly able to win three in a row. In this do-or-die game, Cincinnati sent out second-year hurler Mike LaCoss to face the Pirates' Bert Blyleven who was coming off a 12–5 regular season.

Rain delayed the start of the game, but when it got under way, it was apparent early on that Game Three would not resemble the first two. LaCoss was wild from the beginning, walking Pirates center fielder Omar Moreno to lead off the bottom of the first. Moreno then stole second, went to third base on a fielder's choice, and came home on a sacrifice fly by Dave Parker to give the Bucs a 1–0 lead.

In the second, things were no better for LaCoss as Phil Garner led off the inning with a triple to right, coming home on a Tim Foli sacrifice fly to make the score 2–0. Not wanting to let the game get out of hand, Reds manager John McNamara quickly went to his bullpen and pulled LaCoss in favor of Fred Norman.

With Blyleven dominating the Reds through the first three innings, the Pirates' offense broke the game open, scoring twice each in the third and fourth innings. Pittsburgh slugger Willie Stargell, who was about to be named National

League MVP in 1979, crushed a home run in the third to make it 3–0 and then received a standing ovation from the adoring crowd. "If they took a picture of my body," a touched Stargell said later on, "they would show Goosebumps everywhere. The Good Lord lets us shed tears at touching moments and that's what transpired with me. I wish there was a way to thank every fan individually."[1] Two batters later, Bill Madlock followed suit as he hit a home run of his own, increasing the Pirates' advantage to four. The rout was on.

Stargell rose to the occasion again in the fourth with a two-out, two-run double and put the icing on the cake in the eighth with another run on a Garner RBI single. The Bucs were up 7–1.

Blyleven finished up his dominating nine-strikeout performance in the ninth, getting Driessen and Knight to ground out before striking out Cesar Geronimo for the final out of the Pirates' National League Championship Series sweep and setting off a wild celebration in the Steel City. "There's something about ending it with a strikeout," Blyleven said. "There's something about seeing the last pitch go past the batter and watch the catcher jump up in the air."[2]

For the Reds, they knew it was not only the end of their dominance over the Pirates but also the end of their championship run. Foster gave credit to the trade that brought Bill Madlock from the Giants in late June as the move that made the Bucs champions. "They're a better team with Bill Madlock. He helped them both defensively and offensively," Foster said.[3]

Beyond Madlock, what also inspired the team was a less than stellar evaluation of the Bucs' chances to win the NL championship by Detroit Tigers scout Jack Tighe. An article in a Cincinnati newspaper had Tighe rating the Reds superior in six out of eight positions. "The story in Cincinnati ticked us off," Madlock said following the victory. "It's like Cincinnati has such a better team, that we should have stayed in Pittsburgh."[4]

Blyleven's impressive showing was an appropriate finish to a series defined by stellar Pirates pitching. Pittsburgh limited the Reds to only five runs in 30 innings of play for a sparkling 1.50 ERA. Combined with the timely hitting of Stargell and the others, the Pirates would now face the Baltimore Orioles, an honor they earned by achieving the decade-long challenge of finally beating the Cincinnati Reds.

CIN N	0	0	0		0	0	1		0	0	0	—	1	8	1
PIT N	1	1	2		2	0	0			0	1	x	—	7	7	0

BATTING

Cincinnati Reds	AB	R	H	RBI
Collins rf	4	0	2	0
Morgan 2b	4	0	0	0
Concepcion ss	4	0	2	0
Foster lf	4	0	0	0
Bench c	4	1	1	1
Driessen 1b	4	0	0	0
Knight 3b	4	0	2	0
Geronimo cf	4	0	1	0
LaCoss p	0	0	0	0
Norman p	1	0	0	0
Leibrandt p	0	0	0	0
Auerbach ph	1	0	0	0
Soto p	0	0	0	0
Spilman ph	1	0	0	0
Tomlin p	0	0	0	0
Hume p	0	0	0	0
Totals	35	1	8	1

FIELDING—E: Geronimo (1).
BATTING—2B: Knight (1,off Blyleven).
HR: Bench (1,6th inning off Blyleven 0 on 1 out).
Team LOB: 7.

Pittsburgh Pirates	AB	R	H	RBI
Moreno cf	2	1	0	0
Foli ss	4	0	0	1
Parker rf	3	1	1	1
Stargell 1b	4	1	2	3
Milner lf	2	0	0	0
B. Robinson lf	1	0	0	0
Madlock 3b	2	1	1	1
Ott c	4	0	0	0
Garner 2b	4	2	2	0
Blyleven p	3	1	1	0
Totals	29	7	7	6

BATTING—**2B:** Stargell (2,off Norman).
3B: Garner (1,off LaCoss).
HR: Stargell (2,3rd inning off Norman 0 on 0 out); Madlock (1,3rd inning off Norman 0 on 1 out).
SH: Moreno (1,off Norman); Blyleven (1,off Tomlin).
SF: Parker (1,off LaCoss); Foli (2,off LaCoss).
IBB: Madlock (1,by Tomlin).
Team LOB: 8.
BASERUNNING—**SB:** Moreno (1,2nd base off LaCoss/Bench); Parker (1,2nd base off Tomlin/Bench).

PITCHING

Cincinnati Reds	IP	H	R	ER	BB	SO
LaCoss L(0–1)	1.2	1	2	2	4	0
Norman	2	4	4	4	1	1
Leibrandt	0.1	0	0	0	0	0
Soto	2	0	0	0	0	1
Tomlin	1.2	2	1	0	1	1
Hume	0.1	0	0	0	0	0
Totals	**8**	**7**	**7**	**6**	**6**	**3**

IBB: Tomlin (2,Madlock).

Pittsburgh Pirates	IP	H	R	ER	BB	SO
Blyleven W(1–0)	9	8	1	1	0	9

Umpires: HP—Jerry Dale, 1B—Frank Pulli, 2B—Dick Stello, 3B—Jim Quick, LF—John Kibler, RF—Ed Montague
Time of Game: 2:45 **Attendance:** 42,240

PIRATES 7, ST. LOUIS CARDINALS 5
APRIL 6, 1973

Celebrating a Fallen Icon

It had been a difficult four-month period for the Pittsburgh Pirates to start 1973. Their beloved leader, Roberto Clemente, was tragically killed in a plane crash on New Year's Eve while delivering much-needed supplies to earthquake-ravaged Nicaragua. While losing Clemente as a player certainly hurt the team, losing Clemente the man and the unquestioned leader of the team was devastating.

"He died caring," exclaimed Pirates general manager Joe L. Brown. "I'm sorry about baseball last. The big thing is losing Roberto Clemente the man." Closer Dave Giusti was equally stunned. "I still can't believe it," he said. "I've been around other superstars. I never saw any of them have as much compassion for his teammates like Clemente did. He would treat a rookie like he was Willie Stargell."[1]

Probably the player who was most shattered by Clemente's death was his close friend and fellow Latino Manny Sanguillen. To Sanguillen, Clemente was the hero and leader of all Latin ballplayers, and he appreciated every moment he spent with the Pirates' Hall of Famer. "[That's why] I thank God I played with him," he said. "Because I saw the sacrifices he made to help Latinos. He said he . . . was going to do everything possible for Puerto Rico and Latin America to be the best ball players in the world. He sacrificed for that and he always said that in a few years there were going to be many Puerto Rican and Latino ball players in the Hall of Fame . . . He was our leader, like Jackie Robinson."[2]

Sanguillen was crushed. He was the only member of the team not to attend Clemente's funeral in Puerto Rico, opting instead to dive in the shark-infested waters near the beach where the plane crashed in an attempt to recover Clemente's body, but it was never found.

Perhaps symbolically, Pirates manager Bill Virdon chose Sanguillen to replace their fallen leader in right field on opening day. While moving Sanguillen to right would serve as a tribute, it would also allow Virdon to insert another potent bat, catcher Milt May, into the Bucs' already powerful lineup.

As the opening game was about to begin, Sanguillen was thinking less about his new position and more about his fallen friend who he was about to replace. "I dreamt of Roberto last night," he said. "I dreamt I was diving and looking for his body in the water."[3] Still struggling to overcome his sorrow, he would take the field and do his best to replace Clemente, who was honored in a touching pregame ceremony.

A then record opening day crowd of 51,695 emotional fans stood and offered a respectful ovation as Clemente's widow, Vera, came on the field with her three small sons, Roberto Jr., Enrique, and Luis, along with Roberto's mother, Luisa Walker. Vera accepted his uniform as the team retired his number 21. She was also given the Gold Glove Award, his 12th, which he earned in 1972, and a lifetime pass to major-league baseball games. When she accepted the uniform, Vera broke down in tears, as did a good percentage of the fans in attendance.

Pittsburgh's Steve Blass got the start that day after back-to-back sterling seasons, but his career would begin to take a sudden downturn that day, a downturn that saw Blass's pinpoint control mysteriously leave him, becoming uncontrollably wild and inconsistent. He would no longer be known for his 103 victories or his historic World Series win in 1971 but for his sudden loss of control, a malady that has since been named "Steve Blass Disease," a condition that began to surface on this day.

He gave up five runs in the third inning, putting the Cardinals up 5–0, before eventually calming down and retiring St. Louis in order in the fourth and fifth. But the damage was done, and the veteran hurler was replaced in the sixth.

What had begun as a day of somber reflection had turned into a debacle. But then the Pirates began a memorable and emotional comeback. Even without their beloved leader, the Bucs' lineup remained one of the most dangerous in the game, and despite facing the great Bob Gibson their talent began to showcase itself in the sixth. They scratched out a run in the sixth, and third baseman Richie Hebner then led off the seventh with a home run after missing a take sign.

While the Bucs' offense was beginning to come alive, the bullpen was shutting down the St. Louis offense. Luke Walker had tossed two innings of one-hit ball, and Jim Rooker then struck out a pair in a scoreless eighth, bringing the Pirates up to bat down 5–2. With one out, Sanguillen and Al Oliver singled, putting men on first and third, and then slugger Willie Stargell walked to load the bases.

Veteran hurler Diego Segui came on to try to stop the Pirates' attack. He quickly struck out Bob Robertson for the second out before Hebner continued his heroics with his third hit of the contest, a broken bat blooper into short left field for a two-run double.

Gene Clines, sent up by Virdon next to pinch-hit for Rooker, ripped a line drive into the gap in left center. Lou Brock, the speedy Cardinals' left fielder, almost made a spectacular catch to end the inning, but the ball bounced off his glove as Clines strolled into third with a two-run triple giving the Pirates their first lead of the day 6–5. They would tack on one more on a Milt May grounder that St. Louis shortstop Ray Busse failed to come up with, allowing Clines to score.

Pittsburgh reliever Ramon Hernandez came in to pitch in the top of the ninth and, after a leadoff walk, set down the Cardinals in order to end the contest and to complete the Pirates' dramatic comeback victory.

Despite the win and the excitement that the large throng was now embracing, most understood it was a hollow victory. When the joy of the victory was over, the sober reality set in: they would never again get to witness one of the franchise's greatest players. It was a win under such sorrowful circumstances that no one could have imagined it only four months before.

STL N	0	3	2		0	0	0		0	0	0	—	5	7	2
PIT N	0	0	0		0	0	1		1	5	x	—	7	8	0

BATTING

St. Louis Cardinals	AB	R	H	RBI
Brock lf	4	0	1	1
Sizemore 2b	4	1	1	0
J. Cruz cf	2	1	0	0
Torre 1b	3	0	1	0
Simmons c	3	1	0	1
Reitz 3b	4	0	1	1
Carbo rf	3	1	2	1
Melendez ph	0	0	0	0
Busse ss	4	1	1	0
Gibson p	2	0	0	1
Segui p	0	0	0	0
Stein ph	1	0	0	0
Totals	30	5	7	5

FIELDING—DP: 2. Busse-Sizemore-Torre, Gibson-Busse-Torre.
E: Busse 2 (2).
PB: Simmons (1).
BATTING—2B: Busse (1,off Blass).
SF: Gibson (1,off Blass).
HBP: Torre (1,by Blass).
Team LOB: 5.
BASERUNNING—CS: Brock (1,2nd base by Blass/May).

Pittsburgh Pirates	AB	R	H	RBI
Stennett 2b,ss	4	1	0	0
Sanguillen rf	4	1	2	0
Oliver cf	3	1	2	1
Stargell lf	2	1	0	0
R. Hernandez p	0	0	0	0
Robertson 1b	4	0	0	0
Hebner 3b	4	2	3	3
Alley ss	2	0	0	0
Rooker p	0	0	0	0
Clines ph,lf	1	1	1	2
May c	3	0	0	0
Blass p	1	0	0	0
Davalillo ph	1	0	0	0
Walker p	0	0	0	0
Cash ph,2b	2	0	0	0
Totals	31	7	8	6

BATTING—2B: Hebner (1,off Segui).
3B: Oliver (1,off Gibson); Clines (1,off Segui).
HR: Hebner (1,7th inning off Gibson 0 on 0 out).
SF: Oliver (1,off Gibson).
GDP: Sanguillen (1,off Gibson); Robertson (1,off Gibson).
IBB: May (1,by Segui).
Team LOB: 6.

PITCHING

St. Louis Cardinals	IP	H	R	ER	BB	SO
Gibson	7.1	6	5	4	4	4
Segui L(0–1)	0.2	2	2	1	1	1
Totals	8	8	7	5	5	5

IBB: Segui (1,May).

Pittsburgh Pirates	IP	H	R	ER	BB	SO
Blass	5	5	5	5	4	1
Walker	2	1	0	0	0	0
Rooker W(1–0)	1	1	0	0	0	2
R. Hernandez SV(1)	1	0	0	0	1	0
Totals	9	7	5	5	5	3

WP: Blass (1).
HBP: Blass (1,Torre).
Umpires: HP—Ed Vargo, 1B—Paul Pryor, 2B—Bruce Froemming, 3B—Terry Tata
Time of Game: 2:02 Attendance: 51,695

PIRATES 9, HOUSTON ASTROS 8
JULY 28, 2001

Comeback for the Ages

As the Pirates entered the 2001 campaign, there was hope for the franchise. The club thought it had pieced together one of the best young starting rotations in the majors, led by Francisco Cordova, Jason Schmidt, and Kris Benson. Add to the mix the signing of free-agent slugger Derek Bell, and the hopes for a promising season seemed justified. As it turned out, they weren't.

Cordova and Schmidt were still working their way back from injuries and weren't ready to start the season, while Benson hurt his arm and would miss the entire campaign. This left new manager Lloyd McClendon with a raw, untested pitching staff made up of players either before or after their prime. What's more, Bell was having a miserable year, hitting .173. The promise of a competitive team was vanishing; now they were just trying to avoid losing 100 games as they began to play in their sparkling new home, PNC Park.

Despite their losing ways, more than 2.4 million fans would see the Pirates play in the inaugural season at PNC Park, and on July 28, the 32,977 in attendance to see Pittsburgh host the Houston Astros would witness the high point of the season.

For the first eight innings, the script unfolded much as it had for the 2001 Pirates. On the strength of three home runs by Houston's Vinnie Castillo, narrowly missing a record-tying fourth homer on a spectacular over-the-fence catch by Pirates left fielder Brian Giles in the fourth, the Astros took an 8–2 lead into the bottom of the ninth. The victory appeared imminent as the Houston bullpen led the team to a 49–0 record when going into the ninth with a lead.

Not surprisingly, Astros reliever Mike Jackson retired the first two Pirates in the ninth, but the Pirates hadn't quit yet. "Guys were still peppy," McClendon would say later. "I just told them to swing the bats and see what happens. Surely, we have nothing to lose in that case."[1] They certainly didn't have anything to lose and began to prove it.

Kevin Young kept the Pirates alive with a double to left. Second baseman Pat Meares then cut the Astros' lead to four when he parked a homer over the left field fence to make it 8–4. What remained of the large crowd stirred, appreciating that the home team would go down fighting. The fans became even more thrilled when pinch hitter Adam Hyzdu stroked a single to left, and Tyke Redman followed with a walk with shortstop Jack Wilson coming to the plate. Wilson then singled in Hyzdu to reduce the deficit to three runs and brought the tying run to the plate.

Astros manager Larry Dierker had seen enough and called for his closer, Billy Wagner, to stop the Pirates' rally in its tracks and allow the Astros to escape with what only moments ago seemed like a certain victory. Instead of squashing the rally, Wagner hit catcher Jason Kendall to load the bases. That brought up the Bucs' most potent hitter, Brian Giles, as the potential winning run. Wagner fired a smoking fastball, but Giles walloped it over the fence for a dramatic walk-off grand slam, giving the Bucs an improbable 9–8 victory.

The seven-run, two-out comeback in the bottom of the ninth equaled a National League mark for greatest comeback in that situation, matching the 1952 Cubs, who also pulled out a 9–8 victory against the Cincinnati Reds.

"I was just trying to put it in play and hit it hard," Giles said. "I don't think you ever go there expecting to go deep. You want to be short to the ball, and he's going to supply the power."

McClendon was equally amazed. "Lefty on lefty. Their guy's throwing 100 mph, and you turn that fastball around. That's pretty good. Surely you don't think I'm going to sit here and try to explain it."[2] It was a finish that certainly was difficult to explain, a shining moment in a dark season. And it remains the most exciting contest that the Pirates have played in their dazzling home.

| HOU N | 0 | 1 | 0 | 0 | 3 | 0 | 0 | 2 | 2 | — | 8 | 12 | 0 |
| PIT N | 0 | 1 | 0 | 0 | 0 | 0 | 1 | 0 | 7 | — | 9 | 12 | 0 |

BATTING

Houston Astros	AB	R	H	RBI
Biggio 2b	5	2	3	0
Lugo ss	4	0	1	1
Berkman cf,lf	5	1	1	1
Castilla 3b	5	3	3	5
Alou rf	4	0	0	0
Ward 1b	3	1	1	0
Hidalgo cf	1	0	0	0
Eusebio c	3	0	1	0
Merced lf	3	0	1	1
Jackson p	0	0	0	0
Wagner p	0	0	0	0
Oswalt p	3	0	0	0
Villone p	0	0	0	0
Bagwell ph,1b	1	1	1	0
Totals	**37**	**8**	**12**	**8**

BATTING—2B: Lugo (14,off Olivares).
HR: Castilla 3 (13,2nd inning off Arroyo 0 on 0 out,5th inning off Arroyo 2 on 1 out,8th inning off Olivares 0 on 0 out).
SH: Lugo (7,off Arroyo).
IBB: Merced (1,by Arroyo).
Team LOB: 7.
BASERUNNING—CS: Merced (1,2nd base by Olivares/Kendall).

Pittsburgh Pirates	AB	R	H	RBI
Redman cf	4	1	1	0
J. Wilson ss	5	1	1	1
Kendall c	4	1	0	0
Giles lf	5	2	3	4
Ramirez 3b	4	1	1	0
Vander Wal rf	4	0	1	0
Young 1b	3	1	2	2
Meares 2b	4	1	2	2
Arroyo p	2	0	0	0
Morris ph	0	0	0	0
C. Wilson ph	1	0	0	0
Olivares p	0	0	0	0
Hyzdu ph	1	1	1	0
Totals	**37**	**9**	**12**	**9**

BATTING—2B: Giles (30,off Oswalt); Vander Wal (22,off Oswalt); Young (23,off Jackson).

HR: Meares (4,9th inning off Jackson 1 on 2 out); Giles (25,9th inning off Wagner 3 on 2 out).

SF: Young (3,off Oswalt).

HBP: Kendall (12,by Wagner).

Team LOB: 5.

PITCHING

Houston Astros	IP	H	R	ER	BB	SO
Oswalt	6.1	7	2	2	0	6
Villone	0.2	0	0	0	0	1
Jackson	1.2	4	5	5	1	0
Wagner L(2–4)	0	1	2	2	0	0
Totals	8.2	12	9	9	1	7

HBP: Wagner (1,Kendall).

Pittsburgh Pirates	IP	H	R	ER	BB	SO
Arroyo	7	7	4	4	2	4
Olivares W(5–7)	2	5	4	4	2	1
Totals	9	12	8	8	4	5

WP: Arroyo (3).

IBB: Arroyo (3,Merced).

Umpires: HP—John Hirschbeck, 1B—Jay Klemm, 2B—Brian O'Nora, 3B—Bill Welke

Time of Game: 2:30 **Attendance:** 32,977

PIRATES 9, CINCINNATI REDS 6
OCTOBER 1, 1927

The Prize
Murderers' Row

Though the prize for victory was an even more daunting challenge for the 1927 Pittsburgh Pirates, a win over the Cincinnati Reds at Redland Field would conclude what had been a brilliant three-team race for the National League pennant among the Pirates, St. Louis Cardinals, and New York Giants.

Going into the contest, Pittsburgh enjoyed a two-game lead with two left to play. The Giants had lost to Brooklyn 10–5 that day, which officially eliminated New York, and the Cardinals were hanging on by a thread. A loss by St. Louis or a win by the Pirates would give the Bucs their second senior circuit championship in three years—and this time, a trip to the 1927 World Series to face "Murderers' Row," the powerful 1927 New York Yankees, arguably the greatest team in the history of the game.

Pirates manager Donie Bush gave the ball to one of his aces, 34-year-old Ray Kremer, who needed one more victory to clinch his second straight 20-win season.

Pittsburgh took charge early with a two-run single by Glenn Wright in the first inning, followed by a George Grantham triple and another RBI hit by Earl Smith to make it 5–0 before the Reds even came to bat. Up by five runs and with the red-hot Kremer on the mound, the Bucs looked to have the pennant wrapped up before the game was an inning old. But Cincinnati soon made things interesting.

The Reds plated one run in the bottom of the first and three more in the fourth to cut the Pirates' advantage to a mere run. Bush pulled Kremer for his other ace, 22-game-winner Carmen Hill, who stopped the bleeding. Unfortunately, the damage had already been done, and the Reds were now firmly back in the ball game.

In the top of the sixth, the Pirates were able to put some separation between themselves and the Reds when future Hall of Famer Pie Traynor ripped a single, scoring two runs and giving the Bucs a 7–4 lead. Cincinnati once again battled back, chipping away with a run in each of the sixth and seventh innings to cut the lead to one.

With their lead—and their chance to win the pennant—again in danger of disappearing, the Pirates' offense came through to put away this game in the ninth. Grantham walked with one out and scored all the way from first when Smith singled to right. Pittsburgh tacked an insurance run, and in the bottom of the ninth, Pirates reliever John Miljus made quick work of the Reds, retiring the side in order to secure the sixth National League pennant in the franchise's history.

Soon after the joy had dissipated, the Bucs did indeed get their prize for winning the title: the right to face the legendary Yankees lineup. The New York team made quick work of the Bucs, sweeping them in four straight games to win their second world championship. But the lopsided Fall Classic couldn't erase the jubilation the Pirates experienced on this October afternoon in Cincinnati, when Pittsburgh earned the right to face one of the greatest teams of all time.

PIT N	5	0	0	0	0	2	0	0	2	—	9	17	3
CIN N	1	0	0	3	0	1	1	0	0	—	6	16	1

BATTING

Pittsburgh Pirates	AB	R	H	RBI
L. Waner cf	5	1	3	0
Barnhart lf	5	2	2	0
P. Waner rf	5	1	2	0
Wright ss	4	1	1	2
Traynor 3b	5	1	3	2
Grantham 2b	4	2	1	2
Rhyne 2b	0	0	0	0
Harris 1b	5	0	1	0
Smith c	5	1	3	2
Kremer p	2	0	0	0
Hill p	1	0	0	0
Miljus p	2	0	1	1
Totals	**43**	**9**	**17**	**9**

FIELDING—DP: 1. Grantham-Wright-Harris.

E: Grantham 2 (35), Hill (4).

PB: Smith 2 (7).

BATTING—2B: Barnhart (23); Harris (27).

3B: Grantham (11).

SH: Barnhart (21).

HBP: L. Waner (6).

Team LOB: 11.

Cincinnati Reds	AB	R	H	RBI
Dressen 3b	5	2	1	1
Walker rf	5	1	3	1
Pipp 1b	5	0	1	2
Bressler lf	5	0	3	0
Allen cf	4	0	0	0
Ford ss	5	0	0	0
Critz 2b	5	2	4	0
Hargrave c	2	1	1	1
Picinich c	2	0	1	0
Lucas ph	1	0	0	0
Donohue p	0	0	0	0
Kolp p	2	0	2	0
May p	2	0	0	0
Totals	**43**	**6**	**16**	**5**

FIELDING—DP: 1. Critz-Ford-Pipp.
E: Ford (27).
BATTING—2B: Dressen (36); Bressler 2 (14).
3B: Walker (10).
Team LOB: 11.

PITCHING

Pittsburgh Pirates	IP	H	R	ER	BB	SO
Kremer	3.2	9	4	4	1	0
Hill	2	4	1	1	0	1
Miljus W(8–3)	3.1	3	1	0	0	4
Totals	**9**	**16**	**6**	**5**	**1**	**5**

Cincinnati Reds	IP	H	R	ER	BB	SO
Donohue L(6–16)	0.1	5	5	5	0	0
Kolp	3.2	5	0	0	0	0
May	5	7	4	2	2	3
Totals	**9**	**17**	**9**	**7**	**2**	**3**

WP: May (8).
HBP: May (14).
Umpires: HP—Barry McCormick, 1B—Ernie Quigley, 3B—Beans Reardon
Time of Game: 2:17

#18

PIRATES 1, NEW YORK METS 0
SEPTEMBER 5, 1990

Slaying the Beast

The Pittsburgh Pirates had been battling the beast for the better part of three years, and by the beginning of September 1990, they were finally poised to slay it. The proverbial beast in this scenario was the New York Mets. The Bucs finally had the opportunity to get them in their sights and begin to put an end to their dominance. In a midweek doubleheader at Three Rivers Stadium, just after Labor Day, Pittsburgh would have a chance to topple its rivals.

Since 1984, the Mets had been the dominant team in the National League East, finishing a close second in 1984 and 1985, before crushing the division in their world championship season of 1986 and then capturing another division title two years later. Meanwhile, the Pirates were on the other end of the spectrum, trying their best to stay out of the division cellar. With Pittsburgh on the rise and the Mets beginning their decline, the teams battled for the NL East title throughout the 1990 season.

Going into September, Pittsburgh had been atop the division standings for 120 out of the season's 146 days, but three days later, the Mets overtook the Pirates and held a half-game lead as the final month of the campaign began. The next day the Bucs defeated the Phillies, and the Mets lost to the Cardinals, giving Pittsburgh a razor-thin edge. The following evening, the two rivals met in a doubleheader for the two most important games of the 1990 campaign.

After a decade of futility, Pirates fans knew the importance of this matchup, and, thirsty for their first championship in 11 years, the largest crowd of the season—49,793—showed up at Three Rivers Stadium to watch a critical moment of the pennant race.

In the first game, Pirates manager Jim Leyland tabbed newly acquired pitcher Zane Smith, who'd won his first three games since coming over in a trade with the Montreal Expos in early August. While Smith had been pitching in the final weeks of the summer, as autumn approached, he would toss the game of his life.

Center fielder Keith Miller led off the game with a single for the Mets. Despite the hit against the Pirates' southpaw, Miller's single represented New York's only offense of the day. The Pittsburgh offense was more active, constantly threatening to score against Mets starter Frank Viola, but each time the New York starter battled out of trouble, holding the Bucs scoreless. While Viola was playing with fire, Smith was completely in control.

After the single to Miller in the first and a walk to the Mets' center fielder in the third, Smith retired the next 19 New York batters in order as this unusual pitching duel went into the ninth scoreless.

Smith quickly set down the Mets in order in the top of the ninth, but unless the Bucs could figure out a way to scratch out a run, his efforts might be for naught. Mets manager Bud Harrelson pulled Viola going into the ninth as the New York starter stranded 13 batters in his eight innings of shutout ball.

Mets closer John Franco came on to face the Pirates' Gary Redus who led off the ninth with a sharp single to center. Shortstop Jay Bell came up next and laid down a poor bunt in an attempt to move Redus into scoring position, looking like a sure double play. New York catcher Charlie O'Brien made a bad throw to second and everyone was safe. After Van Slyke moved both runners into scoring position with a sacrifice bunt, Franco intentionally walked Bonilla to load the bases and try to set up a force-out with one out.

Up came the team's best hitter, Barry Bonds, with a chance to win the game and give the Bucs a little breathing room in the standings. With the infield drawn in, Bonds came through as he had so many times before, sending a long fly to left field that dropped in for the game-winning hit, giving the team an exciting 1–0 win.

Smith's masterpiece—nearly wasted—had culminated in a victory. "It was by far the biggest game I've ever pitched," he said. "It was pretty heart-wrenching. I think it was the kind of game everybody likes to watch."[1]

With momentum now on their side, the Pittsburgh hurlers once again handcuffed the Mets' batters in the second game, en route to a 3–1 victory to complete the sweep, building a 2½-game lead in the division.

The next day Pittsburgh put an exclamation point on this important three-game series with their rivals, crushing the floundering Mets, 7–1.

The Pirates were now ready to be champions and were finally able to stand up to the mighty Mets. Smith's and Bonds's superb clutch hits proved to Pittsburgh they could get over the hump and top the Mets in the long pennant race. The win in the first game of this doubleheader was a springboard to three consecutive Eastern Division crowns, while for the Mets it began a long period of struggle.

NY N	0	0	0	0	0	0	0	0	0	—	0	1	2
PIT N	0	0	0	0	0	0	0	0	1	—	1	8	0

BATTING

New York Mets	AB	R	H	RBI
Miller cf	3	0	1	0
Herr 2b	4	0	0	0
Jefferies 3b	3	0	0	0
Strawberry rf	3	0	0	0
McReynolds lf	3	0	0	0
Johnson ss	3	0	0	0
Teufel 1b	3	0	0	0
O'Brien c	3	0	0	0
Viola p	2	0	0	0
Tabler ph	1	0	0	0
Franco p	0	0	0	0
Totals	28	0	1	0

FIELDING—E: Teufel (4), O'Brien (1).
BATTING—Team LOB: 2.

Pittsburgh Pirates	AB	R	H	RBI
Redus 1b	4	1	1	0
Bell ss	4	0	0	0
Van Slyke cf	4	0	1	0
Bonilla rf	4	0	1	0
Bonds lf	3	0	1	1
King 3b	4	0	1	0
Lind 2b	4	0	0	0
LaValliere c	2	0	2	0
Smith p	4	0	1	0
Totals	33	1	8	1

BATTING—2B: LaValliere (12,off Viola); Smith (3,off Viola).
SH: Van Slyke (3,off Franco).
HBP: Bonds (3,by Viola).
IBB: Bonilla (9,by Franco).
Team LOB: 15.
BASERUNNING—CS: Bonds (10,2nd base by Viola/O'Brien).

PITCHING

New York Mets	IP	H	R	ER	BB	SO
Viola	8	6	0	0	5	5
Franco L(4–1)	0.1	2	1	1	1	0
Totals	8.1	8	1	1	6	5

WP: Viola (11).
HBP: Viola (2,Bonds).
IBB: Franco (1,Bonilla).

Pittsburgh Pirates	IP	H	R	ER	BB	SO
Smith W(10–7)	9	1	0	0	1	7

Umpires: HP—Harry Wendelstedt, 1B—Joe West, 2B—Tom Hallion, 3B—Randy Marsh
Time of Game: 2:32 Attendance: 49,793

The Candy Man Can

Despite the fact that Forbes Field was a spacious, pitcher-friendly ballpark, no pitcher had ever tossed a no-hitter there. While the Cardinals' Bob Gibson was able to break the 64-year Steel City no-hitterless streak in 1971 when he pitched a no-hitter against the soon-to-be world champions at Three Rivers Stadium, the streak remained for the hometown pitchers. Finally in 1976, a 22-year-old pitcher by the name of John Candelaria ended the 69-year streak in front of a national TV audience.

The young pitcher was in his second year with the Pirates and had made a name for himself as a rookie the year before, going 8–6 with a 2.76 ERA, then fanning a record 14 Cincinnati Reds in game three of the National League Championship Series. His second season was even better as he roared to a 10–4 mark and had become the team's best pitcher. The 1976 team, though, was not having a stellar campaign, as it was unable to continue the success it had enjoyed in the 1970s and had fallen well back of the front-running Philadelphia Phillies by August. The Bucs were in need of a quick spark, and their young phenom was just about to give them that.

Facing the Los Angeles Dodgers on "Candy Night" at Three Rivers (every fan in the park received a candy bar in honor of the star pitcher), Candelaria started off sharp, although his date with destiny almost ended before it began. After retiring Davey Lopes on a flyout to center, L.A. second baseman Ted Sizemore lifted a lazy fly to right field that looked like it was going to drop in for a hit. Pirates right fielder Dave Parker came out of nowhere to make a fantastic knee-high catch to rob Sizemore. It didn't seem like a big deal at the time, but by game's end it would prove huge.

After setting down the Dodgers in order once again in the second frame, Candelaria got into his only trouble of the evening in the third when the Dodgers loaded the bases on a walk and two errors. Candelaria then retired Bill Russell to end the threat.

As good as Candelaria was, so was Dodgers starter Doug Rau, who gave up only two hits. Both teams were scoreless through four innings.

After Candelaria retired Los Angeles in order over the next two innings, the Pirates would generate all the offense they would need in the bottom of the fifth. With two outs and two on, Pittsburgh third baseman Bill Robinson stroked a two-run double to left to put the Bucs up 2–0. Now that the Pirates had the lead, Candelaria would go into high gear as he hadn't allowed a base runner since the third inning going into the ninth.

The 9,860 fans at the stadium were on the edge of their seats as they were about to get more than just a candy bar. Candelaria retired the first two batters on three pitches in the ninth. Bill Russell would be the Dodgers' last chance to break up the gem. After firing a strike to Russell, Candelaria got him to loft the next offering into center field. When Al Oliver cradled the ball in his glove, Candelaria leaped into the air as his teammates surrounded him to celebrate the first Pirates' no-hitter pitched in Pittsburgh in 69 years.

While the young southpaw was thrilled with his memorable accomplishment, it came at a price. Even though he was only 22, the chronic back problems that would plague him throughout his career bothered him greatly after the game. "The back hurts," he said. " It would hurt if I had been knocked out in the first inning or if I had just pitched five or six innings."[1] It was an injury he suffered while still in the minors, and he told the press that while there was an operation that could ease some of his pain, it would most likely end his baseball career.

Despite the fact that he suffered constantly, Candelaria went on to enjoy a 19-year career, where he compiled a fine 177–129 record with a 3.33 ERA. But for all his success, it was the night when he ended one of the strangest streaks in Pirates history that he would be truly remembered for.

LA N	0	0	0	0	0	0	0	0	0 —	0	0	1
PIT N	0	0	0	0	2	0	0	0	x —	2	5	2

BATTING

Los Angeles Dodgers	AB	R	H	RBI
Lopes cf	4	0	0	0
Sizemore 2b	4	0	0	0
Russell ss	4	0	0	0
Garvey 1b	3	0	0	0
Cey 3b	3	0	0	0
Baker rf	3	0	0	0
Buckner lf	1	0	0	0
Lacy ph,lf	2	0	0	0
Yeager c	2	0	0	0
Rau p	2	0	0	0
Auerbach ph	1	0	0	0
Hough p	0	0	0	0
Totals	**29**	**0**	**0**	**0**

FIELDING—DP: 1. Sizemore-Garvey.
E: Russell (14).
BATTING—Team LOB: 3.

Pittsburgh Pirates	AB	R	H	RBI
Taveras ss	4	0	1	0
Stennett 2b	4	0	0	0
Oliver cf	2	0	1	0
Stargell 1b	3	0	0	0
Zisk lf	3	1	1	0
Parker rf	3	1	1	0
Robinson 3b	3	0	1	2
Dyer c	3	0	0	0
Candelaria p	3	0	0	0
Totals	**28**	**2**	**5**	**2**

FIELDING—E: Taveras (22), Robinson (4).
BATTING—2B: Robinson (20,off Rau).
GDP: Stargell (3,off Rau).
Team LOB: 3.
BASERUNNING—SB: Stennett (14,2nd base off Rau/Yeager).

PITCHING

Los Angeles Dodgers	IP	H	R	ER	BB	SO
Rau L(10–9)	7	5	2	2	1	6
Hough	1	0	0	0	0	0
Totals	**8**	**5**	**2**	**2**	**1**	**6**

Pittsburgh Pirates	IP	H	R	ER	BB	SO
Candelaria W(11–4)	9	0	0	0	1	7

Umpires: HP—Nick Colosi, 1B—Ed Montague, 2B—Lee Weyer, 3B—Paul Runge

Time of Game: 1:45 **Attendance:** 9,860

PIRATES 22, CHICAGO CUBS 0
SEPTEMBER 16, 1975

The Perfect Day

On June 10, 1892, Wilbert Robinson drove in 11 runs in a single game, going a perfect seven for seven. The performance vaulted him into the record books for most hits in a nine-inning game, a record that for 83 years had been approached but never equaled.

Many players had come close by garnering six hits in a game. For the Pirates alone, 10 players had rapped a half-dozen hits in a game, including such notables as Max Carey, Carson Bigbee, Dick Groat, Kiki Cuyler, Paul Waner, and his brother, Lloyd. In 1975, Pirates second baseman Rennie Stennett would surpass all those former Pirates, as his team would put on a memorable offensive display in the friendly confines of Wrigley Field.

A native of Colon, Panama, Stennett was signed by Pirates super scout Howie Haak in 1969 and rose quickly through the Bucs' minor-league system. On his way, he won the Carolina League batting crown in 1970 and was hitting .344 in AAA with Columbus in 1971 before he was called up to the Pirates in the midst of their world championship campaign. Stennett shocked everyone by hitting .353 for the remainder of the season, and while he was controversially left off the postseason roster in favor of veteran Jose Pagan, it was apparent he was in the majors to stay. While not reaching the lofty offensive numbers he put up his rookie season, the Panamanian nevertheless had become the Bucs' starting second baseman by 1975.

As the 1975 campaign was coming to a close, the Bucs were waltzing to their fifth division crown in six seasons, and a mid-September contest against the Cubs seemed relatively meaningless. In the first inning, though, it quickly became apparent that this contest would be anything but meaningless as the powerful Pirates' offense put on a show.

Fewer than 5,000 fans filed into Wrigley Field to see this game, not knowing they would be witnessing history. Pittsburgh peppered the Cubs' starter for nine runs in their first at bat. It began with Stennett smacking a double into right field to lead off the contest. He came home moments later on a single by third baseman Richie Hebner for the first run of the game. The Pirates scored five more runs before Stennett came up again in the opening inning, ripping an RBI single to extend the lead to seven. If the Pirates were shooting bazookas with their offense, the Cubs had a popgun; they were able to muster up only a single in the first two innings to keep the score 9–0.

As the Cubs' offense was silent, the Pittsburgh bats caught fire again in the third. With one out, Stennett slashed his third hit of the day, a single to center against Dettore, and then Hebner followed with his 15th home run of the season to make it 11–0. After tacking on another run in the fourth, the Bucs plated six more in the fifth with the Bucs' second baseman collecting two more hits, including an RBI single, to make him five for five on the day. The hit also put Stennett in the record books as he tied the major-league mark with two hits in an inning twice in the same game.

Though Stennett didn't bat in the sixth, the team scored two more to increase the score to 20–0. An inning later the second baseman led off the frame with a single, his sixth hit of the contest, and scored on a Dave Parker single. The Pirates added one more to close out the scoring at 22–0.

For his part, Candelaria completed his day after setting down the Cubs in order in the bottom of the seventh, turning over the game to Ken Brett in the eighth. The only suspense left in the game would be if Stennett could match the 83-year-old record. He faced Paul Reuschel in the eighth and rifled a long shot to right field that fell in the gap for a triple. It was Stennett's seventh hit, tying the record.

A game that began as "meaningless" turned out to be historical. Not only did Stennett match an impressive major-league mark but the 22–0 victory broke the all-time record for biggest run advantage by a team in a shutout, originally set by the 1901 Tigers and the 1939 Yankees, who both won games 21–0.

For Stennett it was a perfect day, seven for seven with five runs and two RBIs. He remains the only player alongside Robinson to achieve a seven-hit performance. It remains not only one of the greatest performances in the long history of the Pittsburgh Pirates but in the annals of major-league baseball.

PIT N	9	0	2	1	6	2	2	0	0	—	22	24	0
CHI N	0	0	0	0	0	0	0	0	0	—	0	3	3

BATTING

Pittsburgh Pirates	AB	R	H	RBI
Stennett 2b	7	5	7	2
Randolph pr,2b	0	0	0	0
Hebner 3b	7	3	2	3
Oliver cf	4	2	1	1
Dilone cf	1	0	0	0
Stargell 1b	4	2	3	3
Robertson 1b	3	1	1	0
Parker rf	4	3	2	5
Zisk lf	5	2	2	1
Sanguillen c	5	2	2	1
Brett p	1	0	0	0
Hernandez p	0	0	0	0
Taveras ss	6	1	3	3
Candelaria p	5	1	1	2
Ott ph,c	1	0	0	0
Totals	53	22	24	21

BATTING—2B: Stennett 2 (24,off R. Reuschel, off Dettore).

3B: Stennett (6,off P. Reuschel).

HR: Hebner (15,3rd inning off Dettore 1 on 1 out); Parker (24,5th inning off Zamora 2 on 0 out).

SF: Parker (1,off R. Reuschel).

HBP: Parker (5,by Dettore).

Team LOB: 12.

Chicago Cubs	AB	R	H	RBI
Kessinger 3b	3	0	0	0
Dunn 3b	1	0	0	0
Tyrone lf	4	0	0	0
Morales cf	3	0	0	0
LaCock rf,1b	1	0	0	0
Cardenal rf	2	0	1	0
Harris cf	1	0	0	0
Thornton 1b	3	0	1	0
P. Reuschel p	0	0	0	0
Trillo 2b	2	0	0	0
Sperring 2b	1	0	0	0
Mitterwald c	3	0	0	0
Rosello ss	3	0	1	0
R. Reuschel p	0	0	0	0
Dettore p	1	0	0	0
Zamora p	0	0	0	0
Hosley ph	1	0	0	0
Schultz p	0	0	0	0
Summers rf	1	0	0	0
Totals	30	0	3	0

FIELDING—E: Dunn (1), Rosello (3), Dettore (2).
BATTING—Team LOB: 3.

PITCHING

Pittsburgh Pirates	IP	H	R	ER	BB	SO
Candelaria W(8–5)	7	3	0	0	0	5
Brett	1	0	0	0	0	2
Hernandez	1	0	0	0	0	0
Totals	9	3	0	0	0	7

Chicago Cubs	IP	H	R	ER	BB	SO
R. Reuschel L(10–16)	0.1	6	8	8	2	0
Dettore	3.2	7	8	7	2	1
Zamora	1	4	2	2	0	2
Schultz	2	6	4	2	1	2
P. Reuschel	2	1	0	0	1	0
Totals	9	24	22	18*	6	5

*—Team earned runs does not equal the composite totals for all pitchers due to instances in which provisions of Section 10.18 (i) of the Scoring Rules were applied.

Dettore faced 4 batters in the 5th inning

WP: Dettore (5).

HBP: Dettore (9,Parker).

Umpires: HP—Harry Wendelstedt, 1B—Bob Engel, 2B—Dutch Rennert, 3B—Doug Harvey

Time of Game: 2:35 **Attendance:** 4,932

PIRATES 13, CHICAGO CUBS 12
APRIL 21, 1991

Ain't No Mountain High Enough

In 1991, the sports world in the Steel City was the polar opposite of what it would be two decades later. The Steelers were suffering through their worst stretch since the 1960s, while the Pirates were going through a renaissance that resulted in three consecutive Eastern Division crowns.

On a memorable afternoon in 1991, as the Steelers were mistakenly celebrating what turned out to be arguably the worst first-round draft pick in team history (Florida defensive end Huey Richardson), the Pirates pulled one of the most incredible comebacks in major-league history. After they surprised the baseball world with a division crown in 1990, nothing short of a repeat performance in 1991—if not a world championship—was expected of them. With a young base of players that included Bobby Bonilla, Barry Bonds, Andy Van Slyke, Doug Drabek, and John Smiley, the optimism was justified.

One characteristic they carried over from 1990 was their ability to fight through adversity. They never felt they were out of the game—a trait that would be exemplified against the Chicago Cubs. Ironically, considering what was to come, the first 4½ innings became a pitcher's duel between Pittsburgh's Randy Tomlin and the Cubs' Mike Harkey. Neither team had scored, as both teams combined for two hits, both by Chicago.

The Bucs finally broke through with two runs in the fifth, but the Cubs bounced back with three in their next at bat to take the lead. And the slugfest was on.

An inning later, Chicago seemed to put the game away as it exploded for four more runs—aided by a two-run throwing error by Pittsburgh—to extend its lead to 7–2. With a fine mist falling, this gritty Pirates team bolted back to cut the lead to one in the eighth, as Orlando Merced ripped a two-run triple, and then Bonilla blasted a home run to make it 7–6.

An inning later, in the bottom of the ninth, the Pirates made the comeback complete when Gary Varsho, who was batting for reliever Bill Landrum, smacked a two-out RBI double to tie the game. Jay Bell then came up with a chance to win the contest, but as he had in the sixth with a runner in scoring position, the Bucs' shortstop was unsuccessful with a groundout too short to send the game in extra innings. "I was mad," Bell said. "I had my chance to drive in the winning run."[1]

Pittsburgh had another opportunity to win the game in the 10th but stranded a runner on third. When the Cubs erupted for five runs in the top of the 11th—four on a grand slam by Andre Dawson to take a 12–7 lead—it looked like the Bucs had finally run out of chances

It was all but over. No team in the history of the game had ever come back from a five-run deficit twice to win a game. But the Pirates didn't quit. They loaded the bases, and Cubs manager Don Zimmer called on the Pirates' Mike Bielecki to nail down the game for Chicago. The next batter was Jay Bell, whose error and lack of clutch batting had haunted the Pirates earlier. This time he finally came through, lacing a double into the left field corner, scoring two to make it 12–9. Van Slyke then lofted a sacrifice fly to bring home the third run of the inning.

The Cubs' once comfortable lead was now in peril. Bielecki made things even more difficult when he walked Bonilla, bringing up defending National League MVP Barry Bonds. Bonds was off to a slow start in 1991 and had been mired in an 0-for-22 slump, which he snapped out of in the fifth inning, and had yet to deliver a hit with a man in scoring position so far in the young season. Bonds came through with a single to cut the lead to one. Bielecki's nightmare continued as he walked Gary Redus to load the bases.

Up next was catcher Don Slaught looking for redemption after failing to come through offensively earlier in the game with men in scoring position and calling the change up in the top of the 11th that Dawson launched for the grand slam. He sent a long fly ball to center. "I thought it was at least a sacrifice fly, that at least we had tied the game," Slaught said. But it proved to be more than a sacrifice as it went over the head of Cubs center fielder Jerome Walton for a double that scored Bonilla and Bonds to deliver the incredible 13–12 victory.

"I had a chance to win it before that inning, but how many times do you get a second chance to win it?" a delighted Slaught said afterward. "I'm thankful for that. Otherwise, I'd be beating my head against a wall."[2]

For Pirates manager Jim Leyland, it was an emotional moment that showed just how far his team had come since he was hired in 1987. "I'm real proud of that effort. I'm kind of an emotional guy as you know," he said choking back the tears. "But I just like people who go to work and do their job."[3]

It was certainly a great moment in a season that helped launch the Bucs to their second consecutive Eastern Division championship, winning by 14½ games over the St. Louis Cardinals.

As for their neighbors at Three Rivers Stadium, the Steelers finished off 1991 with a disappointing 7–9, with their top draft pick on their roster for just one season. Less than two years later, their roles would reverse as title contender and disappointment—a trend that continued to the next century. That April day, though, typified the short-lived era in Pittsburgh sports history— the Steelers, the joke, and the Pirates proving there was no mountain too high.

CHI N	0	0	0		0	0	3		0	4	0		0	5 —	12	13	0
PIT N	0	0	0		0	2	0		0	4	1		0	6 —	13	13	1

BATTING

Chicago Cubs	AB	R	H	RBI
Walton cf	5	2	1	0
Sandberg 2b	6	2	3	1
Grace 1b	2	1	0	1
Salazar ph,1b	2	1	0	0
Bell lf	4	0	1	1
Dascenzo pr,lf	2	2	1	1
Dawson rf	6	1	3	5
Dwight Smith rf	0	0	0	0
Dunston ss	4	1	0	0
Scott 3b	5	1	0	0
McElroy p	0	0	0	0
Slocumb p	0	0	0	0
Bielecki p	0	0	0	0
Pappas c	4	0	1	1
Harkey p	2	1	2	0
Assenmacher p	2	0	1	0
Dave Smith p	0	0	0	0
Vizcaino 3b	0	0	0	0
Totals	44	12	13	10

BATTING—2B: Sandberg (3,off Tomlin); Bell (3,off Huismann).
HR: Dawson (3,11th inning off Patterson 3 on 2 out).
SF: Grace (1,off Tomlin).
HBP: Grace (2,by Heaton).
GDP: Walton (1,off Tomlin).
IBB: Dunston (1,by Huismann).
Team LOB: 6.
BASERUNNING—SB: Dunston (4,2nd base off Tomlin/LaValliere).
CS: Dawson (1,2nd base by Tomlin/LaValliere).

Pittsburgh Pirates	AB	R	H	RBI
Merced 1b	4	2	2	2
Bell ss	6	1	1	2
Van Slyke cf	5	0	0	1
Bonilla rf	4	3	2	2
Bonds lf	6	2	2	1
King 3b	4	1	1	0
Patterson p	0	0	0	0
Redus ph	0	0	0	0
LaValliere c	2	0	1	1
Slaught ph,c	3	0	1	2
Lind 2b	3	2	1	1
Tomlin p	2	0	0	0
Heaton p	0	0	0	0
Huismann p	0	0	0	0
McClendon ph	0	1	0	0
Landrum p	0	0	0	0
Varsho ph	1	0	1	1
Kipper p	0	0	0	0
Wilkerson 3b	1	1	1	0
Totals	41	13	13	13

FIELDING—DP: 1. Lind-Bell-Merced.
E: Bell (2).
BATTING—2B: LaValliere (1,off Harkey); Varsho (3,off Dave Smith); Bonilla (3,off McElroy); Bell (3,off Bielecki); Slaught (3,off Bielecki).
3B: Merced (1,off Assenmacher).
HR: Bonilla (2,8th inning off Assenmacher 1 on 2 out).
SH: Slaught (1,off Dave Smith).

SF: Lind (1,off Harkey); Van Slyke (4,off Bielecki).
IBB: Merced (1,by Dave Smith); King (2,by McElroy).
Team LOB: 8.
BASERUNNING—CS: Merced (1,2nd base by Assenmacher/Pappas).

PITCHING

Chicago Cubs	IP	H	R	ER	BB	SO
Harkey	5.1	2	2	2	2	7
Assenmacher	2.2	3	4	4	1	5
Dave Smith	1	2	1	1	1	0
McElroy	0.2	1	0	0	1	2
Slocumb	0.1	2	3	3	1	0
Bielecki L(2–1)	0.1	3	3	3	2	0
Totals	10.1	13	13	13	8	14

Slocumb faced 3 batters in the 11th inning
WP: Assenmacher (1), Slocumb (1).
IBB: Dave Smith (3,Merced); McElroy (1,King).

Pittsburgh Pirates	IP	H	R	ER	BB	SO
Tomlin	6	7	3	3	1	2
Heaton	1	1	1	1	1	0
Huismann	1	2	3	1	1	2
Landrum	1	0	0	0	0	1
Kipper	1	0	2	2	2	1
Patterson W(1–0)	1	3	3	3	0	0
Totals	11	13	12	10	5	6

Heaton faced 1 batter in the 8th inning
Kipper faced 2 batters in the 11th inning
HBP: Heaton (1,Grace).
IBB: Huismann (1,Dunston).
Umpires: HP—Mike Winters, 1B—Paul Runge, 2B—Charlie Reliford, 3B—
Jerry Layne
Time of Game: 4:10 Attendance: 10,860

#14

The Freak Show

It had been one of the strangest yet most satisfying seasons the Pittsburgh Pirates had experienced in their long and illustrious history. To describe the unique ways this young, underdog team went about surprising the baseball world, Pirates broadcaster Greg Brown dubbed the club "The Freak Show."

During the off-season, general manager Cam Bonifay decided to purge the roster, trading veterans Jeff King, Jay Bell, Orlando Merced, and Carlos Garcia for a group of prospects. The team's payroll had been reduced to a meager $9 million, roughly a million less than star outfielder Albert Belle was being paid by the Chicago White Sox.

Predictions of doom and gloom were rampant. The Bucs were called no more than a Class AAA team. So when Pirates manager Gene Lamont claimed that the team would win at least 70 games, he was thought to be foolish.

Instead, a bunch of youngsters stepped up. An aggressive second-year catcher led the Pirates into battle. Jason Kendall, who hit .300 in his rookie season, was joined by an unlikely lineup, consisting of Tony Womack, Kevin Polcovich, and Jermaine Allensworth. The pitching staff would be pieced together by young prospects that included a trio of pitchers from the Mexican League, led by Francisco Cordova, a nonroster player who was signed before the 1996 campaign. Cordova proved to be impressive from the onset, tossing 59 games (mostly relief) his rookie season before becoming the club's ace in the rotation during this strange 1997 campaign.

As the season went on, Lamont's prediction of 70 wins looked brilliant as the Pirates continued to defy expectations. Pittsburgh wound up winning 79 games and continued to stun the baseball nation. What's more, the Bucs were competing in the lackluster National League Central Division. They spent 40 days in first place, finding ways to win games they had no business competing in.

Perhaps the one game that epitomized the freakish ride that the 1997 Pirates were on occurred just after the All-Star break against their division rivals, the Houston Astros. In the first two games of the series, the Astros brought the Pirates down to earth, thrashing them 7–0 and 10–0. Cordova would take the mound this night hoping to get the club back on track in front of the largest crowd of the season, as 44,119 fans filed into Three Rivers Stadium.

Cordova took control early, retiring six of the first seven Astros he faced, with Jeff Bagwell being the only one to reach base with a two-out walk in the first. The major obstacle in Cordova's quest for victory in this contest wasn't Houston's offense; it was his own.

Going into the game, the Pirates' bats had gone 19 consecutive innings without scoring a run, and Astros rookie pitcher Chris Holt continued that streak. While Pittsburgh had more offensive success in the first few innings than Houston, it was meaningless as the Bucs stranded runners in the first two frames.

After the Bucs' streak of ineptitude stretched to 22 scoreless innings, Cordova continued his dominance. After retiring Chuck Carr and Bagwell, Houston nearly got its first hit of the game in the fourth when left fielder Luis Gonzales smashed a liner down the first base line that Kevin Young grabbed spectacularly to keep the no-hitter alive.

Holt matched Cordova almost pitch for pitch over the next three innings, giving up only a single to Womack in the sixth as the teams were still scoreless going into the eighth. With two outs, Houston shortstop Tim Bogar hit a flair into short right field that looked like it might drop in for a single, but once again Young came to the rescue with a fine running catch to end the inning.

While Cordova was flirting with history, the Pirates' offense was continuing its ineptness, giving the hurler absolutely no support. They had a chance to end their streak in the eighth, but Womack struck out with two aboard to send the game into the ninth, still scoreless.

Cordova completed his nine innings, holding the Astros hitless, but after the Pirates couldn't score against the Houston closer Billy Wagner in the bottom of the frame, Lamont ended Francisco Cordova's phenomenal evening, pulling the hurler in favor of his countryman Ricardo Rincon. The team was still in the hunt for the division crown that superseded Cordova's quest for history. "It was not a difficult decision," Lamont said. "He threw a few too many pitches [121]. I let him stay in the game to bat in the eighth inning, but felt he had thrown too many pitches to pitch in the tenth."[1]

Cordova was disappointed he wasn't able to continue the classic but seemed to understand it was best for the team. "I wanted to stay in the game if he [Lamont] let me," he said. "But I was getting a little tired."[2]

In the history of baseball, there had never been a combined extra-inning no-hitter. Rincon kept the gem alive in the top half of the 10th, allowing only a two-out walk. With their scoreless streak now at 28 innings, the Pirates came to bat in the bottom of the 10th.

Dale Sveum struck out to open the frame, then Jason Kendall walked, and Jose Guillen struck out. Lamont sent up Turner Ward to pinch-hit, and Ward was able to work a walk, putting two Pirates on base for just the second time in the game. It would be up to another pinch hitter, Mark Smith, who was coming to the plate for Rincon. Let the freak show begin.

The large crowd—which represented the first nonopening day sellout in 20 years at Three Rivers—buzzed with anticipation. Smith fell behind 0–1 before sending the second pitch into the left field seats for a dramatic 3–0 victory.

The crowd went berserk, having witnessed not only an exciting contest but baseball history. Smith was ecstatic for his part in this classic contest. "It's the greatest feeling in the world," he said. "It's like the whole ballpark went silent when I swung. I know the crowd was cheering very loud, but I didn't hear anything."[3] It capped an exciting week for Smith as it was his second extra-inning game-winning homer in the time period, the first being the St. Louis Cardinals' 7–5 victory eight days before.

For Cordova, he was proud that he could share this historic moment, baseball's first combined extra-inning no-hitter, with his countryman Rincon. "It's the first no-hitter I've ever thrown," Cordova said. "And to have Ricardo finish the game makes it even more special."[4] It was indeed a special moment in a special season—the greatest episode that the 1997 freak show would orchestrate.

HOU N	0	0	0	0	0	0	0	0	0	0 —	0	0	0
PIT N	0	0	0	0	0	0	0	0	0	3 —	3	6	0

BATTING

Houston Astros	AB	R	H	RBI
Biggio 2b	4	0	0	0
Carr cf	3	0	0	0
Bagwell 1b	3	0	0	0
Gonzalez lf	3	0	0	0
Bell rf	3	0	0	0
Spiers 3b	4	0	0	0
Ausmus c	4	0	0	0
Bogar ss	3	0	0	0
Wagner p	0	0	0	0
Hudek p	0	0	0	0
Holt p	2	0	0	0
Gutierrez ss	1	0	0	0
Totals	30	0	0	0

FIELDING—DP: 1. Spiers-Biggio-Bagwell.
BATTING—HBP: Carr (1,by Cordova).
Team LOB: 4.

Pittsburgh Pirates	AB	R	H	RBI
Womack 2b	4	0	2	0
Allensworth cf	4	0	0	0
Martin lf	4	0	0	0
Young 1b	4	0	0	0
Sveum 3b	4	0	0	0
Kendall c	2	1	1	0
Guillen rf	4	0	0	0
Collier ss	3	0	0	0
Ward ph	0	1	0	0
Cordova p	3	0	2	0
Rincon p	0	0	0	0
Smith ph	1	1	1	3
Totals	33	3	6	3

BATTING—HR: Smith (3,10th inning off Hudek 2 on 2 out).
GDP: Allensworth (3,off Holt).
Team LOB: 4.
BASERUNNING—CS: Womack (3,2nd base by Holt/Ausmus).

PITCHING

Houston Astros	IP	H	R	ER	BB	SO
Holt	7.2	5	0	0	1	1
Wagner	1.1	0	0	0	0	4
Hudek L(0–1)	0.2	1	3	3	2	1
Totals	9.2	6	3	3	3	6

Pittsburgh Pirates	IP	H	R	ER	BB	SO
Cordova	9	0	0	0	2	10
Rincon W(3–4)	1	0	0	0	1	1
Totals	10	0	0	0	3	11

HBP: Cordova (8,Carr).
Umpires: HP—Tom Hallion, 1B—Jerry Crawford, 2B—Ed Montague, 3B—Wally Bell
Time of Game: 2:39 **Attendance:** 44,119

PIRATES 5, CINCINNATI REDS 2
OCTOBER 2, 1979

The Hurdle

Every championship team has its own symbolic hurdle—an opponent who always seems to prevent them from reaching their ultimate goal. For the Pittsburgh Pirates of the 1970s, the Cincinnati Reds proved to be their Mount Everest.

Five times in the first six years of the decade, the Pirates captured the NL Eastern Division crown. In three of those seasons—1970, 1972, and 1975—the Pirates and Reds met in the National League Championship Series, with the Reds winning each time. Four years after their last October encounter, Pittsburgh and Cincinnati won their respective divisions once again and would meet for the 1979 pennant.

Despite the fact that the faces on the teams had changed and the Reds were no longer the "Big Red Machine" that they had been earlier in the decade, the Pirates, nonetheless, had a difficult task ahead of them. That task would begin in Game One at Cincinnati's Riverfront Stadium where Pittsburgh would face the Reds' future Hall of Fame pitcher Tom Seaver. To counter, Pirates manager Chuck Tanner threw his top hurler, John Candelaria, who'd won 14 games during the 1979 regular season.

Following a 45-minute rain delay, the game finally started and became the pitchers' duel that most had expected. The Reds had the first opportunity in the second, but Candelaria got out of the jam, striking out Ray Knight and Dan Driessen after a one-out triple by Johnny Bench.

Moments later, Pirates second baseman Phil Garner lifted a home run to put Pittsburgh up 1–0. A batter later, Omar Moreno lifted a line drive to right field that the Reds' Dave Collins unsuccessfully attempted to catch. The ball bounced over the right fielder's head, sending Moreno into third with a one-out triple. Moreno came home with the second run when shortstop Tim Foli hit a sacrifice to right.

In the bottom of the fourth, Reds slugger George Foster blasted a two-run homer to tie the game at two. At that point, the pitchers hit their stride over the next three innings with the teams combining for three base runners as the game went into the eighth still tied 2–2.

It looked like Cincinnati might take the lead when they put two on with one out in the bottom of the eighth, but Pittsburgh closer Kent Tekulve got Reds shortstop Dave Concepcion to hit into an inning-ending double play.

Pittsburgh nearly pulled ahead in the top of the ninth when Bill Madlock launched a long fly ball to center where Hector Cruz leaped against the wall to make a brilliant catch. Tekulve retired the Reds in order the bottom half of the ninth to plunge this playoff opener into extra innings.

After a scoreless 10th, the Bucs started a rally in the 11th with back-to-back singles. Up to the plate came Willie Stargell, who was enjoying a renaissance season that would see him be named the National League MVP. Stargell extended his performance into the postseason by ripping a three-run homer to put the Pirates ahead 5–2. While things looked good for the Bucs, they were not out of the woods yet.

The bottom of the 11th started off well enough as Pirates reliever Grant Jackson retired the first two Reds. Concepcion then singled and Foster walked. With the tying run coming up to the plate in future Hall of Famer Johnny Bench, Tanner brought in right-handed Don Robinson to close the door on the Reds. With the Riverfront crowd roaring, Bench worked a full count, but Robinson remained calm. "I grew up watching Johnny Bench hit too many clutch home runs," the pitcher said. "And I wasn't going to let him hit a three-run home run off me."[1] He didn't give up a homer, but Robinson threw his curve out of the strike zone, loading the bases for Ray Knight, who was having a great season hitting .318.

Robinson bore down and struck out Knight to end the long, tense game and give the Bucs the very important road victory. With the final three games of the best-of-five series in Pittsburgh, clinching at least a split in Cincinnati gave the Bucs a huge advantage. More importantly, the win was a big step in the Pirates overcoming the hurdle that was the Cincinnati Reds, a step that would lead them back to the World Series.

PIT N	0	0	2	0	0	0	0	0	0	0	3 —	5 10	0
CIN N	0	0	0	2	0	0	0	0	0	0	0 —	2 7	0

BATTING

Pittsburgh Pirates	AB	R	H	RBI
Moreno cf	5	1	1	0
Foli ss	4	0	2	1
Alexander pr	0	1	0	0
B. Robinson lf	0	0	0	0
Parker rf	4	1	1	0
Stargell 1b	4	1	1	3
Milner lf	5	0	0	0
Stennett 2b	0	0	0	0
Madlock 3b	5	0	2	0
Ott c	5	0	1	0
Garner 2b,ss	4	1	2	1
Candelaria p	3	0	0	0
Romo p	0	0	0	0
Tekulve p	0	0	0	0
Easler ph	1	0	0	0
Jackson p	1	0	0	0
D. Robinson p	0	0	0	0
Totals	41	5	10	5

FIELDING—DP: 2. Garner-Foli-Stargell, Madlock-Garner-Stargell.
BATTING—3B: Moreno (1,off Seaver).
HR: Garner (1,3rd inning off Seaver 0 on 0 out); Stargell (1,11th inning off Hume 2 on 0 out).
SF: Foli (1,off Seaver).
GDP: Parker (1,off Seaver).
IBB: Garner (1,by Tomlin).
Team LOB: 7.
BASERUNNING—SB: Madlock 2 (2,2nd base off Seaver/Bench,2nd base off Tomlin/Bench).

Cincinnati Reds	AB	R	H	RBI
Collins rf	5	0	2	0
Morgan 2b	4	0	0	0
Concepcion ss	5	1	2	0
Foster lf	3	1	1	2
Bench c	3	0	2	0
Knight 3b	5	0	0	0
Driessen 1b	4	0	0	0
Cruz cf	4	0	0	0
Seaver p	2	0	0	0
Auerbach ph	1	0	0	0
Hume p	1	0	0	0
Tomlin p	0	0	0	0
Totals	**37**	**2**	**7**	**2**

FIELDING—DP: 1. Concepcion-Morgan-Driessen.
BATTING—3B: Bench (1,off Candelaria).
HR: Foster (1,4th inning off Candelaria 1 on 0 out).
GDP: Knight (1,off Candelaria); Concepcion (1,off Tekulve).
Team LOB: 7.
BASERUNNING—SB: Collins (1,2nd base off Romo/Ott).
CS: Bench (1,2nd base by Tekulve/Ott).

PITCHING

Pittsburgh Pirates	IP	H	R	ER	BB	SO
Candelaria	7	5	2	2	1	4
Romo	0.1	1	0	0	1	1
Tekulve	1.2	0	0	0	1	0
Jackson W(1–0)	1.2	1	0	0	1	2
D. Robinson SV(1)	0.1	0	0	0	1	1
Totals	**11**	**7**	**2**	**2**	**5**	**8**

Cincinnati Reds	IP	H	R	ER	BB	SO
Seaver	8	5	2	2	2	5
Hume L(0–1)	2.1	5	3	3	0	1
Tomlin	0.2	0	0	0	1	1
Totals	**11**	**10**	**5**	**5**	**3**	**7**

IBB: Tomlin (1,Garner).

Umpires: HP—John Kibler, 1B—Ed Montague, 2B—Jerry Dale, 3B—Frank Pulli, LF—Dick Stello, RF—Jim Quick

Time of Game: 3:14 **Attendance:** 55,006

PIRATES 4, BALTIMORE ORIOLES 3
OCTOBER 13, 1971

Turn On the Lights

For 70 years, the World Series had been a matinee affair. Generations of fans, old and young alike, would tell stories of missing school or work for the opportunity to experience what was then America's most anticipated sporting event of the year.

While Game Five of the 1949 Fall Classic ended in darkness and the lights being turned on for the ninth inning, there had never been a game scheduled to start in the evening. In 1971, baseball commissioner Bowie Kuhn sold the idea of nighttime games to NBC on the theory that more people would watch and the ratings would soar. Needless to say, he was right.

It was a festive atmosphere on October 13, 1971, as 51,378 fans crammed into Three Rivers Stadium on a balmy autumn evening for Game Four of the 1971 World Series. With all the hoopla surrounding this game, perhaps the biggest centered on Pittsburgh manager Danny Murtaugh's controversial decision to start Luke Walker instead of his ace, Dock Ellis. Walker had a career year in 1970 with a 15–6 mark, but while he had a sore arm in 1971, he was able to turn it around, winning his last five starts. The only problem going into Game Four of the World Series was that Walker hadn't pitched for three weeks.

Other than the historical aspect, the game was important for another reason. After Baltimore had taken a commanding two-games-to-none lead in the series, Pittsburgh won Game Three, and a victory here would allow them to tie a series that only days before no one had given them much of a chance in.

Not surprisingly, Walker started off rusty and loaded the bases on a leadoff single and two infield hits. Then a passed ball by Manny Sanguillen put the Orioles up 1–0. After intentionally walking Frank Robinson, Walker surrendered back-to-back sacrifice flies to up the Baltimore lead to 3–0.

Twenty-two pitches in and Walker's day was over as he was pulled for rookie hurler Bruce Kison, who had already been through a whirlwind season. Kison began the year on the Bucs' AAA team in Charleston, where he was an impressive 10–1 with a 2.86 ERA, and ended up securing a spot in Pittsburgh's starting rotation down the stretch. While showing promise, Kison also had a penchant for being wild, which was on display during this historic contest.

The Pirates' rookie pitcher got them out of the first inning without further damage. Then Baltimore's starting pitcher Pat Dobson, one of the Orioles' 20-game winners in 1971, started off just as shaky as Walker had. He walked second baseman Dave Cash to open the frame, and after getting Richie Hebner on a popup and striking out Roberto Clemente, he faced the most dangerous hitter in the National League in 1971: Willie Stargell. The Bucs' left fielder did not disappoint, slashing a long line drive to the gap in right center to score Cash from first, cutting the Orioles' advantage to two runs. Al Oliver then followed with a bloop double to plate Stargell and make the score now 3–2.

When Kison gave up a one-out double in the second, Pirates fans feared another big Baltimore inning. As it turned out, it was not only the last Orioles hit of the inning but the final one a Pirates pitcher would give up this game.

Fireworks erupted in the bottom of the third as the Pirates' offense once again caught fire. Richie Hebner started it off with a one-out single, and then Roberto Clemente seemed to put the Pirates ahead when he lashed a long drive to right field that appeared to hit the foul pole. But right field umpire John Rice called it a foul ball, as Pittsburgh coach Don Leppert and manager Danny Murtaugh stormed out to argue. The argument proved fruitless, but Clemente would not be denied, slapping a sharp single to right to put men on first and second. Oliver brought home Hebner with a liner to right for his second RBI, tying the game.

With the score remaining tied, Kison found his groove as he mowed down the Orioles in impressive fashion. But his control problem reared its ugly head as he hit three more batters—the only base runners he would allow after the second inning.

In the seventh, the Pirates threatened to take the lead with two on and one out when pinch hitter Vic Davalillo lofted a fly ball to the usually reliable Paul Blair in center, but he dropped the ball. Blair made up for the error when Manny Sanguillen, who was going into second, made too wide a turn past the base and was out on a throw, apparently squashing the rally. It would be up to another rookie, 20-year-old catcher Milt May, who was batting for Kison.

The son of former major-leaguer Pinky May, Milt had batted only 126 times during the season. In the first true pressure at bat of his major-league career, May responded with a single to right center to score the go-ahead run.

Murtaugh called on Dave Giusti to close out the victory, which he did, retiring the last six Orioles in order, bringing the Pirates' fans to their feet to celebrate an exciting victory on this historic evening and tie the World Series at two games apiece.

The night was bigger than just a Pirates win though; it was an evening that eventually changed the face of the Fall Classic. Kuhn was correct: night games had an incredible effect on the ratings, and within a few years, daytime World Series, even on weekends, would become ancient history. Night games soon became the norm, ending the practice of skipping school and work during the Fall Classic. That night in Pittsburgh, a new tradition of baseball began.

BAL A	3	0	0	0	0	0	0	0	0	—	3	4	1
PIT N	2	0	1	0	0	0	1	0	x	—	4	14	0

BATTING

Baltimore Orioles	AB	R	H	RBI
Blair cf	4	1	2	0
Belanger ss	4	1	1	0
Rettenmund lf	4	1	1	0
F. Robinson rf	2	0	0	0
B. Robinson 3b	3	0	0	1
Powell 1b	3	0	0	1
Johnson 2b	3	0	0	0
Etchebarren c	2	0	0	0
Dobson p	2	0	0	0
Jackson p	0	0	0	0
Shopay ph	1	0	0	0
Watt p	0	0	0	0
Richert p	0	0	0	0
Totals	28	3	4	2

FIELDING—DP: 1. Belanger-Johnson-Powell.

E: Blair (1).

BATTING—2B: Blair (1,off Kison).

SF: B. Robinson (1,off Walker); Powell (1,off Walker).

HBP: Johnson (1,by Kison); F. Robinson (1,by Kison); Etchebarren (1,by Kison).

GDP: Etchebarren (1,off Kison).

IBB: F. Robinson (1,by Walker).

Team LOB: 4.

Pittsburgh Pirates	AB	R	H	RBI
Cash 2b	4	1	1	0
Hebner 3b	5	1	1	0
Clemente rf	4	0	3	0
Stargell lf	5	1	2	1
Oliver cf	4	0	2	2
Robertson 1b	4	1	1	0
Sanguillen c	4	0	2	0
Hernandez ss	3	0	1	0
Davalillo ph	1	0	0	0
Giusti p	0	0	0	0
Walker p	0	0	0	0
Kison p	2	0	0	0
May ph	1	0	1	1
Alley pr,ss	0	0	0	0
Totals	37	4	14	4

FIELDING—DP: 1. Hernandez-Cash-Robertson.
PB: Sanguillen (1).
BATTING—2B: Stargell (1,off Dobson); Oliver (1,off Dobson).
GDP: Cash (1,off Dobson).
IBB: Oliver (1,by Dobson).
Team LOB: 13.
BASERUNNING—SB: Sanguillen (1,2nd base off Dobson/Etchebarren);
Hernandez (1,2nd base off Dobson/Etchebarren).

PITCHING

Baltimore Orioles	IP	H	R	ER	BB	SO
Dobson	5.1	10	3	3	3	4
Jackson	0.2	0	0	0	1	0
Watt L(0–1)	1.1	4	1	1	0	1
Richert	0.2	0	0	0	0	1
Totals	8	14	4	4	4	6

IBB: Dobson (1,Oliver).

Pittsburgh Pirates	IP	H	R	ER	BB	SO
Walker	0.2	3	3	3	1	0
Kison W(1–0)	6.1	1	0	0	0	3
Giusti SV(1)	2	0	0	0	0	1
Totals	9	4	3	3	1	4

HBP: Kison 3 (3,Johnson,F. Robinson,Etchebarren).

IBB: Walker (1,F. Robinson).

Umpires: HP—Ed Vargo, 1B—Jim Odom, 2B—John Kibler, 3B—Nestor Chylak, LF—Ed Sudol, RF—John Rice

Time of Game: 2:48 **Attendance:** 51,378

PIRATES 5, CHICAGO CUBS 4
OCTOBER 2, 1974

On the Back of Robertson

He was supposed to be the Pirates' next superstar, a player who was compared to Mickey Mantle. After the Bucs' 1971 championship campaign, Bob Robertson appeared to have the world in front of him. He'd hit 53 home runs in his first two full major-league seasons, so no one could have guessed his career would go downhill from there.

Robertson slumped badly in 1972 and 1973, hitting .193 and .239, respectively. The burly redhead had two knee operations in 1974 as his slump continued, hitting a mere .229. While his numbers deteriorated and he was a shadow of his former self, one of his greatest contributions in a Pirates uniform was yet to come.

Pittsburgh enjoyed a renaissance in 1974, bouncing back from a subpar 1973 campaign with a late-season surge that had them in position to win their fourth division title in five years. A game up on St. Louis, the first-place Pirates would take on the last-place Chicago Cubs. With a win they would go to the National League Championship Series. A loss would mean that the Cardinals would have the opportunity to play the Bucs in a one-game playoff to determine the NL East championship.

The game itself would be known not only for the memorable way it ended but for the inappropriate way that some of the 22,725 Pirates fans in attendance acted, nearly forcing the umpires to call a forfeit in this important contest.

Veteran Jim Rooker started the game for the Pirates and struggled in the first, giving up a Cubs run after a walk and two singles. An error by third baseman Richie Hebner opened the floodgates, and all of a sudden Pittsburgh was behind 4–0.

Things looked even worse for the Bucs when Cubs starter Rick Reuschel cruised through the first two innings. It looked like Pittsburgh's fate would be in the hands of the Montreal Expos to beat the Cardinals in their scheduled makeup game the next day. While it looked grim, the Pirates would not go down without a fight. Unfortunately, neither would some of the fans.

Pittsburgh picked up its first run in the bottom of the third when shortstop Frank Taveras scored on a ground ball by Hebner. An inning later they almost added a second run, but when Richie Zisk, who was on third base, broke for home on a fly ball by Ed Kirkpatrick to center, the Cubs' Rick Monday made a perfect throw to catcher Steve Swisher, who put the tag on Zisk to complete the inning-ending double play. The fans, believing it was a bad call, were incensed and let home plate umpire John Kibler know just how they felt. It began a series of disturbing interruptions by the fans that threatened to cost the Pirates the game.

When Chicago came onto the field to begin the bottom of the fifth, a fan tossed a bottle at Jose Cardenal as he took his place in left field. Despite the fact that the Bucs were making a game of it and cut the lead to two, some members of the crowd remained unruly.

In the top of the sixth, another bottle came down, bouncing off the Cubs' dugout onto the field. Two innings later, another bottle landed right next to Morales in right, and Chicago manager Jim Marshall pulled his team off the field for three minutes until the crowd got somewhat under control. Announcements about the threat of a forfeit by Art McKennan, the Pirates' longtime public address announcer, seemed to go on deaf ears.

An uneasy calm was over the ballpark as the Pirates headed into the ninth, still down by two runs. Zisk and catcher Manny Sanguillen walked to open up the frame. Pittsburgh manager Danny Murtaugh sent the speedy Miguel Dilone to run for Zisk, and then Kirkpatrick sacrificed both runners into scoring position. Dave Parker then grounded out to Sperring at second, which scored Dilone and sent Sanguillen to third, 90 feet away from tying the game.

With two out, Murtaugh sent up his once-promising slugger Bob Robertson to bat for Giusti. This was a situation that Robertson thrived on three years earlier when he was a different player. He worked the count to 3–2 when Reuschel launched a slider that was outside and looked like ball four. Robertson nonetheless swung at the pitch and missed for what looked like the last out of the game, but Cubs rookie catcher Steve Swisher dropped the pitch. The slow, lumbering Robertson took off for first. The ball hadn't rolled far, and it looked like it would be an easy out. With victory within his grasp, Swisher made a poor throw to first and hit Robertson in the back, scoring Sanguillen with the tying run as Robertson was safe at first. The Pittsburgh dugout turned from frustration into joy in a matter of seconds. "I was swearing and cussing," Giusti said. "I was walking down the runway. The next thing I know I'm yelling, run you SOB."[1]

Despite the jubilation, the fans had a different reaction. They littered the field with debris and bottles, apparently in celebration. Veteran umpire Shag Crawford, who was at third base in this game, considered ruling the game a forfeit, later claiming that this was the worst crowd he had ever seen. Murtaugh helped the situation by running onto the field and imploring the fans to stop. Seeing Murtaugh, Crawford reconsidered his original thought as he let the game continue.

It took four minutes for the grounds crew to clean up the mess before the game could continue. Once it did, Rennie Stennett grounded out, and what was once a certain Cubs' victory would now go to extra innings. In the top half of the 10th, Chicago could muster up only a single, which let the Pirates have another chance to win this strange game.

With one out, Al Oliver crushed a line drive into the left field corner and hustled his way to third with a triple. The Cubs then intentionally walked Willie Stargell and Gene Clines to load the bases and set up a force at home. This brought up Sanguillen with a chance to win the division. Sangy hit a slow roller to the Cubs' Bill Madlock at third. The third baseman rushed the ball, trying to pick it up with his bare hand and toss it to Swisher at home for the force-out. But Madlock was unable to snag the ball as Oliver came across the plate with the tally that gave the Bucs the division title.

For Robertson, he had accomplished much in his Pirates career, delivering a handful of memorable hits; yet one of his biggest accomplishments was a strikeout that wound up winning the division and making him a hero once again.

CHI N	4 0 0	0 0 0	0 0 0	0 — 4 10 3
PIT N	0 0 1	0 1 0	0 0 2	1 — 5 7 1

BATTING

Chicago Cubs	AB	R	H	RBI
Monday cf	3	1	2	0
Kessinger ss	4	1	1	0
Cardenal lf	5	1	2	1
Madlock 3b	5	1	1	1
Morales rf	4	0	1	1
Fanzone 1b	4	0	1	0
Swisher c	4	0	0	0
Sperring 2b	4	0	2	1
Reuschel p	3	0	0	0
Frailing p	0	0	0	0
Zamora p	0	0	0	0
Totals	**36**	**4**	**10**	**4**

FIELDING—DP: 3. Fanzone-Kessinger-Fanzone, Monday-Swisher, Kessinger-Fanzone.
E: Swisher (7), Reuschel 2 (5).
PB: Swisher (6).
BATTING—SH: Reuschel (9,off Rooker); Kessinger (7,off Rooker).
GDP: Morales (14,off Hernandez).
Team LOB: 7.
BASERUNNING—CS: Morales (12,3rd base by Rooker/Sanguillen); Sperring (2,Home by Rooker/Sanguillen).

Pittsburgh Pirates	AB	R	H	RBI
Stennett 2b	4	0	1	0
Hebner 3b	5	0	0	1
Oliver cf	5	1	1	0
Stargell lf	3	0	0	0
Zisk rf	2	0	0	0
Dilone pr,rf	0	1	0	0
Clines ph	0	0	0	0
Sanguillen c	4	1	3	1
Kirkpatrick 1b	3	0	0	0
Taveras ss	2	2	1	0
Parker ph	1	0	0	1
Mendoza ss	0	0	0	0
Rooker p	2	0	1	0
Popovich ph	1	0	0	0
Giusti p	0	0	0	0
Robertson ph	1	0	0	0
Augustine pr	0	0	0	0
Hernandez p	0	0	0	0
Totals	33	5	7	3

FIELDING—DP: 1. Stennett-Mendoza-Kirkpatrick.
E: Hebner (28).
BATTING—3B: Oliver (12,off Frailing).
SH: Kirkpatrick (4,off Reuschel).
GDP: Hebner (13,off Reuschel); Zisk (12,off Reuschel).
IBB: Stargell (21,by Frailing); Clines (2,by Frailing).
Team LOB: 9.

PITCHING

Chicago Cubs	IP	H	R	ER	BB	SO
Reuschel	9	5	4	2	6	6
Frailing L(6–9)	0.1	1	1	1	2	1
Zamora	0	1	0	0	0	0
Totals	9.1	7	5	3	8	7

IBB: Frailing 2 (10,Stargell,Clines).

Pittsburgh Pirates	IP	H	R	ER	BB	SO
Rooker	7	9	4	2	2	4
Giusti	2	0	0	0	1	4
Hernandez W(5–2)	1	1	0	0	0	0
Totals	**10**	**10**	**4**	**2**	**3**	**8**

Umpires: HP—John Kibler, 1B—Terry Tata, 2B—Dutch Rennert, 3B—Shag Crawford

Time of Game: 2:57 **Attendance:** 22,725

#10

PIRATES 9, SAN FRANCISCO GIANTS 5
OCTOBER 6, 1971

It Takes a Team to Win a Title

As most Pirates fans remember, it was Roberto Clemente who put the Bucs on his back and led them to the 1971 world championship. While Clemente certainly had a wonderful World Series and deserved the MVP award, the Pirates never would have captured their first National League pennant in 11 years if not for the stellar play of his teammates. This teamwork never was more evident than in Game Four of the 1971 National League Championship Series when Pittsburgh pulled together to overcome its opponents from the City by the Bay.

The Bucs came into this game on a roll, winning the second and third games of the series to put San Francisco on the brink of elimination. While there had been many Pirates heroes in the series thus far, Steve Blass wasn't one of them. Blass had enjoyed a wonderful regular season with a 15–8 mark and team-low 2.85 ERA. But he faltered horribly in Game One of the National League Championship Series, giving up five runs in five innings. Making his hopes for a victory even longer was the fact he would face future Hall of Famer Gaylord Perry in Game Four.

Blass's woes continued in the top of the first, thanks in part to an error by second baseman Dave Cash, who booted a ground ball by Ken Henderson to lead off the game. San Francisco took advantage of the miscue as Willie McCovey singled to bring home Henderson. After the Giants loaded the bases, Blass was able to get out of the jam with only a single run surrendered.

Perry was no better in the bottom half of the first as he allowed a single to Cash and a double to third baseman Richie Hebner. Up to the plate strolled Clemente, who came through with a ringing single to give the Bucs a 2–1 lead. It would not last for long.

Blass's championship nightmare continued in the second. To lead off the frame, he gave up a home run to shortstop Chris Speier, who had hit only eight homers all year. After getting an out, the Pirates' pitcher surrendered back-to-back singles and then struck out the dangerous Willie Mays for the inning's second out. With the equally menacing Willie McCovey coming to the plate, Blass would not be so lucky. McCovey parked a Blass pitch—a pitch that the Bucs' hurler called "ignorant"—over the right field fence for a three-run homer to put the Giants ahead comfortably 5–2.

With Clemente having come through with the heroics in the first inning, it would be up to the rest of the lineup to lift the club out of this mess. With two on and two out, Richie Hebner, who hit an important homer in Game Three, came up to the plate and quickly fell behind 0–2. Perry then threw a breaking ball out of the strike zone, but Hebner swung anyway. The Bucs' third baseman surprisingly made solid contact, sending the ball over the right center field wall to tie this game once again at 5–5.

Having pulled Blass in the second, Murtaugh chose a rookie hurler, right-handed Bruce Kison, to try to halt the hot Giants' offense. It proved to be a wise choice as Kison tossed 4⅔ innings of scoreless ball, giving up only two hits and two walks. With Kison quieting the Giants' bats, Pittsburgh took control of the game in the sixth.

Cash came through with a one-out single and got into scoring position when Hebner grounded out to McCovey. Once again Clemente came up to bat in a clutch situation. He seemed surly when the home plate umpire first glared at him to hurry up and then when Olsen called a strike on a pitch that Clemente felt was outside. With a steely determination, the greatest right fielder in Pirates history ripped a single into center that scored Cash with the go-ahead run as the crowd roared.

The Giants called on reliever Jerry Johnson, who intentionally walked Willie Stargell after Clemente went to second on a wild pitch. With two on, Johnson would now have to face the Pirates' dangerous center fielder Al Oliver. Johnson tried to sneak a fastball around Oliver's waist, but the center fielder turned on the pitch and sent it deep into the right field seats, sending the Three Rivers Stadium crowd into hysterics. The jubilant Oliver pumped his fists, jogging around the bases with his team now up 9–5. Murtaugh then called on his closer Dave Giusti, who cruised through the final two innings, making the victory merely a formality.

Pittsburgh made it official when a Bobby Bonds ground ball rolled to Hebner at third who tossed it to Robertson at first for the final out. For the first time in more than a decade, the Pirates were National League champions.

The town and the team were jubilant at their title. The Pirates won as a team, overcoming much adversity in both the regular season and the playoffs.

Yes, Clemente was at his best, but his back would be safe. There were plenty of heroes on this Pirates team taking turns leading the way to ensure Pittsburgh would continue its championship run.

SF N	1	4	0		0	0	0		0	0	0 —	5	10	0
PIT N	2	3	0		0	0	4		0	0	x —	9	11	2

BATTING

San Francisco Giants	AB	R	H	RBI
Henderson lf	5	2	1	0
Fuentes 2b	4	1	2	0
Mays cf	4	0	0	0
McCovey 1b	5	1	3	4
Bonds rf	4	0	1	0
Dietz c	4	0	1	0
Hart 3b	3	0	0	0
Gallagher 3b	1	0	0	0
Speier ss	4	1	1	1
Perry p	3	0	1	0
Johnson p	0	0	0	0
Kingman ph	1	0	0	0
McMahon p	0	0	0	0
Totals	38	5	10	5

FIELDING—PB: Dietz (1).

BATTING—HR: Speier (1,2nd inning off Blass 0 on 0 out); McCovey (2,2nd inning off Blass 2 on 2 out).

GDP: McCovey (1,off Kison).

Team LOB: 9.

Pittsburgh Pirates	AB	R	H	RBI
Cash 2b	5	2	3	0
Hebner 3b	5	2	2	3
Clemente rf	5	1	2	3
Stargell lf	2	1	0	0
Oliver cf	4	1	1	3
Robertson 1b	4	0	0	0
Sanguillen c	3	0	1	0
Hernandez ss	4	1	1	0
Blass p	0	0	0	0
Mazeroski ph	1	1	1	0
Kison p	2	0	0	0
Giusti p	1	0	0	0
Totals	36	9	11	9

FIELDING—DP: 1. Cash-Hernandez-Robertson.

E: Cash (1), Hernandez (1).

BATTING—2B: Hebner (1,off Perry).

HR: Hebner (2,2nd inning off Perry 2 on 2 out); Oliver (1,6th inning off Johnson 2 on 2 out).

IBB: Stargell 2 (2,by Perry,by Johnson).

Team LOB: 6.

BASERUNNING—SB: Cash (1,2nd base off Perry/Dietz).

PITCHING

San Francisco Giants	IP	H	R	ER	BB	SO
Perry L(1–1)	5.2	10	7	7	2	6
Johnson	1.1	1	2	2	1	2
McMahon	1	0	0	0	0	1
Totals	8	11	9	9	3	9

WP: Perry (1).

IBB: Perry (1,Stargell); Johnson (1,Stargell).

Pittsburgh Pirates	IP	H	R	ER	BB	SO
Blass	2	8	5	4	0	2
Kison W(1–0)	4.2	2	0	0	2	3
Giusti	2.1	0	0	0	1	2
Totals	**9**	**10**	**5**	**4**	**3**	**7**

WP: Kison (1).

Umpires: HP—Andy Olsen, 1B—Dick Stello, 2B—Satch Davidson, 3B—Tom Gorman, LF—Shag Crawford, RF—Lee Weyer

Time of Game: 3:00 **Attendance:** 35,487

PIRATES 5, NEW YORK METS 0
SEPTEMBER 30, 1972

3,000

There has never been an athlete in the history of Pittsburgh who has been respected, not just as an athlete but as a man and a hero. Decades after his tragic death, Roberto Clemente is still revered.

On New Year's Eve 1972, Clemente was traveling in an ill-equipped plane filled with relief supplies earmarked for earthquake-ravaged Nicaragua. Angry at rumors that the leaders of that country were reportedly stealing the relief supplies from their desperate citizens who needed them so badly, Clemente decided to accompany the supplies himself to make sure they went to where they were needed. Soon after takeoff, the overloaded plane crashed into the Atlantic Ocean. There were no survivors.

Just three months earlier, Clemente had been on top of the world, playing in what would prove to be his last regular-season game. That day he unknowingly capped his Hall of Fame career by becoming the 11th player ever to reach the 3,000-hit plateau.

By the end of his career, the Pirates' right fielder had gone from a misunderstood and underappreciated talent to team leader and beloved icon. He had risen to a legendary status in most Latino countries and was finally appreciated by U.S. baseball fans after he put his immense talent on display in the 1971 World Series.

Clemente's focus in 1972 was clearly on the quest for 3,000. He entered the campaign 118 short of the magical mark.

While it seemed like a sure thing as the season began, Clemente's aging body was beginning to break down, and for much of the season, fans wondered whether he'd reach the milestone by the end of 1972.

A combination of rheumatic heels, inflammation in both Achilles tendons, and tendonitis in his ankles limited his season. To top it off, he suffered from a viral infection that caused him to lose 15 pounds. All of this resulted in a stretch where he didn't start 39 out of 40 games.

Through it all, the great right fielder still had a fine season, committing no errors and winning his 12th consecutive Gold Glove. He was also productive in his limited plate appearances, hitting .312, but the hits weren't adding up fast enough, and Clemente went into late September still short of his ultimate goal.

The fact that most of the team's September games were meaningless—the Bucs had already run away with the Eastern Division crown—made the pursuit more difficult for Clemente. "What made it hard for me was that we already clinched the title," he said. "I hate to play exhibition games and these games to me are exhibitions. I can't get all keyed up for them."[1]

As September wound down, he came tantalizingly close. He got his 2,999th hit in Philadelphia in the last contest of a three-game series with the Phillies. Manager Bill Virdon then pulled him from the game to give him the opportunity to get the historic hit in front of his hometown fans, against the Mets in the next-to-final series of the season.

His first opportunity came in the opener against future Hall of Famer Tom Seaver. Clemente came up in the first inning with Vic Davalillo on first, and the right fielder hit a shot up the middle that bounded off the glove of New York second baseman Ken Boswell into center field. The 24,193 fans that were on hand at Three Rivers Stadium that night erupted as Clemente's chase appeared to be over. The ball was thrown in to be kept as a memento when all of the sudden an E flashed on the scoreboard, signaling that the official scorer ruled the play as an error on Boswell and not the 3,000th hit. With his historic moment now gone, Clemente was unable to have any success against Seaver for the rest of the evening, with a strikeout, groundout, and fly out in the Mets' 1–0 victory.

The next day Rookie of the Year candidate Jon Matlack would be on the mound to face Clemente. In the first inning, Matlack struck out the Hall of Fame right fielder and continued his mastery over the Pirates' veteran as Clemente failed to collect a hit on the rookie during the season. Clemente got another opportunity in the fourth inning when Matlack quickly got ahead of him with a strike. He then fired a curveball that Clemente ripped into the left center field gap for a clean double—no controversy attached.

The quest for hit number 3,000 was now officially in the books. Clemente stood there at second base staring into the crowd, proud of his accomplishment as the more than 13,000 fans who came to Three Rivers Stadium on this day were on their feet showing their appreciation. Moments later Clemente came home on a Manny Sanguillen single and was mobbed by his teammates, who congratulated him on his accomplishment.

"I dedicate this hit to the fans of Pittsburgh," Clemente said later. "They have been wonderful. And to the people back home in Puerto Rico, but especially to the fellow who pushed me to play baseball, Roberto Marin. He made me play. He carried me around looking for the man to sign me."[2]

Clemente went to right field after the inning was over, tipped his hat to the cheering fans, and then when it was his turn to bat in the fifth, Virdon inserted Bill Mazeroski, who had spent so many years as Clemente's teammate, to pinch-hit for him.

The Pirates went on to win the game 5–0, and that was it for the Pirates' right fielder as Virdon chose to rest Clemente the remainder of the campaign so he would be fresh for the playoffs. While no one knew it at the time, the 3,000 hit would turn out to be the last regular-season at bat in his epic 18-year career. Just over three months later, the Pirates' legend was no more, etching his name as the greatest icon this city has ever known.

NY N	0	0	0		0	0	0		0	0	0	— 0	2	1
PIT N	0	0	0		3	0	2		0	0	x	— 5	6	0

BATTING

New York Mets	AB	R	H	RBI
Garrett 3b	4	0	0	0
Boswell 2b	4	0	1	0
Milner lf	3	0	0	0
Staub rf	3	0	0	0
Rauch p	0	0	0	0
Marshall ph	1	0	0	0
Kranepool 1b	3	0	1	0
Fregosi ss	3	0	0	0
Schneck cf	3	0	0	0
Dyer c	1	0	0	0
Nolan ph,c	2	0	0	0
Matlack p	2	0	0	0
Hahn rf	0	0	0	0
Totals	29	0	2	0

FIELDING—DP: 3. Boswell-Fregosi-Kranepool, Boswell-Fregosi-Kranepool, Fregosi-Kranepool.

E: Garrett (14).

PB: Dyer (3), Nolan (2).

BATTING—Team LOB: 5.

Pittsburgh Pirates	AB	R	H	RBI
Goggin 2b	4	0	2	0
Stennett cf	4	0	0	0
Clemente rf	2	1	1	0
Mazeroski ph	1	0	0	0
Davalillo rf	1	0	0	0
Stargell 1b	3	1	1	0
Zisk lf	1	2	0	0
Sanguillen c	3	1	1	1
Pagan 3b	3	0	0	0
J. Hernandez ss	3	0	1	2
Ellis p	2	0	0	0
Clines ph	1	0	0	0
Johnson p	0	0	0	0
Totals	**28**	**5**	**6**	**3**

BATTING—2B: Clemente (19,off Matlack).

3B: J. Hernandez (1,off Matlack).

GDP: Stennett (16,off Matlack); Pagan (1,off Matlack).

Team LOB: 4.

PITCHING

New York Mets	IP	H	R	ER	BB	SO
Matlack L(14–10)	6	5	5	3	5	5
Rauch	2	1	0	0	0	1
Totals	**8**	**6**	**5**	**3**	**5**	**6**

Pittsburgh Pirates	IP	H	R	ER	BB	SO
Ellis W(15–7)	6	1	0	0	2	4
Johnson SV(3)	3	1	0	0	1	2
Totals	**9**	**2**	**0**	**0**	**3**	**6**

Umpires: HP—John Kibler, 1B—Frank Pulli, 2B—Doug Harvey, 3B—Shag Crawford

Time of Game: 2:10 **Attendance:** 13,117

And a Babe Shall Lead Them

It was billed as a battle between two of the game's titans: Ty Cobb of the Detroit Tigers and the Pirates' Honus Wagner. A Fall Classic of two baseball icons looking for redemption. Appropriately, the two teams matched each other through the first six games of the 1909 World Series, forcing a seventh and deciding game, marking the first time a Fall Classic came down to a do-or-die contest.

Cobb had led the Tigers to the previous two American League pennants, but on each occasion they were defeated in the World Series, losing both times at the hands of the Chicago Cubs. This time Cobb's task would be even more difficult.

For all his brilliance, Cobb spent the better part of his career battling teammates, fans, and the authorities alike. Earlier in the 1909 campaign, he had a violent altercation with a house detective in Cleveland, and police were waiting for Cobb to enter Ohio so they could charge him for the offense. To avoid this, Cobb would drive back and forth between Pittsburgh and Detroit during the series, going through Canada and then Buffalo. It was an exhausting trek that put the Georgia native at less-than-peak performance. Through six games, he was batting a modest .272 and was hoping to improve that drastically in the final contest held in his own home stadium, Bennett Park.

Honus Wagner also had a bad taste in his mouth, left over from a tough World Series six years earlier in the first Fall Classic. Wagner batted just .222 and was blamed by both the media and fans alike for costing Pittsburgh the championship against their American League counterparts from Boston. It was a stain on his magnificent career and one that he was hoping to wipe clean against the Tigers. Unlike Cobb, Wagner was having an outstanding series through the first six games, hitting .333 with six stolen bases.

With all eyes focused on Cobb and Wagner, a pair of unheralded pitchers turned out to be the key component of the series. Detroit veteran George Mullin had won two games, dominating the potent Pirates lineup, while Pittsburgh rookie Charles "Babe" Adams had emerged victorious in both of his series starts.

Mullin had kept the Tigers alive in Game Six with a complete-game 5–4 victory but would only be available in relief for Detroit in Game Seven. Adams, however, got the opportunity not only to win his third game of the series but to bring Wagner and his teammates their long-awaited championship.

The Bucs threatened in the first when Bobby Byrne was hit by a "Wild" Bill Donovan pitch to lead off the game and was sacrificed to second. Byrne then tried to steal third off the questionable arm of Detroit catcher Boss Schmidt and collided into third baseman George Moriarty, who was 40 pounds heavier. Both men were rolling in pain on the ground as Byrne was called out on the steal attempt and had to be carried to the locker room after badly injuring his ankle. It was an ominous start for the Pirates.

In the second, Donovan would not be so lucky. Bill Abstien walked to open the inning and then tried to atone for the five errors he committed in the series thus far by stealing second. Chief Wilson then tried to sacrifice Abstien over to third, laying down a bunt right in front of the plate. But he was safe at first when Tigers catcher Boss Schmidt tried to unsuccessfully throw out the lead runner. Bucs catcher George Gibson was unable to bring home a run as he popped out to short, bringing up Adams. Donovan showed why he was nicknamed "Wild" by walking the Pirates' pitcher and loading the bases. Ham Hyatt, who came into the game to play center when Tommy Leach had to move to third to replace the injured Byrne, lifted a long fly ball to center, scoring Abstien with the first run. The Tigers' hurler then walked Leach and Fred Clarke forcing another run to give Pittsburgh a 2–0 lead.

Trying once again to come back as they had in Game Six when they rallied from three runs behind, the Tigers threatened in the third, putting runners on second and third with one out. But Adams stopped Detroit cold, getting Tom Jones on a pop-up to short and Schmidt on a groundout to keep the American League champions off the board.

With Adams in control, the Pirates' offense gave him more support in the fourth. For the Tigers, Jennings had pulled Donovan following the third inning in favor of the Tigers' series star George Mullin. Mullin was tired, though, following his three series starts and gave up a walk to Hyatt, a single to Leach, and then intentionally walked Wagner. Pirates rookie second baseman Dots Miller followed with a single, which scored two more runs, making it 4–0. It was more than enough for Adams, but the Pirates' offense wasn't done.

In the sixth, Leach hit a one-out double, and Clarke walked, bringing up Wagner once again with a man in scoring position. He laced a triple to left field, scoring both runners and then himself to give the Bucs a seven-run lead.

Pittsburgh added a final run in the eighth making it 8–0, thoroughly extinguishing Detroit's hopes for its first world championship. Adams finished the game and the series strong, capturing his third victory of the Fall Classic with a six-hit shutout.

It was the battle between good and evil that made this series so appealing. For Wagner, it was the ultimate redemption after his embarrassing series in 1903. He was now a hero, the ultimate sportsman whom fans idolized, soundly defeating Cobb, the man who was his opposite in just about every way.

As compelling as the battle between the two superstars was, in the end, though, it was a young hurler by the name of Babe Adams who overshadowed Cobb and Wagner and was the true hero in the Pirates' first World Series championship.

PIT N	0	2	0	2	0	3	0	1	0 —	8	7	0
DET A	0	0	0	0	0	0	0	0	0 —	0	6	3

BATTING

Pittsburgh Pirates	AB	R	H	RBI
Byrne 3b	0	0	0	0
Hyatt cf	3	1	0	1
Leach cf,3b	3	2	2	0
Clarke lf	0	2	0	1
Wagner ss	3	1	1	2
Miller 2b	5	0	2	2
Abstein 1b	4	1	1	0
Wilson rf	4	1	0	0
Gibson c	5	0	1	0
Adams p	3	0	0	0
Totals	30	8	7	6

BATTING—2B: Abstein (2,off Donovan); Leach (4,off Mullin); Gibson (2,off Mullin).

3B: Wagner (1,off Mullin).

SH: Leach (1,off Donovan); Wilson (2,off Donovan); Clarke (4,off Mullin); Adams (2,off Mullin).

SF: Hyatt (1,off Donovan).

HBP: Byrne (2,by Donovan).

Team LOB: 11.

BASERUNNING—SB: Clarke 2 (3,2nd base off Donovan/Schmidt,2nd base off Mullin/Schmidt); Abstein (1,2nd base off Donovan/Schmidt); Miller (3,2nd base off Mullin/Schmidt).

CS: Byrne (1,3rd base by Donovan/Schmidt).

Detroit Tigers	AB	R	H	RBI
D. Jones lf	4	0	1	0
Bush ss	2	0	0	0
Cobb rf	4	0	0	0
Crawford cf	4	0	0	0
Delahanty 2b	3	0	2	0
Moriarty 3b	1	0	1	0
O'Leary pr,3b	3	0	0	0
T. Jones 1b	4	0	1	0
Schmidt c	3	0	1	0
Donovan p	0	0	0	0
Mullin ph,p	3	0	0	0
Totals	31	0	6	0

FIELDING—DP: 1. Bush-Schmidt-Delahanty.

E: D. Jones (1), Bush (5), Crawford (2).

BATTING—2B: Moriarty (1,off Adams); Schmidt (3,off Adams); Delahanty (5,off Adams).

SH: Bush (3,off Adams).

HBP: Bush (2,by Adams).

Team LOB: 7.

BASERUNNING—CS: Bush (2,2nd base by Adams/Gibson).

PITCHING

Pittsburgh Pirates	IP	H	R	ER	BB	SO
Adams W(3–0)	9	6	0	0	1	1

HBP: Adams (1,Bush).

Detroit Tigers	IP	H	R	ER	BB	SO
Donovan L(1–1)	3	2	2	2	6	0
Mullin	6	5	6	4	4	1
Totals	**9**	**7**	**8**	**6**	**10**	**1**

HBP: Donovan (1,Byrne).
Umpires: HP—Silk O'Loughlin, 1B—Jim Johnstone, LF—Billy Evans, RF—Bill Klem
Time of Game: 2:10 **Attendance:** 17,562

PIRATES 10, PHILADELPHIA PHILLIES 7
SEPTEMBER 1, 1971

Breaking Barriers

Breaking racial barriers in sports are moments for the ages, ones that often mix a wide range of emotions.

Twenty-four years after Jackie Robinson became the first African American to play in the majors, there was another more subtle moment but just as telling. September 1, 1971, was the first time the entire lineup for one major-league team was made up solely of men of color. There was no fanfare, no reporters to cover the event. In reality, not even the players, the fans, or the manager truly understood the significance of the moment. It was the greatest racial barrier ever broken that nobody knew about.

The Pirates of 1971 were a diverse team, particularly in a conservative era in the game's history. Their roster included 13 players of either African American or Latin decent, composing nearly half of the team. On September 1, 1971, in a game against the Philadelphia Phillies, Pirates manager Danny Murtaugh handed home plate umpire Stan Landes the following lineup:

2B-Rennie Stennett
CF-Gene Clines
RF-Roberto Clemente
LF-Willie Stargell
CA-Manny Sanguillen
3B-Dave Cash
1B-Al Oliver
SS-Jackie Hernandez
PI-Dock Ellis

While it turned out to be a day to remember, the players on the field didn't notice what was happening until after the game had started. According to Al Oliver's autobiography, *Baseball's Best Kept Secret*, it was shortly after the game began that Dave Cash said to him, "Hey, Scoop, we've got all brothers out there." Starting pitcher Dock Ellis was also caught by surprise, later saying he was certain it had been a mistake on Murtaugh's part.

As amazing as it was, Ellis's wildness threatened to quickly break up the historic lineup. In the top of the first, he walked the first two batters he faced. Both eventually came in to score as the Phillies opened up an early 2–0 lead.

The powerful Pirates lineup turned things around in the bottom of the first by scoring five runs of their own knocked in by five different players.

Ellis was no better in the second, giving up a two-run homer to Philadelphia's Ron Stone and cutting the lead to one. Murtaugh had seen enough, replacing Ellis with Bob Moose, pulling the plug on the all-minority lineup before the game was two innings old.

Ellis was angry and felt at the time that the umpires were conspiring against him once they realized the nature of the Pirates' lineup. "The umpire knew who we had on the field and he was trying to get me out of there," Ellis said. "I was throwing balls down the middle of the plate and he was calling balls." In Oliver's book, Ellis said that he was so angry after leaving the game that he immediately boarded a plane because he was afraid he'd kill the umpire. Ellis, who had a history of drug abuse, was high and ended up in the house of Dodgers great Willie Crawford where he collapsed on the living room floor and slept until the next day.

Whether or not Ellis was accurate in his suspicions, Moose was no better, surrendering a two-run shot to slugger Deron Johnson, giving the Phillies the lead, 6–5. But the lead proved temporary, as the Bucs came back to recapture their advantage in the bottom half of the second. After an RBI sacrifice fly by Willie Stargell, Manny Sanguillen smashed a two-run homer to make it 8–6 Pittsburgh.

Following the offensive outburst in the first two innings, both bullpens settled down to bring order to the chaos. Eventually, Murtaugh brought reliever Bob Veale into the game, and the Pirates once again sported an all-minority lineup.

Pittsburgh tacked on two more runs to the Phillies as the Bucs held on for a 10–7 win. As nice as a victory was, it was the broken barrier that not only made this contest significant but made the players who participated in it proud. "I was proud of that day," Cash said. "We accomplished something that may never be done again."[1]

Murtaugh downplayed the moment. "Did I have nine blacks out there?" he mused. "I thought I had nine Pirates out there on the field. Once a man puts on a Pirate uniform I don't notice the color of their skin."[2] It was a sentiment most of his players would have agreed with.

Like most important moments in the fight for racial equality, controversy followed. The media made little of it at first, but Pirates general manager Joe L. Brown was besieged with negative letters, with many fans blaming the team's less-than-stellar attendance on the fact they had "too many blacks" on the team.

Regardless of the negative outcry, the racial and ethnic mix is what made the 1971 Pirates so special. From the front office to the dugout, this franchise was only interested in putting players on the field who could help it win no matter what the color of their skin was or where they were born. It's what made their championship that same year so cherished by all who experienced it. It was truly a team that changed baseball.

PHI N	2	4	0	1	0	0	0	0	0	—	7	7	1
PIT N	5	3	1	0	0	1	0	0	x	—	10	13	1

BATTING

Philadelphia Phillies	AB	R	H	RBI
Stone rf	4	2	1	2
Bowa ss	2	2	0	0
McCarver c	4	1	1	0
Johnson 1b	4	1	1	2
Montanez cf	3	0	0	1
Gamble lf	4	0	1	1
Harmon 2b	4	0	1	0
Vukovich 3b	3	1	0	0
Fryman p	0	0	0	0
Brandon p	2	0	1	0
Selma p	1	0	1	0
Lis ph	1	0	0	0
Champion p	0	0	0	0
Totals	32	7	7	6

FIELDING—E: McCarver (6).

BATTING—HR: Stone (2,2nd inning off Ellis 1 on 1 out); Johnson (29,2nd inning off Moose 1 on 2 out).

SF: Montanez (10,off Walker).

GDP: Johnson (14,off Walker); Stone (3,off Walker).

Team LOB: 6.

Pittsburgh Pirates	AB	R	H	RBI
Stennett 2b	5	1	2	1
Clines cf	5	2	2	0
Clemente rf	4	2	2	2
Stargell lf	3	1	2	2
Sanguillen c	4	2	2	2
Cash 3b	3	1	1	1
Oliver 1b	4	0	2	1
J. Hernandez ss	2	1	0	1
Ellis p	1	0	0	0
Moose p	0	0	0	0
Veale p	0	0	0	0
Walker p	2	0	0	0
Totals	**33**	**10**	**13**	**10**

FIELDING—DP: 3. Clines-Cash, Cash-Stennett-Oliver, Stennett-J. Hernandez-Oliver.
E: J. Hernandez (15).
PB: Sanguillen (11).
BATTING—2B: Stargell (24,off Fryman); Oliver (24,off Fryman); Clines (11,off Selma).
HR: Sanguillen (6,2nd inning off Brandon 1 on 2 out).
SH: Veale (1,off Brandon).
SF: J. Hernandez (3,off Brandon); Stargell (5,off Brandon).
Team LOB: 5.
BASERUNNING—SB: Clines (10,2nd base off Brandon/McCarver); Cash (13,2nd base off Selma/McCarver).
CS: J. Hernandez (2,2nd base by Selma/McCarver).

PITCHING

Philadelphia Phillies	IP	H	R	ER	BB	SO
Fryman	0.1	6	5	5	0	0
Brandon L(6–6)	2.1	4	4	4	1	1
Selma	4.1	3	1	1	2	3
Champion	1	0	0	0	0	1
Totals	**8**	**13**	**10**	**10**	**3**	**5**

WP: Selma (2).

Pittsburgh Pirates	IP	H	R	ER	BB	SO
Ellis	1.1	2	5	3	4	2
Moose	1.1	3	1	1	0	1
Veale	0.1	0	0	0	0	1
Walker W(7–8)	6	2	1	1	3	1
Totals	**9**	**7**	**7**	**5**	**7**	**5**

Umpires: HP—Stan Landes, 1B—Shag Crawford, 2B—Mel Steiner, 3B—Satch Davidson
Time of Game: 2:44 **Attendance:** 11,278

MILWAUKEE BRAVES 1, PIRATES 0
MAY 26, 1959

The Greatest Game Ever Pitched

Every so often there comes a moment when the ordinary becomes extraordinary, when what should have been a routine episode instead becomes once in a lifetime. On a May night in 1959, a diminutive southpaw from Medway, Ohio, named Harvey Haddix experienced such an evening. On this fateful evening, Haddix took "perfect" to a level never seen before or since as he threw arguably the greatest game a pitcher has ever thrown in the history of the game.

While Haddix was exceptional, there's an ironic twist to his tale. Generally when an athlete accomplishes such greatness, there is joy and euphoria. He is lifted on the shoulders of his teammates and paraded around in a celebration befitting kings. In Haddix's case, afterward he sat dejectedly in his locker room stall, drinking a beer and trying to shake away the thought of what might have been. No pitcher had ever been perfect past nine innings in a single game, much less taking a perfect game into the 13th. Haddix did that, but his teammates were unable to get the one run that would have made him a legend. Instead, he sat in his locker room stall, knowing the 13th inning was not kind to him. For Harvey Haddix had pitched maybe the greatest game ever, and lost.

Out of all the pitchers who stepped on the mound in the annals of the game, Haddix was one of the least likely to throw such a gem. He was acquired from the Reds in January 1959, along with Smoky Burgess and Don Hook, and, at 33, was the oldest member of a young Pirates starting rotation. Haddix had been excellent in the mid-1950s, winning 20 and 18 games in 1953 and 1954, respectively, but was a mere 47–46 since.

The Pirates' offense established a disturbing trend in the first two innings, when it threatened to score against Milwaukee Braves hurler Lew Burdette. Each time they were unable to deliver the clutch hit. The second inning saw the Bucs squander their best chance to score when right fielder Roman Mejias was thrown out at trying to advance to third after a single by Haddix. Shortstop Dick Schofield followed with a hit that would have easily scored Mejias had he stayed at second. The Braves escaped unscathed, and Mejias's overaggressiveness would haunt Haddix and the Pirates the rest of the game.

Haddix was dominant, easily retiring the Braves' lineup. The only threat was a line drive by Milwaukee's Johnny Logan, which was speared by Schofield in the third inning. Burdette had given up some hits to the Bucs but was still effective as the game went into the ninth still scoreless.

In the top of the ninth, Pittsburgh almost pushed across the winning run. Bill Virdon singled to center with one out and went to third when Rocky Nelson singled to right. With two out and men at the corners, Skinner had a chance to be a true hero but instead grounded out to Burdette to end the inning.

Even though he couldn't win it, Haddix would now try to become the first man since Don Larsen in the 1956 World Series to toss a perfect nine-inning game. He struck out Andy Pafko, got Logan on a fly to left, and then fanned Lew Burdette to become only the eighth man since 1880 to pitch a perfect game in the majors and the first to toss a perfect game in the regular season since Charles Robinson of the White Sox in 1922. Yet Haddix's day wasn't done. To collect a historic victory, Haddix would have to do what no pitcher had done: go beyond nine innings of perfection.

Naturally as the game went on, the Bucs' southpaw began to tire. In the 10th inning he gave up long drives to Del Rice and Eddie Mathews, which were caught by Virdon in front of the warning track in center. Catcher Del Crandall crushed another to Virdon in the 11th. Through it all, the perfect game remained intact: 33 Braves up and 33 Braves down.

While Haddix's game remained unblemished, his teammates did him no favors offensively, managing only singles by Hoak and Schofield in the 10th and 11th. After the Bucs came up empty again in the top of the 12th, Haddix retired the side in the bottom half to extend his streak to 36.

In the top of the 13th, Burdette gave up his 12th hit of the contest, Schofield's third hit, but it came with two outs. Virdon then grounded to second to end the inning, and the crowd of 19,194 was now focused on the five-foot-nine, 150-pound southpaw to see if this incredible pitching performance would continue.

So focused was Haddix that he had no idea how good he had truly been. "Sure, I knew I had the no-hitter," he said later. "Now and then I would look at the scoreboard what the count was on the hitter. I had to see that zero back of the Braves. I didn't know about the perfect game, though. I thought that maybe back there in the early innings I might have walked a man."[1]

Unfortunately, perfection can't last forever. The first batter in the unlucky 13th, Felix Mantilla, got aboard when Don Hoak's throw to first base on a grounder to third went low and got away from Nelson. Eddie Mathews sacrificed Mantilla into scoring position, but the no-hitter had reached 12⅓ innings. After walking Hank Aaron intentionally, Haddix now faced Joe Adcock, for an at bat that would forever live in infamy for the Pirates nation.

Haddix made his only mistake of the night firing a slider that was too high in the strike zone, and Adcock sent it over the right center field wall to give the Braves a sudden win. In the hysteria, Adcock passed Aaron on the base paths; thus the game-winning home run was changed to a double and only Mantilla's run counted.

It was of little consequence to Haddix, as this incredible night was nothing more than his third loss of the season. Of course it was more than that. Until he faced Andy Pafko in the 12th, he hadn't fallen behind a batter in the contest. Only 12 of the 36 consecutive batters he retired got the ball out of the infield. It was an incredible yet tragic performance, one that manager Danny Murtaugh described as "a damn shame."[2]

It wasn't the way that the greatest-pitched game ever was supposed to end. At least at the time, Haddix was officially acknowledged in the record book as having thrown a perfect nine-inning game. But even that designation would be taken away from the Pirates' southpaw. To add insult to injury, in September 1991 major-league baseball created a new definition of what a no-hitter was. It now was a complete game of nine innings or more in which a pitcher did not allow a hit. Thus "greatest game ever pitched" was removed from the record books. A damn shame, indeed.

PIT N	0	0	0	0	0	0	0	0	0	0	0	0	0 —	0	12	1
MIL N	0	0	0	0	0	0	0	0	0	0	0	0	1 —	1	1	0

BATTING

Pittsburgh Pirates	AB	R	H	RBI
Schofield ss	6	0	3	0
Virdon cf	6	0	1	0
Burgess c	5	0	0	0
Nelson 1b	5	0	2	0
Skinner lf	5	0	1	0
Mazeroski 2b	5	0	1	0
Hoak 3b	5	0	2	0
Mejias rf	3	0	1	0
Stuart ph	1	0	0	0
Christopher rf	1	0	0	0
Haddix p	5	0	1	0
Totals	47	0	12	0

FIELDING—E: Hoak (5).
BATTING—GDP: Skinner (2,off Burdette); Haddix (1,off Burdette);
Burgess (4,off Burdette).
Team LOB: 8.

Milwaukee Braves	AB	R	H	RBI
O'Brien 2b	3	0	0	0
Rice ph	1	0	0	0
Mantilla 2b	1	1	0	0
Mathews 3b	4	0	0	0
Aaron rf	4	0	0	0
Adcock 1b	5	0	1	1
Covington lf	4	0	0	0
Crandall c	4	0	0	0
Pafko cf	4	0	0	0
Logan ss	4	0	0	0
Burdette p	4	0	0	0
Totals	38	1	1	1

FIELDING—DP: 3. Adcock-Logan-Adcock, Mathews-O'Brien-Adcock,
Adcock-Logan.

BATTING—**2B:** Adcock (3,off Haddix).
SH: Mathews (1,off Haddix).
IBB: Aaron (2,by Haddix).
Team LOB: 1.

PITCHING

Pittsburgh Pirates	IP	H	R	ER	BB	SO
Haddix L(4–3)	12.2	1	1	0	1	8

IBB: Haddix (5,Aaron).

Milwaukee Braves	IP	H	R	ER	BB	SO
Burdette W(8–2)	13	12	0	0	0	2

Umpires: HP—Vinnie Smith, 1B—Frank Dascoli, 2B—Frank Secory, 3B—Hal Dixon
Time of Game: 2:54 **Attendance:** 19,194

PIRATES 7, BOSTON AMERICANS 3
OCTOBER 1, 1903

An American Tradition Begins

An exhausting two-year war in the national pastime was about to end. Few expected the upstart American League to truly challenge the more established National League. After all, the senior circuit had already fended off the American Association, the Union Association, and the Players League. This time, though, the new circuit had what the others did not: strong leadership in the name of their founder and president, Ban Johnson, the man who would become known as the "Czar of Baseball." Johnson was very successful in his endeavor, stealing several of the National League's best players for his fledgling league.

Before the 1903 season, the two circuits signed a pact, agreeing that both would recognize the other's contracts, in effect ending the raiding of players. They established a three-man commission to resolve all disputes. The other development occurred when Pirates president Barney Dreyfuss sent a letter to Henry Killilea, president of Boston's American League club. Dreyfuss proposed a series of games at the end of the year between the two league champions to keep baseball interest alive among the fans.

Dreyfuss said in his letter, "The time has come for the National League and American League to organize a World Series. It is my belief that if our clubs played a series on a best-of-9 basis, we would create great interest in baseball, in our leagues, and in our players. I also believe it would be a financial success." Thus was born one of the most anticipated events on the American sports calendar: the World Series.

While many of its fellow franchises were devastated by Johnson's raid, the Pirates went relatively untouched by the American League. It seemed appropriate that the Pirates would meet the AL champion Boston Americans in the first Fall Classic, the team that had benefited the most from the deflections of the National League stars.

Despite the fact that the new postseason series was a last-minute venture, excitement in both cities was high. Ticket prices had quadrupled in some cases, but more than 16,000 jammed into Boston's Huntington Avenue Grounds for this momentous first contest, with fans filing in more than three hours before the first pitch.

On the mound were two of the greatest hurlers of the decade: Pittsburgh's Deacon Phillippe, a 25-game winner in 1903, and Boston's Cy Young, who won 28.

The Bucs entered this series shorthanded with their other star hurlers out. Sam Leever suffered a shoulder injury during a trap-shooting contest, and Ed Doheny had been committed to an insane asylum due to an extreme case of paranoia. To add to the Pirates' troubles, Honus Wagner was hampered by a leg injury but decided to play through the pain.

Regardless of the injuries and the fact the Americans were an early 5–4 favorite in the opening contest, the Pirates were still the defending three-time National League champions and would make sure the upstart American League pennant winners were aware of that from the onset.

After Young retired the first two batters in the first, Pirates third baseman Tommy Leach ripped a shot into the fans standing behind a rope in right field for a triple. Honus Wagner then brought him home with a single to left, scoring the first run in World Series history. It was only the beginning for Pittsburgh.

Wagner promptly stole second and moved to third when Kitty Bransfield was safe on a grounder that Boston second baseman Hobe Ferris bobbled. Bransfield then tried to steal second in an attempt to put both men in scoring position. Boston catcher Lou Criger fired the ball into center field, allowing Wagner to score and sending Bransfield to third.

A frustrated Young then walked Claude Ritchey, who also stole second. Jimmy Sebring popped a line drive into left, scoring two more runs and extending the Pirates' lead to 4–0. Criger's first inning problems continued when Young struck out catcher Eddie Phelps for the apparent last out of the frame. Criger let strike three get by him, and Phelps was safe at first on the error. Young finally was able to end the long first inning when he struck out his mound opponent Phillippe, but the damage had been done, giving the Pirates' pitcher all the support he would need. Phillippe was dominant from the beginning, striking out five of the first seven batters he faced and holding Boston scoreless for the first six innings.

By the top of the seventh, Pittsburgh's lead had swelled to 7–0, the final run off the bat of Sebring, who hit the first home run ever in World Series play. The Pirates' right fielder hit a ball over Boston right fielder Buck Freeman's head. Thinking it would roll into the crowd for a ground rule triple, Freeman did not hustle after the ball. Sebring kept running and beat the delayed throw home to give the Bucs a commanding seven-run advantage.

Boston was able to score three runs in the final three innings, but the Pirates closed out the initial game of the Fall Classic as 7–3 victors. The fans of the more established National League were beside themselves, thinking that the opener was a harbinger of things to come, especially after Pittsburgh took a commanding three-to-one lead in the best-of-nine series, with Phillippe winning all three games. But things would change quickly. Boston dominated the final four contests outscoring the Bucs 27–8 to win the series and secure the honor of becoming baseball's first World Series champion.

Regardless of the eventual outcome, for one day when the entire baseball world was looking on, the Pirates came up big in the historic first contest, capturing the victory in the first chapter of what would become an American epic.

PIT N	4	0	1		1	0	0		1	0	0	—	7	12	2
BOS A	0	0	0		0	0	0		2	0	1	—	3	6	4

BATTING

Pittsburgh Pirates	AB	R	H	RBI
Beaumont cf	5	1	0	0
Clarke lf	5	0	2	0
Leach 3b	5	1	4	1
Wagner ss	3	1	1	1
Bransfield 1b	5	2	1	0
Ritchey 2b	4	1	0	0
Sebring rf	5	1	3	4
Phelps c	4	0	1	0
Phillippe p	4	0	0	0
Totals	40	7	12	6

FIELDING—E: Leach (1), Wagner (1).
BATTING—3B: Leach 2 (2,off Young 2); Bransfield (1,off Young).
HR: Sebring (1,7th inning off Young 0 on 1 out).
Team LOB: 9.
BASERUNNING—SB: Wagner (1,2nd base off Young/Criger); Bransfield (1,2nd base off Young/Criger);
Ritchey (1,2nd base off Young/Criger).
CS: Leach (1,Home by Young/Criger).

Boston Americans	AB	R	H	RBI
Dougherty lf	4	0	0	0
Collins 3b	4	0	0	0
Stahl cf	4	0	1	0
Freeman rf	4	2	2	0
Parent ss	4	1	2	1
LaChance 1b	2	0	0	2
Ferris 2b	3	0	1	0
Criger c	3	0	0	0
O'Brien ph	1	0	0	0
Young p	3	0	0	0
Farrell ph	1	0	0	0
Totals	**33**	**3**	**6**	**3**

FIELDING—E: Ferris 2 (2), Criger 2 (2).
BATTING—3B: Freeman (1,off Phillippe); Parent (1,off Phillippe).
SF: LaChance 2 (2,off Phillippe 2).
HBP: Ferris (1,by Phillippe).
Team LOB: 6.

PITCHING

Pittsburgh Pirates	IP	H	R	ER	BB	SO
Phillippe W(1–0)	9	6	3	2	0	10

HBP: Phillippe (1,Ferris).

Boston Americans	IP	H	R	ER	BB	SO
Young L(0–1)	9	12	7	3	3	5

Umpires: HP—Hank O'Day, 1B—Tommy Connolly
Time of Game: 1:55 Attendance: 16,242

#4

Pops Becomes an Icon

It had been a long, wild ride for the Pittsburgh Pirates in 1979. They had overcome several obstacles, overtaking the Montreal Expos in the final week of the season to capture the division crown, and then they finally knocked off their rivals the Cincinnati Reds for the first time after three losses in the National League Championship Series. It seemed like their joyride had finally come to an end when the Baltimore Orioles took three of the first four games in the World Series. Down but not out, the Bucs defeated Baltimore 7–1 and 4–0 in Games Five and Six to bring them to the ultimate climax of this memorable campaign: Game Seven of the World Series.

While Dave Parker said that he could "feel something dramatic building" after the Bucs fell behind three games to one, most figured the Pirates were finished.[1] Two key factors helped Pittsburgh turn the tide. First, after Game Four, pitcher Jim Rooker confided that the scouting reports the team was getting on the Baltimore hitters seemed incorrect. The pitchers decided to disregard the reports and gave up only two runs in the final three games. The second unforeseen catalyst was the emotion brought about by the passing of manager Chuck Tanner's mother after the fourth game. Tanner decided to remain with the team following her death, saying that he knew his mother would have wanted him to make that decision and lead his club to the World Series title.

Fueled by emotion and strategic adjustments, the Pirates knew if they wanted to win the title, they'd have to figure out Orioles hurler Scott McGregor. McGregor was having a tremendous postseason and had defeated the Pirates in Game Three. Facing McGregor would be the Bucs' powerful 35-year-old right-hander Jim Bibby, who was signed as a free agent by the Pirates in 1978 and had a 12–4 record with a 2.81 ERA in 1979.

As this dramatic game began to unfold, it was apparent early on that the pitchers were in control. Bibby gave up only a single over the first two frames, and McGregor shut down a Pirates threat in the second.

Baltimore second baseman Rich Dauer led off the bottom of the third with a long shot that cleared the left field fence for his first homer of the series to give the Orioles an early 1–0 lead. Pittsburgh squandered another scoring opportunity in the fourth, and the Bucs went into the top of the sixth still scoreless.

During the Pirates' magical run during the 1979 campaign, there had been one constant that kept them afloat in tough times—their leader, first baseman Willie Stargell. This decisive game would be no different. Stargell already had a single and a double as he stepped to the plate with a man on first in the sixth. Stargell once again etched his name in Pirates lore.

In the right field bullpen, catcher Ed Ott and Rooker discussed whether Stargell would come through in clutch once again. As if on cue, the man nicknamed "Pops" blasted a McGregor breaking ball toward right field where the Orioles' Ken Singleton jumped at the wall, almost making a fantastic catch. The ball just eluded his glove and landed right beside Ott and Rooker to give the Bucs a dramatic lead. "At first I didn't think it would travel that far," Stargell said later. "When it did I was just thrilled."[2]

With the Bucs now ahead, Tanner was confident his bullpen could hold it. His confidence may have been shaken in the eighth, though, when Baltimore got two on with one out. The Pirates' manager called on his closer Kent Tekulve, who had been bombed in the fourth game of the series, to get the team out of this jam. Before Tekulve's first pitch, Stargell came over from first to talk to his reliever and make sure that his poor performance of a few days before was out of his head. He told Teke to relax and show the Orioles how good he really was. "And if you don't think you can do that," Stargell quipped. "You play first and I'll pitch."[3]

The talk did the trick. He got Terry Crowley to bounce out to second, moving the base runners into scoring position. Tanner chose to intentionally walk Singleton, so Tekulve could face the future Hall of Famer Eddie Murray, who was mired in an 0-for-20 slump. The move worked as the Pirates' reliever got Murray to fly out to right, where Dave Parker slipped three times on the poor Memorial Stadium turf before he made the inning-ending catch.

Still clinging to a one-run lead, Phil Garner led off the ninth with a double to left field, and then Omar Moreno smacked a one-out single to center, scoring Garner. After Tim Foli singled, sending Moreno to third, both Parker and Bill Robinson were hit by Orioles relievers Tippy and Dennis Martinez, respectively, to force home the Pirates' fourth run.

Tekulve made short work of the Orioles in the ninth, striking out Ron Roenicke and Doug DeCinces before pinch hitter Pat Kelly lifted a fly ball that ended up cradled in the glove of Moreno to end the game and the series, completing a remarkable comeback.

Appropriately Willie Stargell was named series MVP, hitting .415 with three homers and seven RBIs. It was a clean sweep for the future Hall of Famer who also was awarded the regular season and National League Championship Series MVP, ensuring his place in Pittsburgh lore as one of the town's greatest sports icons. It was a season for the ages for both Stargell and the Pirates as they put an exclamation point on one of the most exciting campaigns in franchise history.

PIT N	0	0	0	0	0	2	0	0	2	— 4	10	0
BAL A	0	0	1	0	0	0	0	0	0	— 1	4	2

BATTING

Pittsburgh Pirates	AB	R	H	RBI
Moreno cf	5	1	3	1
Foli ss	4	0	1	0
Parker rf	4	0	0	0
B. Robinson lf	4	1	1	1
Stargell 1b	5	1	4	2
Madlock 3b	3	0	0	0
Nicosia c	4	0	0	0
Garner 2b	3	1	1	0
Bibby p	1	0	0	0
Sanguillen ph	1	0	0	0
D. Robinson p	0	0	0	0
Jackson p	1	0	0	0
Tekulve p	1	0	0	0
Totals	**36**	**4**	**10**	**4**

BATTING—2B: Stargell 2 (4,off McGregor 2); Garner (4,off Stoddard).
HR: Stargell (3,6th inning off McGregor 1 on 1 out).
SH: Foli (1,off McGregor).
HBP: Parker (1,by T. Martinez); B. Robinson (1,by D. Martinez).
GDP: Stargell (1,off D. Martinez).
IBB: Garner (2,by McGregor); Madlock (2,by McGregor).
Team LOB: 10.

Baltimore Orioles	AB	R	H	RBI
Bumbry cf	3	0	0	0
Garcia ss	3	0	1	0
Ayala ph	0	0	0	0
Crowley ph	1	0	0	0
Stoddard p	0	0	0	0
Flanagan p	0	0	0	0
Stanhouse p	0	0	0	0
T. Martinez p	0	0	0	0
D. Martinez p	0	0	0	0
Singleton rf	3	0	0	0
Murray 1b	4	0	0	0
Lowenstein lf	2	0	0	0
Roenicke ph,lf	2	0	0	0
DeCinces 3b	4	0	2	0
Dempsey c	3	0	0	0
Kelly ph	1	0	0	0
Dauer 2b	3	1	1	1
McGregor p	1	0	0	0
May ph	0	0	0	0
Belanger pr,ss	0	0	0	0
Totals	**30**	**1**	**4**	**1**

FIELDING—DP: 1. Belanger-Murray.

E: Garcia (1), Lowenstein (1).

BATTING—HR: Dauer (1,3rd inning off Bibby 0 on 0 out).

IBB: Singleton (1,by Tekulve).

Team LOB: 6.

BASERUNNING—CS: Garcia (1,2nd base by Bibby/Nicosia).

PITCHING

Pittsburgh Pirates	IP	H	R	ER	BB	SO
Bibby	4	3	1	1	0	3
D. Robinson	0.2	1	0	0	1	0
Jackson W(1–0)	2.2	0	0	0	2	1
Tekulve SV(3)	1.2	0	0	0	1	2
Totals	9	4	1	1	4	6

IBB: Tekulve (2,Singleton).

Baltimore Orioles	IP	H	R	ER	BB	SO
McGregor L(1–1)	8	7	2	2	2	2
Stoddard	0.1	1	1	1	0	0
Flanagan	0	1	1	1	0	0
Stanhouse	0	1	0	0	0	0
T. Martinez	0	0	0	0	0	0
D. Martinez	0.2	0	0	0	0	0
Totals	9	10	4	4	2	2

HBP: T. Martinez (1,Parker); D. Martinez (1,B. Robinson).
IBB: McGregor 2 (2,Garner,Madlock).
Umpires: HP—Jerry Neudecker, 1B—Bob Engel, 2B—Russ Goetz,
3B—Terry Tata, LF—Jim McKean, RF—Paul Runge
Time of Game: 2:54 **Attendance:** 53,733

PIRATES 2, BALTIMORE ORIOLES 1
OCTOBER 17, 1971

Rule 801

Rule 801, an obscure notation in major-league baseball's official rule book, simply states the pitcher must throw from in front of the pitching rubber, but in Game Seven of the 1971 World Series, Rule 801 was about to become the talk of the nation.

Baltimore manager Earl Weaver noticed that Pirates pitcher Steve Blass seemed to be throwing from the side of the rubber and not the front. Never mind that Blass was already throwing wild; Weaver was the master of the mind game. He figured this was a chance to get inside Blass's head. Weaver decided to go out and argue with the umpire and in the process send the nervous Blass over the edge. With 20-game winner Mike Cuellar on the mound for Baltimore, it could be the move that would give Weaver's Orioles the win and a second consecutive world championship. As it turned out, it was a maneuver that backfired dramatically.

After pitching a two-hit masterpiece in Game Three, Blass was Pirates manager Danny Murtaugh's choice to start the deciding Game Seven. The Bucs' hurler, while honored to get the rare opportunity to start Game Seven of the World Series, was a little nervous before the contest and admitted that he would have trouble sleeping the night before. Murtaugh was not concerned, claiming that he should be nervous and that admitting it would help him adjust.

From the outset, Blass appeared anything but focused, walking Buford to start the game and then allowing Boog Powell to hit a long drive down the right field line that drifted foul. It was after Powell's second stinging foul ball that Weaver exited the dugout to argue Rule 801 with home plate umpire Nestor Chylak. Chylak motioned for Murtaugh to join them on the mound and pointed out that Blass must start from the front of the rubber, his foot touching it, instead of the side. There was a long delay as Weaver's strategy appeared to be working.

After the discussion, Blass asked Chylak for time to warm up, and his first toss flew high over catcher Manny Sanguillen's glove, sailing to the backstop. Clearly, Blass appeared rattled. Weaver came out one more time to protest to Chylak, this time arguing that Blass was going to his mouth too much. His first official pitch after the debate bounced in front of the plate, and the next was high and outside. On the brink of unraveling, Blass's third pitch was a perfect slider that struck out Powell. It seemed to settle Blass down, and he got out of the inning unscathed. As it turned out, Weaver's intrusion was exactly what the pitcher needed. "I thank Earl every time I see him," Blass said. "I was all over the place until Earl came out and it calmed me down with his nonsense. As the game went on, I got settled into the contest."[1]

Blass got out of a jam in the second inning, enticing a double play after the Orioles put two men on base with one out. Meanwhile, Cuellar was cruising through the Pirates' lineup in the first three innings. As the game went into the fourth, Cuellar faced the Hall of Fame Pirates right fielder Roberto Clemente. Cuellar and Clemente did not have the best relationship as Cuellar had played on a winter league team where Roberto was managing the year before. Clemente had a strict style of managing, which Cuellar felt was abrasive, and the Bucs' right fielder did not appreciate that the Orioles' hurler would not take any suggestions. The relationship ended quickly as Cuellar quit the team. Clemente got his revenge, hitting Cuellar's first pitch over the left center field fence to give Pittsburgh the lead.

Over the next four innings, Blass got stronger, surrendering only one hit, and he was enjoying the moment. "I took a moment in the bottom of the seventh after I warmed up and before the first pitch," he said. "I took the baseball and went to the back of the mound to take in the whole scene. You don't know if you'll ever get back again and I wanted to soak in the atmosphere and have an image to bring up whenever I need it. I made everyone wait until I soaked in my mental image, then we went back to work."[2]

As good as Blass was, he wasn't getting much support from the Pirates' offense. That changed in the top of the eighth when Pittsburgh gave its star pitcher the breathing room he needed. Willie Stargell led off the inning with a walk and aggressively tried to score after Jose Pagan ripped a double to left center, where Baltimore's Merv Rettenmund picked up the ball and threw it toward home with a very realistic chance to retire the hustling Stargell. Surprisingly, first baseman Boog Powell cut off the throw, trying to keep Pagan from going to third. Stargell slid in safely with the Bucs' insurance run. Pittsburgh now had a 2–0 advantage.

It was all the support Blass needed. The Orioles cut the lead back to one in their half of the eighth when Don Buford grounded to Robertson, scoring Elrod Hendricks, who led off the inning with a single to center.

Blass got out of the eighth with no further damage and then retired the first two Baltimore hitters in the bottom of the ninth. Rettenmund then stroked a shot up the middle, but Pirates shortstop Jackie Hernandez moved quickly to his left, snagging the ball behind second base, and tossed it to Bob Robertson at first to begin the wild celebration. The joyous Blass, with his second complete game of the series, leaped into the first baseman's arms.

What started out looking like a game that would end badly for the Pirates with Weaver's argument about Rule 801 ended happily because of it. It was Weaver's miscalculation that helped make the Bucs the world champions.

PIT N	0	0	0	1	0	0	0	1	0	— 2	6	1
BAL A	0	0	0	0	0	0	0	1	0	— 1	4	0

BATTING

Pittsburgh Pirates	AB	R	H	RBI
Cash 2b	4	0	0	0
Clines cf	4	0	0	0
Clemente rf	4	1	1	1
Robertson 1b	4	0	1	0
Sanguillen c	4	0	2	0
Stargell lf	4	1	1	0
Pagan 3b	3	0	1	1
Hernandez ss	3	0	0	0
Blass p	3	0	0	0
Totals	33	2	6	2

FIELDING—DP: 1. Cash-Robertson.
E: Robertson (1).
BATTING—2B: Pagan (2,off Cuellar).
HR: Clemente (2,4th inning off Cuellar 0 on 2 out).
Team LOB: 4.

Baltimore Orioles	AB	R	H	RBI
Buford lf	3	0	1	1
Johnson 2b	4	0	0	0
Powell 1b	4	0	0	0
F. Robinson rf	4	0	0	0
Rettenmund cf	4	0	0	0
B. Robinson 3b	2	0	0	0
Hendricks c	3	1	2	0
Belanger ss	3	0	1	0
Cuellar p	2	0	0	0
Shopay ph	0	0	0	0
Dobson p	0	0	0	0
McNally p	0	0	0	0
Totals	29	1	4	1

BATTING—2B: Hendricks (1,off Blass).
SH: Shopay (1,off Blass).
GDP: Belanger (1,off Blass).
Team LOB: 4.

PITCHING

Pittsburgh Pirates	IP	H	R	ER	BB	SO	HR	BFP
Blass W(2–0)	9	4	1	1	2	5		

Baltimore Orioles	IP	H	R	ER	BB	SO
Cuellar L(0–2)	8	4	2	2	0	6
Dobson	0.2	2	0	0	0	1
McNally	0.1	0	0	0	0	0
Totals	9	6	2	2	0	7

Umpires: HP—Nestor Chylak, 1B—Ed Sudol, 2B—John Rice, 3B—Ed Vargo, LF—Jim Odom, RF—John Kibler
Time of Game: 2:10 **Attendance:** 47,291

PIRATES 9, WASHINGTON SENATORS 7
OCTOBER 15, 1925

The Glorious Downpour

The odds were clearly against the Pirates. They had fought back valiantly from a three-to-one deficit to send the series to a deciding Game Seven. In the process they were trying to pull off a feat that had never been accomplished before: win a World Series after falling behind by such a margin.

The Bucs did have the home-field advantage for Game Seven, but they would need more than just that to defeat the defending world champion Washington Senators. Making matters worse, Pittsburgh would face perhaps the greatest hurler in baseball history, Walter Johnson.

In his first two starts in this World Series, Johnson had completely stymied the Pirates' bats, including a dominant six-hit shutout in Game Four, to give the Senators a seemingly invincible series lead. To complete the comeback, the Pirates would have to find a way to solve Johnson, a feat that precious few hitters had ever been able to do.

One other factor would play an important part in this game: the weather. A light mist was falling at the beginning of the contest, but it would soon turn into a hard, driving rain. Despite the ominous forecast, commissioner Kenesaw Landis wanted to finish the series, so he started the game on time.

While the odds were stacked against them, this was still a quality Pirates team. Led by Max Carey, Kiki Cuyler, and Pie Traynor, Pittsburgh comfortably won the National League crown by 8½ games over the New York Giants. Pirates manager Bill McKechnie felt his club had a superstitious advantage going in—he had worn the same undershirt, underwear, and socks since Pittsburgh won Game Five.

Early on it seemed like momentum, and McKechnie's familiar wardrobe would be nonfactors as Washington surged to a quick 4–0 lead in the top of the first inning. Pirates starter Vic Aldridge was having difficulty with his footing on the wet pitching rubber and was wild, walking in the first run. After giving up another, McKechnie called on reliever Johnny Morrison. Morrison fared no better, giving up two more runs on a catcher's interference, after what would have been a groundout, and an error by Pirates second baseman Eddie Moore.

Before the Pirates even came to bat, it looked like Johnson would have all the run support he would need as he continued his dominance in the bottom of the frame, retiring the Bucs in order. When it appeared that the Pittsburgh magic had run out, they showed just how tough they were.

As the 4–0 lead still held up into the third and the rain was turning from drizzle to downpour, the Bucs finally broke through against Johnson after 20 inept innings. The weather seemed to affect the veteran pitcher who had trouble with his footing. Morrison led off the inning with a single to center, and then Moore smacked a long double to left, scoring Morrison with the first run. Carey followed with a single to score Moore and, after moving to second on a groundout by Cuyler, took third on an uncontested steal. He then came home on a Clyde Barnhart single to cut the Washington lead to 4–3.

Just as quickly as Pittsburgh grabbed the momentum, the defending world champions took it back, scoring two runs in the top of the fourth off a two-run double by Joe Harris.

Pittsburgh made it 6–4 on back-to-back doubles by Carey and Cuyler in the bottom of the fifth but was unable to inflict any more damage as the game went into the seventh inning stretch. The Senators only needed nine more outs to defend their championship.

The Bucs' bats once again came alive, with an assist from Washington short-stop Roger Peckinpaugh, who dropped a fly off the bat of Moore, allowing the Pirates' second baseman to go to second. Carey then laced his third double of the game to cut the lead to one once again. With two out, Traynor tied the contest with a long triple to right that scored Carey. The Bucs' star third base-man wasn't satisfied with a triple and tried to stretch it to an inside-the-park homer. Traynor came sliding into what was now a very muddy home plate and was tagged out, but it was a brand-new game.

Moments later Peckinpaugh went from goat to hero when he smacked a long shot over the screen in front of the scoreboard in left field to put Washington in the lead once again, 7–6.

Johnson seemed to be laboring in the eighth but was able to get the first two Pirates' hitters out. Pittsburgh catcher Earl Smith, who was responsible for a Senators run in the first with a catcher's interference call, made up for it with a double to right field. After he was replaced on the base paths by pitcher Emil Yde, Carson Bigbee followed with a double to left to score Yde and tie the game at seven. Johnson then walked Moore and had to face Carey, who had dominated Johnson in this game. The Washington hurler seemingly got the best of Carey on this play as he softly grounded to Peckinpaugh. But as the shortstop threw to Stan Harris at second for the apparent inning-ending out, he stumbled on the muddy infield and rushed his throw, which sailed high as Moore slid under the ball. For Peckinpaugh, it was his eighth error in what was an embarrassing World Series for him. Instead of the Pirates being retired with the game tied, Kiki Cuyler stepped to the plate with a chance to make himself a Pittsburgh legend.

With the afternoon turning into dusk and the rain falling harder, Cuyler sliced a shot down the right field line into the dusk that cleared the bases in what appeared to be an inside-the-park grand slam. The now ecstatic Forbes Field crowd was quieted somewhat when the umpires, who lost sight of the ball, ruled that it had rolled into the bullpen and therefore was a ground-rule double. Cuyler and Carey were sent back to second and third, but the damage was done on one of the most controversial hits in World Series history. While Pittsburgh argued it should be a homer, the Senators claimed that it was in fact a foul ball. Because the rain and fog had settled over the ballpark, no one seemed to know for sure what happened. Regardless, it went in the books as a two-run double, and the Pirates had their first lead of the game, 9–7, with one inning to play.

McKechnie, with not much left to choose from, selected pitcher Red Oldham to close it out. Though Oldham had only been called on 11 times in 1925, he was up to the challenge. He struck out Sam Rice and got Bucky Harris on a liner to second. It would be up to Goslin to keep the flickering Washington hopes alive. He let the first pitch go past for a called strike before swinging hopelessly at the second pitch to make the count 0–2. Oldham's third offering caught Goslin off guard, and he watched the game-ending third strike go past him to end the game, giving the Bucs an improbable 9–7 victory and a second world championship.

Pittsburgh had beaten the Senators and the odds. Pitcher Babe Adams, the only player on the roster from their last title in 1909, said the players knew all along they could win. "I might remark that I was confident ever since the series started that they [the Pirates] had it in them," he said. "Even when the outlook was bleakest, I was sure they had the stuff in them to bring victory in the end."[1]

As proud as McKechnie was, he said he couldn't wait to get home and get into some new clothes. Not only dirty, McKechnie's outfit was also soaked, thanks to the glorious downpour that helped the Bucs rally back on this unforgettable day.

WAS A	4	0	0	2	0	0	0	1	0	—	7	7	2
PIT N	0	0	3	0	1	0	2	3	x	—	9	15	3

BATTING

Washington Senators	AB	R	H	RBI
Rice cf	5	2	2	0
B. Harris 2b	5	0	0	0
Goslin lf	4	2	1	0
J. Harris rf	3	1	1	2
Judge 1b	3	1	1	1
Bluege 3b	4	0	1	1
xPeckinpaugh ss	3	1	1	2
Ruel c	4	0	0	1
Johnson p	4	0	0	0
Totals	35	7	7	7

x—reached first on interference.

FIELDING—DP: 1. B. Harris-Judge.
E: Peckinpaugh 2 (8).
BATTING—2B: J. Harris (2,off Morrison).
HR: Peckinpaugh (1,8th inning off Kremer 0 on 1 out).
Team LOB: 5.

Pittsburgh Pirates	AB	R	H	RBI
Moore 2b	4	3	1	1
Carey cf	5	3	4	2
Cuyler rf	4	0	2	3
Barnhart lf	5	0	1	1
Oldham p	0	0	0	0
Traynor 3b	4	0	1	1
Wright ss	4	0	1	0
McInnis 1b	4	0	2	0
Smith c	4	0	1	0
Yde pr	0	1	0	0
Gooch c	0	0	0	0
Aldridge p	0	0	0	0
Morrison p	1	1	1	0
Grantham ph	1	0	0	0
Kremer p	1	0	0	0
Bigbee ph,lf	1	1	1	1
Totals	38	9	15	9

FIELDING—E: Moore (1), Cuyler (1), Smith (1).

BATTING—2B: Carey 3 (4,off Johnson 3); Moore (1,off Johnson); Cuyler 2 (3,off Johnson 2); Smith (1,off Johnson); Bigbee (1,off Johnson).

3B: Traynor (2,off Johnson).

SH: Cuyler (3,off Johnson).

GDP: Smith (2,off Johnson).

Team LOB: 7.

BASERUNNING—SB: Carey (3,3rd base off Johnson/Ruel).

PITCHING

Washington Senators	IP	H	R	ER	BB	SO
Johnson L(2–1)	8	15	9	5	1	3

Pittsburgh Pirates	IP	H	R	ER	BB	SO
Aldridge	0.1	2	4	4	3	0
Morrison	3.2	4	2	2	0	2
Kremer W(2–1)	4	1	1	1	0	1
Oldham SV(1)	1	0	0	0	0	2
Totals	9	7	7	7	3	5

WP: Aldridge 2 (2).

Umpires: HP—Barry McCormick, 1B—George Moriarty, 2B—Cy Rigler, 3B—Brick Owens

Time of Game: 2:31 Attendance: 42,856

PIRATES 10, NEW YORK YANKEES 9
OCTOBER 13, 1960

The True Shot Heard Round the World

For years, baseball historians have debated what was the most dramatic home run in the history of the game. There was Bobby Thompson's three-run shot in the final game of the 1951 National League Playoff, the "Shot Heard Round the World," and Joe Carter's dramatic game-ending home run in Game Six of the 1993 Fall Classic. Then, of course, there was the hobbling Kirk Gibson coming off the bench in the bottom of the ninth of the opening contest in the 1988 World Series, smacking a two-run homer to set up the Dodgers' improbable five-game defeat of favored Oakland A's. For many historians, though, the discussion begins and ends with one moment: 3:37 P.M. on October 13, 1960, when a second baseman from West Virginia launched a magnificent blast over the left field fence at Forbes Field. It remains the only time a World Series has ended with a Game Seven walk-off home run.

Not only is that moment revered, but the game itself is considered by many to be the greatest ever played. With four lead changes, quirky plays, improbable heroes etching their names in history, and, of course, the dramatic ending, the game truly had it all. It was an unlikely end to what had been a very lopsided World Series. The Yankees clobbered the Pirates in three games, 16–3, 10–0, and 12–0, but somehow the Bucs stayed in it, squeaking by in Games One, Four, and Five by the scores of 6–4, 3–2, and 5–2. Game Seven would see another Yankee outburst, but this time the Pirates would keep pace.

Twenty-two times during the 1960 season, the Pirates won a game in their last at bat. "We did it so many times it became contagious," Pittsburgh shortstop Dick Groat noted. "It got to the point where we thought we weren't supposed to lose. We were like a team of destiny."[1]

Early on it looked like Pirates heroics wouldn't be necessary. After Yankees starter Bob Turley put down Bill Virdon and Dick Groat to begin the game, left fielder Bob Skinner walked, and then Glen "Rocky" Nelson hit the lone postseason home run of his career to give Pittsburgh an early 2–0 lead.

Turley struggled and was pulled in the second, but Cy Young Award–winner Vern Law was dominant for the Pirates, putting down the New York lineup in order over the first two frames.

The Pirates added to their lead in the second when catcher Smoky Burgess singled to lead off the inning before new Yankees pitcher Bill Stafford walked third baseman Don Hoak. Then second baseman Bill Mazeroski, trying to move the runners into scoring position with a bunt, loaded the bases when he beat out a throw from the off-balanced Stafford. Law then bounced the next pitch back to Stafford, who forced Burgess at home with a toss to catcher Johnny Blanchard, who threw a strike to first to get Law for the double play.

With two out and a chance to get out of the inning unscathed, Stafford could not retire Virdon, who stroked a long single to right center to score Hoak and Mazeroski, increasing the Bucs' advantage to four. As good as the Pittsburgh start was, anyone who thought that they would just cruise to a Game Seven victory was sorely mistaken.

Down 4–0 going into the fifth, Moose Skowron finally solved the puzzle that was Vern Law as he ripped a shot just inside the right field foul pole to cut the lead to 4–1. An inning later, after New York put two on, Pirates manager Danny Murtaugh pulled Law and inserted perhaps the greatest reliever in Pittsburgh history, Roy Face. While Law would later say that Murtaugh pushed all the right buttons and made great decisions for the team, he listed this as his most disappointing moment of this magical season for Pittsburgh. "It was the toughest moment of my career, being taken out in the seventh game of the World Series," Law said. "I had a 4–1 lead going into the sixth and was in pretty good control of the game. But I pitched the whole Series on a bad ankle [hurt in the celebration after the Bucs clinched the National League crown] and I guess Murtaugh had enough faith in the bullpen."[2]

The Bucs' skipper certainly had reason to have faith in Face. He won a major-league record of 22 consecutive games between 1958 and 1959 and saved a career high 24 games in 1960 along with a save in each of the club's three wins in this Fall Classic. He wouldn't get a fourth.

Face started off fine, getting Roger Maris, but then Mickey Mantle rolled a slow grounder up the middle that just got by Groat, scoring Bobby Richardson. Yankees catcher Yogi Berra came to the plate and blasted a long homer in the upper deck in right field, just inside the foul pole to give New York a sudden lead, 5–4. Two innings later, the Yankees added to their lead, plating two more runs.

Just as the game was looking like the three earlier New York victories, the capacity crowd at Forbes Field was about to witness the most bizarre and exciting two innings in the history of the game.

Pinch hitter Gino Cimoli singled to right to lead off the eighth, and then center fielder Bill Virdon hit a sharp ground ball to Tony Kubek at short. What could have been a double play instead turned into an infield single when the ball took a funny hop off the rocky Forbes Field infield straight into Kubek's throat. Gasping for breath, Kubek was taken out of the game and spent the night in the hospital. The Yankees' shortstop, who would go on to earn a place in Cooperstown as a broadcaster, was definitely not a fan of the Forbes Field infield. He said in an interview with the *New York Times* in 1985, "It was a terrible infield. It was like the beach at Normandy, half sand, half pebbles, and they never dragged it."[3]

Now with runners at first and second, Groat singled to left to score Cimoli and cut the New York lead to 7–5. Bob Skinner then moved both runners into scoring position with a perfect bunt, and Nelson flied to right for the second out.

A young Roberto Clemente hit a slow roller to Skowron at first for what appeared to end the inning, but Yankees pitcher Jim Coates was late getting to the base, and Clemente hustled down the line beating the throw for a single that scored Virdon.

Reserve catcher Hal Smith, who took over for Smoky Burgess in the eighth and was having one of the best seasons of his career in 1960, stepped to the plate. In that moment he etched his name into Pirates history by hitting a three-run homer to miraculously put the Pirates ahead 9–7, sending the stadium, and the city, into hysterics. The Bucs were now somehow only three outs away from the world championship.

Pitcher Bob Friend, who was shelled in Game Six, came in to close out the Yankees but instead threw only four pitches. Those four pitches resulted in two singles that put the tying runs on base with no outs. Murtaugh then called on Harvey Haddix, who got Maris to pop up to Smith before surrendering an RBI single to Mantle. With Gil McDougald, running for Dale Long at third, all eyes were on Berra, who ripped a liner to Nelson at first. The Buccos first baseman snagged the ball, tagged first base to retire Berra, and then looked to second to throw out Mantle for the series-ending play. But Mantle made a magnificent play, diving back into first and beating the tag by Nelson, and McDougald scored on the play, once again tying the game. Skowron then grounded into a force-out, sending this exciting game to the bottom of the ninth.

The emotionally drained Forbes Field crowd was stunned, but in a matter of minutes they would all experience the undisputed greatest moment in Pittsburgh Pirates history. On the mound was Ralph Terry for the Yankees, and at the plate was Bill Mazeroski. With the count 1–0, Mazeroski sent the ball over the left field wall, with Yogi Berra helplessly watching it fly over the fence. Mazeroski—whose nickname, "Maz," was about to become a household name—sprinted around the bases, with delirious Pirates fans chasing him and his teammates excitedly waiting for him to come home. As he touched home plate, the Pirates became world champions, and the Yankees were handed the most stunning defeat in their rich history. Mantle wept in the locker room and the 70-year-old skipper, Casey Stengel, who won seven World Series and 10 American League pennants for the Yankees, would soon be fired as part of the fallout from this surprising defeat.

For the Pirates, there was nothing but euphoria, an incredible way to put an exclamation point on what had been a magical season. Pitcher Vern Law put the game into perspective. "I guess if Murtaugh hadn't taken me out of the game it wouldn't have had that dramatic finish and Maz would have never had the chance to hit in the bottom of the ninth and wouldn't have received all the accolades, and just maybe, wouldn't have been a Hall of Famer. All I can say is I'm glad it ended the way it did." An excited Steel City certainly echoed those sentiments as fans had the pleasure of watching what was truly the "Shot Heard Round the World."[4]

NY A	0	0	0		0	1	4		0	2	2 —	9	13	1
PIT N	2	2	0		0	0	0		0	5	1 —	10	11	0

BATTING

New York Yankees	AB	R	H	RBI
Richardson 2b	5	2	2	0
Kubek ss	3	1	0	0
DeMaestri ss	0	0	0	0
Long ph	1	0	1	0
McDougald pr,3b	0	1	0	0
Maris rf	5	0	0	0
Mantle cf	5	1	3	2
Berra lf	4	2	1	4
Skowron 1b	5	2	2	1
Blanchard c	4	0	1	1
Boyer 3b,ss	4	0	1	1
Turley p	0	0	0	0
Stafford p	0	0	0	0
Lopez ph	1	0	1	0
Shantz p	3	0	1	0
Coates p	0	0	0	0
Terry p	0	0	0	0
Totals	40	9	13	9

FIELDING—DP: 3. Stafford-Blanchard-Skowron, Richardson-Kubek-Skowron, Kubek-Richardson-Skowron.
E: Maris (1).
BATTING—2B: Boyer (2,off Face).
HR: Skowron (2,5th inning off Law 0 on 0 out); Berra (1,6th inning off Face 2 on 1 out).
Team LOB: 6.

Pittsburgh Pirates	AB	R	H	RBI
Virdon cf	4	1	2	2
Groat ss	4	1	1	1
Skinner lf	2	1	0	0
Nelson 1b	3	1	1	2
Clemente rf	4	1	1	1
Burgess c	3	0	2	0
Christopher pr	0	0	0	0
Smith c	1	1	1	3
Hoak 3b	3	1	0	0
Mazeroski 2b	4	2	2	1
Law p	2	0	0	0
Face p	0	0	0	0
Cimoli ph	1	1	1	0
Friend p	0	0	0	0
Haddix p	0	0	0	0
Totals	**31**	**10**	**11**	**10**

BATTING—HR: Nelson (1,1st inning off Turley 1 on 2 out);
Smith (1,8th inning off Coates 2 on 2 out); Mazeroski (2,9th inning off
Terry 0 on 0 out).
SH: Skinner (1,off Coates).
GDP: Law (1,off Stafford); Clemente (1,off Shantz); Mazeroski (2,off
Shantz).
Team LOB: 1.

PITCHING

New York Yankees	IP	H	R	ER	BB	SO
Turley	1	2	3	3	1	0
Stafford	1	2	1	1	1	0
Shantz	5	4	3	3	1	0
Coates	0.2	2	2	2	0	0
Terry L(0–2)	0.1	1	1	1	0	0
Totals	**8**	**11**	**10**	**10**	**3**	**0**

Turley faced 1 batter in the 2nd inning
Shantz faced 3 batters in the 8th inning
Terry faced 1 batter in the 9th inning

Pittsburgh Pirates	IP	H	R	ER	BB	SO
Law	5	4	3	3	1	0
Face	3	6	4	4	1	0
Friend	0	2	2	2	0	0
Haddix W(2–0)	1	1	0	0	0	0
Totals	**9**	**13**	**9**	**9**	**2**	**0**

Law faced 2 batters in the 6th inning

Friend faced 2 batters in the 9th inning

Umpires: HP—Bill Jackowski, 1B—Nestor Chylak, 2B—Dusty Boggess, 3B—Johnny Stevens, LF—Stan Landes, RF—Jim Honochick

Time of Game: 2:36 **Attendance:** 36,683

Notes

#50

1. Dejean Kovacevic, "Three Home Runs Mark History for Pirates McCutchen," *Pittsburgh Post-Gazette,* Aug. 9, 2009.

#49

1. "MARATHON Tired Pirates Outlast Cubs in 20 Innings," *St. Petersburg Times,* June 7, 1980.

#47

1. Phil Musick, "Revenge for Rooker," *Pittsburgh Post-Gazette,* Sept. 26, 1979.

2. Charley Feeney, "Pirates Win 10–4 to Regain 1st," *Pittsburgh Post-Gazette,* Sept. 26, 1979.

#46

1. Paul Meyer, "Drabek Does It Again as Bucs Cut Reds' Playoff Lead to 3–2," *Pittsburgh Post-Gazette,* Oct. 11, 1990.

#45

1. Lester J. Biederman, "Veale's 'Fanning Bee' Shortens Long Night," *Pittsburgh Press,* June 2, 1965.

2. Ibid.

#44

1. Bill Christine, "Bucs Avalanche Buries Braves," *Pittsburgh Press,* Aug. 2, 1970.

#43

1. Dejean Kovacevic, "Michaels' Blast in 10th Caps 'Amazing' Comeback," *Pittsburgh Post-Gazette,* July 13, 2008; Dejean Kovacevic, "Michaels' Two-Run Blast Caps Dramatic Comeback for Pirates," *Pittsburgh Post-Gazette,* July 12, 2008.

#41

1. David Finoli and Bill Ranier, *The Pittsburgh Pirates Encyclopedia* (St. Louis: Sports Publishing Inc., 2003), 259.

#40

1. David Finoli and Bill Ranier, *When Cobb Met Wagner: The Seven Game World Series of 1909* (Jefferson, N.C.: McFarland Publishing, 2011), 145.

2. Phil Musick, "Human Locust Have Their Day," *Pittsburgh Press,* June 29, 1970.

#39

1. Ken Wunderly, "It's a Three-Peat for Pirates in NL East," *Observer Reporter,* Sept. 28, 1992.

2. Ibid.

#38

1. Jack Hernon, "Southpaw Works Masterpiece after Pirates Lose 6–0," *Pittsburgh Post-Gazette,* May 7, 1951.

2. "Biographical Information" on Cliff Chambers, Baseball-Reference.com, accessed Sept. 6, 2012, www.baseball-reference.com:8080/bullpen/Cliff_Chambers.

#37

1. Phil Axelrod, "Phillies Flag Hopes at Half Mast," *Pittsburgh Post-Gazette,* Aug. 6, 1979.

#36

1. "Pirates Win a Great Game," *Pittsburgh Press,* Sept. 21, 1907.

2. Ralph S. Davis, "Fans on Qui Vive," *Sporting News,* Sept. 29, 1910.

#34

1. "19 Innings: Pooped Pirates Prevail in the A.M.," *St. Petersburg Times,* Aug. 27, 1979.

#32

1. "Dock Ellis Hurls Major's First No Hitter of Year to Give Pirates Split," *Youngstown Vindicator,* June 13, 1970.

2. Neille Ilel and Donnell Alexander, "An LSD No-No," American Public Media, Mar. 28, 2008, http://weekendamerica.publicradio.org/display/web/2008/03/28/pitch/.

3. "Dock Ellis Hurls Major's First No Hitter of Year to Give Pirates Split," *Youngstown Vindicator,* June 13, 1970.

4. Ilel and Alexander, "An LSD No-No."

#31

1. Frederick G. Lieb, *The Pittsburgh Pirates* (Carbondale: Southern Illinois Univ. Press, 2003), 171.

#30

1. James Forr, "Bob Prince," *Society for American Baseball Research,* accessed Sept. 6, 2012, http://sabr.org/bioproj/person/0d0c3ddc.

2. Al Abrams, "Prince-King Firings Stir Furor," *Pittsburgh Post-Gazette,* Oct. 31, 1975.

3. Forr, "Bob Prince."

4. Ibid.

5. Bill Modoono, "Gunner Returns with Old Magic," *Pittsburgh Press,* May 4, 1985.

#28

1. Zander Hollander, ed., *1980 Complete Handbook of Baseball* (New York: New American Library 1980), 217.

2. Bob Hertzel, "Pirates Soaked in Joy," *Pittsburgh Press,* Oct. 1, 1990.

3. Ibid.

#25

1. Charley Feeney, "Bucs Win NL East Title," *Pittsburgh Post-Gazette,* Sept. 28, 1970.

2. Jimmy Jordan, "Club Jelled as Times Got Tough," *Pittsburgh Post-Gazette,* Sept. 28, 1970.

#23

1. Jack Hernon, "Long Does It Again—Hits 8th in Eight Games," *Pittsburgh Post-Gazette,* May 29, 1956.

#22

1. Dan Donovan, "Series Bound Pirates Sweep Reds," *Pittsburgh Press,* Oct. 6, 1979.

2. Bob Smizik, "Blyleven Finishes Cincinnati: Big Win Silences Media Critics," *Pittsburgh Press,* Oct. 6, 1979.

3. Dan Donovan, "Real Buc Family Surprises Players With Dance Show," *Pittsburgh Press,* Oct. 6, 1979.

4. Ibid.

#21

1. Charley Feeney, "The Great Roberto Died Caring for Others," *Pittsburgh Post-Gazette,* Jan. 2, 1973.

2. Ibid.

3. Jimmy Jordan, "Misty Scene: Bucs Retire No. 21," *Pittsburgh Post-Gazette,* Apr. 7, 1973.

#20

1. Robert Dvorchak, "Giles' Grand Slam in Ninth Caps Incredible Comeback in 9–8 Victory against Astros," *Pittsburgh Post-Gazette,* July 29, 2001.

2. Ibid.

#18

1. Paul Meyer, "Bucs Extend Lead to 2½," *Pittsburgh Post-Gazette,* Sept. 6, 1990.

#17

1. Charley Feeney, "Candelaria's Refrain Same after No-Hitter," *Pittsburgh Post-Gazette,* Aug. 11, 1976.

#15

1. Paul Meyer, "Pirates Rally from 5 Runs Back in the 11th," *Pittsburgh Post-Gazette,* Apr. 22, 1991.

2. Ibid.

3. Ibid.

#14

1. Ken Wunderly, "Two Pitchers, One No Hitter," *Observer Reporter,* July 13, 1997.

2. Ibid.

3. Ibid.

4. Ibid.

#13

1. Dan Donovan, "Stargell's Long Bomb Puts Pirates Ahead," *Pittsburgh Post-Gazette,* Oct. 3, 1979.

#11

1. Bob Smizik, "Pirates Blunder into Division Title," *Pittsburgh Press,* Oct. 3, 1974.

#9

1. Bob Smizik, "Roberto Gets 3,000th, Will Rest Till Playoffs," *Pittsburgh Press,* Oct. 1, 1972.

2. Ibid.

#7

1. Al Oliver and Andrew O'Toole, *Baseball's Best Kept Secret* (Pittsburgh: City of Champions Publishing, 1997), 54.

2. Ibid., 52.

#6

1. Jack Hernon, "High Slider Cost Me Game, Says Harvey," *Pittsburgh Post-Gazette,* May 27, 1959.

2. Ibid.

#4

1. Dan Donovan "Whew It's Over! Bucs Are Champs," *Pittsburgh Press,* Oct. 18, 1979.

2. Ibid.

3. Ibid.

#3

1. Finoli and Ranier, *The Pittsburgh Pirates Encyclopedia,* 314.

2. Ibid., 548.

#2

1. Babe Adams, "Bucs Real Champions Says Babe," *Pittsburgh Press,* Oct. 16, 1925.

#1

1. Robert Dvorchak, "Pirates' 1960 Champs 'A Team of Destiny,'" *Pittsburgh Post-Gazette,* Apr. 4, 2010.

2. Finoli and Ranier, *The Pittsburgh Pirates Encyclopedia,* 287.

3. David Schoenfield, "The Greatest Game Ever Played," ESPN.com, Oct. 13, 2010.

4. Finoli and Ranier, *The Pittsburgh Pirates Encyclopedia,* 287.